Nation and National Identity

Nation and National Identity

The European Experience in Perspective

edited by
Hanspeter Kriesi
Klaus Armingeon
Hannes Siegrist
Andreas Wimmer

Purdue University Press
West Lafayette, Indiana

First U.S. edition published 2004 by Purdue University Press
www.thepress.purdue.edu

©Verlag Rüegger, Zurich/Chur, 1999. All rights reserved.
website: www.rueggerverlag.ch
email: info@rueggerverlag.ch

This edition not available in Europe.

Printed in the United States of America

ISBN: 1-55753-353-9

Library of Congess Cataloging-in-Publication Data available

Table of Contents

Part II:
Case Studies:
National Identity in a Historical and Comparative Perspective

Part III:
From the Europe of Nations to the European Nation

Preface

The idea of the nation-state is being challenged all over the world today. Nation and nationalism, nationhood and national identity are once more on the agenda in many different countries. The contributions assembled in this volume may be viewed as an attempt to put the contemporary European experience into perspective. These contributions were originally presented at a conference organized by the Priority Program for the Social Sciences of the Swiss National Science Foundation, which took place at Zurich in the Fall of 1998 – the year of the 150th anniversary of the modern Swiss state.

The contributions to this volume are divided into three parts, each introduced by one of the editors, and a general introduction which discusses the peculiarities of the Swiss case of state formation and nation building in relation to the contributions of the three parts. The five chapters of Part I provide an idea of the variety of approaches and perspectives which currently exist in the study of nationhood and national identity. The authors of these contributions clarify basic concepts, show the deep and intractable ambiguity of classic distinctions, and point to new forces within nation-states which have seriously weakened their internal cohesion. All of these considerations give rise to new challenges for nationalist representations of the world and established institutions of social integration. Under present conditions, national identity and political solidarity have to compete with other, cross-cutting ways of creating boundaries: ethnic and cultural fragmentation, gender and sexual divides, divisions in the labor market. In Part II, the recent experiences of a selected number of countries – Belgium, Austria, Germany, Croatia, and Israel – are presented to illustrate the great diversity of current challenges to national identities. Processes such as globalization and European integration have had an impact on all of them, but mobilization by regional movements, reunification of separate territorial parts, the differentiation of formerly homogeneous ethnic identities, the sequels of war, and the country-specific historical legacies, interact with these global processes to constitute so many different challenges for national identities and nationhood. Finally, the two contributions in Part III show that the process of European integration gives rise to different images and fulfills different functions for the various nations involved, but that it has not yet been able to shape a new European identity.

As the editors of this volume, we would like to express our gratitude to the Priority Program for the Social Sciences, which has made possible not only the Zurich conference, but also the publication of the present volume. Peter Farago, Maya Rentsch and Albert Tanner were responsible for the organization of the Zurich conference. Agnes Imhof and Stephen Lake have turned the non-Anglo-Saxons' contributions to this volume into more readable texts. Sylvia Dumons and Priska Kanti have helped us with the administrative details in preparing the present volume. We would like to thank all of them for their precious support.

March 1999   The editors
Hanspeter Kriesi, Klaus Armingeon
Hannes Siegrist, Andreas Wimmer

Authors

Urs Altermatt is professor of Contemporary History at the University of Fribourg/Switzerland. Visiting professor at the Universities of Krakow (Poland), Budapest, Sarajevo and Sofia. He is author and co-author of many books and articles, including his last book *Das Fanal von Sarajevo. Ethnonationalismus in Europa* (Zurich 1996), translated in several languages.

Klaus Armingeon is professor for political science at the University of Berne, Switzerland. His main research areas are: comparative political science, in particular social and economic policy, industrial relations, corporatism and political attitudes; the Swiss political system in comparative perspective; globalization and the latitude of the nation-state; European integration. He published especially on corporatism, unions and industrial relations.

Rogers Brubaker is professor of Sociology at the University of California, Los Angeles. His recent books include *Citizenship and Nationhood in France and Germany* (Harvard, 1992), and *Nationalism Reframed: Nationhood and the National Question in the New Europe* (Cambridge, 1996). He is currently working on an ethnographic study of ethnicity in everyday life in the ethnically mixed Transylvanian city of Cluj/Kolozsvar.

Kas Deprez teaches sociolinguistics at the Universities of Antwerp and Leuven. His main areas of interest are the propagation of Dutch in Flanders, the federalization of Belgium and the position of the Flemings in Brussels, the language policy of the European Union, Europe's minority languages and multilingualism in the new South Africa. He is the editor of *Nationalism in Belgium. Shifting Identities 1780–1995* (London, Macmillan, 1998).

Alain Dieckhoff is research director at CNRS (Centre d'Etudes et de Recherches Internationales, Paris) and teaches at the Institut d'Etudes Politiques in Paris. His main field of research is on politics and society in contemporary Israel and Israeli-Palestinian relations. He is the author of several books on the subject including: *Les espaces d'Israël. Essai sur la stratégie territoriale israélienne* (Presses de la FNSP, 1989); *L'invention d'une nation. Israël et la modernité politique* (Gallimard, 1993); *Israéliens et Palestiniens. L'épreuve de la paix,* Aubier, 1996.

Liah Greenfeld is University professor and professor of political science and sociology at Boston University. She is the author of, among other books, *Nationalism: Five Roads to Modernity* (Harvard University Press, 1992), and numerious articles on the phenomenon of nationalism, as well as other aspects of modern culture, society, and politics. Currently she is concluding a study of the role of nationalism on the emergence of modern economy.

Max Haller is full professor of sociology at the University of Graz. His main research area is the analysis of contemporary societies, comparative theory and research on social structures and values. He published eight monographs, edited nine books, and published about five dozens of articles in Austrian and international social science journals. Recent books include: *Klassenstrukturen und Mobilität in fortgeschrittenen Gesellschaften* (Frankfurt/New York 1989); *Class Structure in Europe*, ed. (New York 1990); *Europa wohin? Wirtschaftliche Integration, soziale Gerechtigkeit und Demokratie*, ed. with P. Schachner-Blazizek (Graz 1994); *Toward A European Nation?* ed., with R. Richter (Armonk, N.Y. 1994); *Identität und Nationalstolz der Österreicher* (Wien/Köln/ Graz 1996).

Robert Hettlage is professor and chair of sociology at the university of Regensburg/Germany. Research and numerous publications in sociological theory, social philosophy, social structure, cooperatives, and various themes of sociology of culture, family, economics and development.

Vjeran Katunaric is professor of sociology, teaching theoretical and historical sociology at the University of Zagreb, Croatia. His empirical studies cover the areas of ethnic relations, interculturalism and cultural policy. Invited professor in the United States, Sweden and Germany. His books include: *Gods, Elites, Peoples* (1994), *The Labyrinth of Evolution* (1994), *Multicultural Reality and Perspectives in Croatia*, ed. (1997, in English), *Cultural Policy of the Republic of Croatia*, ed. (1998,in English).

Hanspeter Kriesi is professor of political science at the University of Geneva. He teaches comparative and Swiss politics. His main research areas include social movements in a comparative perspective, Swiss politics with an emphasis on direct democratic procedures, and public opinion research. He is the author of several books and articles on these topics.

Josef Langer is professor of Sociology, University of Klagenfurt, Austria. Research areas: development and frontiers, culture and identity, modernization theory. Visiting professor among others at universities in Finland, USA, Japan, Czech Republic and India. Selected publications: *Border, Region and Ethnicity in Central Europe* (Klagenfurt, 1996); *Kleine Staaten in grosser Gesellschaft (Small States in the Emerging New Europe)*, (Eisenstadt, 1995), *Emerging Sociology* (Aldershot 1992); *Europe from the Middle of the Continent, Internatio-*

nal Sociology (Europe Beyond Geography), 1992: 12–34; *Identität und Natio-nalstolz der Österreicher* (in cooperation with Max Haller), Wien/Köln/Weimar 1996.

Richard Münch is professor of sociology at the University of Bamberg. Several times visiting professor at the University of California in Los Angeles, USA.

Joane Nagel is professor and Chair of Sociology at the University of Kansas. Her publications include *American Indian Ethnic Renewal* (Oxford University Press, 1996), *Masculinity and Nationalism: Gender and Sexuality in the Making of Nations* (Ethnic and Racial Studies 21, 1998), and *The Color of Sex* (Oxford University Press, 2000).

Hannes Siegrist is professor for comparative European social and cultural history at the Universit of Leipzig. His research areas include the history of management, of employees, of the free professions, of consumption, of property and of nations and regions. He has published several books related to the theme of the present volume: *Nation und Emotion. Deutschland und Frankreich im Vergleich (19. u.20. Jh.)*, Göttingen: Vandenhoeck & Ruprecht 1995 (Hg. zus. mit E. Francois u. J. Vogel); *Amerikanisierung und Sowjetisierung in Deutschland 1945–1970* (Frankfurt am Main: Campus 1997, Hg. zus. mit Konrad H. Jarausch); *Centralismo e federalismo tra Otto e Novecento. Italia e Germania a confronto* (Bologna: Il Mulino 1997, zus. mit O. Janz u. P. Schiera).

Bettina Westle is professor for political science at the University of Bielefeld, Germany, where she teaches political sociology and comparative social research. Recent publications include: *Zur kollektiven Identität der Deutschen*, Opladen 1998; *Konflikt und Konsens als Elemente der pluralistischen Demokratie*, ZUMA-Nachrichten 43; *Nationale Parteien als Vermittlungsinstanzen europäischer Politik?* (with Staeck) in Koenig/Rieger/Schmitt: Europa der Bürger? Opladen 1998.

Andreas Wimmer is director of the Swiss Forum for Migration Studies at the University of Neuchâtel and associate professor (Privatdozent) for Social Anthropology at the University of Zurich. Publications: *Die komplexe Gesellschaft* (Berlin 1995), *Transformationen* (Berlin 1995). Research areas: Ethnicity and nationalism, migration, theory of social change, peasant societies. Regional interests: Mexico and Guatemala, Iraq, Switzerland.

Introduction:
State Formation and Nation Building in the Swiss Case

Hanspeter Kriesi

In 1998, Switzerland commemorated the 150th anniversary of the modern Swiss State. It is against this background that the conference on which the present volume is based, was organized. The anniversary has not mobilized the population, which is not really surprising: at the moment, the Swiss are feeling increasingly insecure about their national identity. This state of mind is not entirely new. As far back as the sixties, some well-known members of the Swiss elite expressed a «malaise helvétique» and an «uneasiness in the small state». At that time, the malaise set in motion a xenophobic movement of impressive proportions, as well as a process of far-reaching reforms, among them a full-scale reform of the Swiss constitution. But somewhere down the line, the spirit of reform evaporated, the reform process got stuck and eventually gave way to an almost purely formal exercise of trimming the existing text of the constitution. The xenophobic movement largely demobilized, although the sentiments which it had drawn upon continued to constitute an important latent potential. Only after the dust had settled at the end of the Cold War in the mid-nineties, did the unfinished business of the past resurface. In a changing international context and under explicit foreign pressure, the Swiss public has been confronted with issues which it had left unanswered in the aftermath of World War II – issues which touch crucially upon the Swiss national identity. The Swiss discovered that for too long, they had believed in the legend of their heroic stand during the war, a legend which they had been only too ready to accept in the immediate post-war period. With this myth, the very experience which, more than anything else, had contributed to forging a common Swiss identity was put into question, dealing a serious blow to Swiss self-consciousness and to the identity the Swiss had come to accept as their own.

In this introduction, I would like to discuss briefly the processes of *state formation and nation building from the perspective of the special case of Switzerland*. The Swiss case is of some interest, because in this country neither state formation nor nation building have gone as far as in the more «typical» European nation-states. In Switzerland, the closure of the political and cultural boundaries has remained strangely ambiguous, which suggests some interesting analogies with the current state formation and nation building at the European level.

State formation and nation building are *two closely related processes*. State formation means above all the creation of a political center, the administrative penetration of the territory dominated by the center, and the consolidation of the political-administrative boundaries. Successful states are sovereign on their territory: there are no internal or external competitors who might make a legitimate claim to share control over their territory. Nation building, in turn, refers to a process of external cultural boundary building and internal cultural standardization (Flora et al. 1983: 16ff.). Nation building has been strongly promoted by the modern states, and the modern nation-state has more or less successfully integrated the various processes of boundary building. Nation-states of the European type are characterized by boundaries which are simultaneously political, military, economic, cultural and functional (Bartolini 1998). Although closely related, the two processes need not always coincide, however. As is pointed out by Rogers Brubaker in his contribution to this volume, there are not only state-framed nations – nations conceived of by the state and institutionally and territorially shaped by it – but also counter-state nations – nations imagined as distinct from, and often in opposition to, the territorial and institutional frame of an existing state[1].

1   The creation of the Swiss federal state and of the Swiss nation

Religion mattered in the process of European nation building, and the Reformation constituted a first major step in that direction. However, language, as the most obvious and pervasive expression of identity and distinctiveness, became even more important for nation building in Europe and elsewhere. Switzerland is one of the few European countries, where religion constituted the crucial issue for the formation of the modern Swiss state, while language hardly mattered at all, and this although it is divided into four different language communities. At the origin of the modern Swiss state was a short and relatively bloodless civil war between the mainly Protestant liberal territories and the Catholic conservative areas. It is very important to understand that the liberals of all the language regions united in order to impose the new federal state – to paraphrase Charlie Brown, they needed all the friends they could get. They won the war, and the Catholics were forced into the federal state by the liberals' military victory. However, the battle had had the effect of considerably

---

1   Tilly (1993: 47ff.) makes a similar distinction between «state-led nationalism» on the one hand, and «state-seeking nationalism» on the other hand. According to Tilly, in state-led nationalism, rulers aggressively pursued a defined national interest while successfully making demands on a broadly defined citizenry in the name of the whole nation and to the exclusion of other loyalties those citizens might have had. In state-seeking nationalism, representatives of some populations that currently did not have collective control of a state claimed a distinctive political status, or even a separate state». See also Calhoun (1993: 218).

calming down the liberals' centralizing impulse. The constitution of 1848 was in fact a compromise between the victorious liberals and the defeated Catholics. The price the victors paid for the acceptance of the new state by their adversaries was a far-reaching decentralization of political authority. The new center was to be weak: the essence of political power rested with the cantonal authorities, which allowed the Catholic losers a large measure of control over their own territories. Correspondingly, the cantonal communities continued to represent the real homelands of the Swiss (de Rougement 1965: 106).

Some authors maintain (Siegenthaler 1993: 323; Ernst 1997: 234) that the successful national integration on the federal level was in fact a precondition for the regional decentralization of the state. This is not only to overestimate the success of the nation building effort of the liberals, but also to entertain a much too harmonious conception of the resulting state. Swiss federalism did allow the two camps to coexist, but it had a defensive character from the start. As Lüthy (1971: 31) has pointed out, Swiss federalism has always been an «anticentralism», which considered the federal state if not as an enemy, then at least as a necessary evil which one had to live with but not to give in to.

Over the course of the past 150 years, both state formation and nation building have made some further progress. Both processes continued to strengthen the federal state and to contribute to the creation of national solidarity. On the one hand, the expansion of state tasks required an increasing legislative activity on the part of the federal state. But the cantons (the constituent parts of the federal state) and the communes kept a large measure of fiscal autonomy and remained largely responsible for the implementation of federal legislation. As a result, the federal bureaucracy remained relatively weak, while the bulk of public employees work in cantonal or local administrations. On the other hand, the industrialization process and the rise of nationalism in the neighboring states (German and Italian unification, and the establishment of large continental and colonial empires) prompted a process of federal nation building (Froidevaux 1997: 35). The new nationalism of the late 19th century had interconfessional characteristics, which now appealed to the Catholics, too (Siegenthaler 1993: 325; Jost 1998: 67). Thus, the year 1891 not only marks the creation and institutionalization of the Swiss national holiday (the 1st of August), commemorating the anniversary of the original pact between the Confederates of 1291, but also the entry of the first Catholic conservative into the Swiss government which, until this date, had been composed entirely of liberals.

The myth of the heroic past of the Swiss was celebrated by historical commemorations, the erection of monuments, and by historical paintings such as the famous Marignano frescos of Hodler in the national museum. Additional icons of the new national myth included the alpine nature – the Swiss Arcadia in the Alps – the direct-democratic tradition, and – Helvetia, the Swiss version of the «maiden with the shield» (see Joane Nagel in this volume) who still today adorns the most frequently used Swiss coins. The ideologues of Swiss nationalism used existing customary practices – folksongs, physical contests, marksmanship – to construct an invented tradition of a novel type for the purposes of uniting the different component parts of the Swiss nation (Hobsbawm 1992: 6). Although a newly invented tradition, it gradually resonated with the Swiss public and served to forge a sense of «unity in diversity». As is pointed out by Smith (1991: 22), «it is myths of common ancestry, not any fact of ancestry (which is usually difficult to ascertain), that are crucial». Liah Greenfeld, in her contribution to this volume, forcefully defends a similar point of view. The question is, of course, as Birnbaum (1997: 28) is careful to add, why some myths and some dreams about common ancestors reinforce nationalist mobilization, while others do not.

Even in its sacralized and mythological form, in the late 19th century, the Swiss federal nation remained imbued with the spirit of *civic nationalism* – for lack of any better alternative, I am using the classic distinction between civic and ethnic nationalism, in spite of its deep ambivalence as pointed out by Rogers Brubaker in his contribution to the present volume. Thus, in 1875, the liberal Swiss constitutional lawyer, Carl Hilty, formulated the nature of the Swiss nation in these terms (quoted by Im Hof 1991: 169; my translation): «Neither race, nor tribal cooperation, neither common language and custom, nor nature or history have created the state of the Swiss Confederation. It has been formed rather as a contrast to all these great powers, originating in an idea, in a political thought and will of increasing clarity and based on it still today after 500 years of existence, just as on the first day». *A nation based on political will* – this was the voluntarist essence of the renewed federal nationalism. Moreover, the reference to a mythical past not only served to forge a community of sentiments between the different parts of the Swiss nation, it also provided the narrative fidelity for the democratic movement which mobilized to radicalize the liberal ideas in the second half of the 19th century. This movement tied its claims for direct democracy to the older heritage of the popular myths about the direct democratic general assemblies («Landsgemeinden») in the alpine cantons and the general councils in city cantons. The protagonists of the democratic movement framed the new paradigm of direct democracy as nothing else but a modernization of tradition (Kriesi and Wisler 1999).

2   The ambiguity of Swiss nationhood

But, as Smith (1986: 149) has pointed out, concrete cases of nationhood and nationalism contain both civic and ethnic elements «in varying proportions at particular moments of their history». Those (including Renan (1991), in his famous speech) who insist on the civic, political or voluntarist nature of the Swiss nation, overlook its double-headed character. The civic conception of Swiss nationhood and pride in one's exceptional political institutions did not preclude *an ethnic conception of citizenship,* which closely resembles that of the Germans (see also Urs Altermatt in this volume). Thus, at the height of European nationalism, in the wake of World War I, the Swiss adopted a naturalization law which has only been marginally modified in 1990 and which renders acquisition of Swiss citizenship very difficult (Froidevaux 1997: 51). The Swiss naturalization procedure is characterized by three particularities (Centlivres and Schnapper 1991: 153; Kleger and D'Amato 1995: 266). First, Swiss citizenship is acquired by becoming a citizen of a local community. Second, while the cantonal and communal naturalization procedures vary from one canton and commune to another, they are never of a purely administrative nature, but always involve a decision by the legislative assemblies of the communes and the cantons. Third, it is the commune's responsibility to assess the suitability of an applicant to become a Swiss citizen. This estimation considers especially the applicant's integration into the local community, his familiarity with the Swiss lifestyle and habits, and his conformity to Swiss law. Still today, the naturalization procedure is notoriously slow, cumbersome and, last but not least, rather costly for the applicant.

It is certainly no accident that the ethnic or communitarian element of the Swiss nation is tied to the local or cantonal level. Just as they have jealously tried to guard their political prerogatives, the cantons have also tried to retain the right to define the national identity of their citizens. Just as Swiss state formation has stopped short of the creation of a strong center, Swiss nation building has not achieved a degree of standardization as we find it in other European nation-states. Thus, the predominantly *civic nationalism at the federal level* goes hand in hand with a predominantly *ethnic nationalism at the cantonal and local level.* As Centlivres and Schnapper (1991: 158) suggest, on the federal level, the political unification preceded and conditioned the development of common sentiments of nationhood, which implies that the federal conception of the Swiss nation is closer to the French republican model. On the cantonal level, by contrast, the sense of belonging to a community with a common culture and a common origin preceded the formation of a political unity, which implies a conception of nationhood and citizenship closer to the German model.

Thus, the multicultural Swiss nation is in fact composed of diverse member «nations», each rather homogeneous within itself. Switzerland constitutes *a successful federation of nations.* Its citizens are welded together by *a common political culture,* i.e. by a common attachment to a set of fundamental political principles – most notably, neutrality, federalism, and direct democracy, buttressed by a set of myths about past heroic struggles to defend these principles against outside aggressors. This common political denominator is minimal, however. Its purpose is precisely to allow the different cultural groups that compose the Swiss nation to be culturally different from one another. In addition to the common political denominator, *external pressure* provided the glue that preserved Swiss unity. It was at its most extreme during World War II – the historic moment which, as I have already observed, more than any other event forged the Swiss nation, although external pressure continued to make for Swiss unity during the Cold War, when the communist threat and the massive immigration of workers from Southern Europe[2] served as functional equivalents of the Nazi menace during World War II. It was only with the fall of the Berlin wall and the dissolution of the communist regimes in Eastern Europe that, in the Swiss perception, the external pressure ceased. The Swiss then found themselves in the geographical heart of a continent which was no longer at war, but which was integrating at a rapid pace. Faced with this new reality, all of a sudden lacking any foreign threat, the Swiss public experienced a sense of loss.

3   The price of Swiss multiculturalism

This surprising reaction has to do with the fact that Swiss multiculturalism within a common institutional framework came with a price attached. Internally, within the common procedural framework, the different component cultures of the Swiss nation lived their own way of life and tended *to mutually ignore each other.* «Live and let live» was the motto, which allowed the coexistence of different religious and language communities. Externally, the minimal common denominator did not allow for more than a *minimal involvement in international affairs.* Swiss neutrality had, not least of all, an internal function: it contributed to the coexistence of the country's various component parts. Mutual ignorance within and abstentionism without – these were the implications of the Swiss national identity. Today, in an increasingly interdependent world, in a world of regional integration, of expanding international regimes and globalizing markets, both of these implications of the Swiss national

---

2   For the role of immigration in the mobilization of the «nationalist/ethnic dialectic», see also Joane Nagel's contribution to this volume.

identity are put into question. That is, at the very same time that they are confronted with the reality of their past, the Swiss have to face the fact that the reality of the present also puts into question the construction of their national identity: they are forced to resituate themselves not only with respect to each other, but also in relation to the rest of the world.

Internally, the increasing need to cooperate makes itself felt in the relations between the different regions. The traditional strategy of mutual ignorance loses much of its validity, given the increasing scale of economic, political, administrative and cultural cooperation. The traditional units of the Swiss confederation – the cantons – have become just too small. There are calls for a rearrangement of Swiss federalism, and an official reform project launched by specialists of public finance is being prepared (see Mottu 1997; Klöti 1997; Meier 1997). But given popular attachment to the federal institutions, the persistence of communal and cantonal identities, and the attachment of the local political elites to their traditional sinecures, major institutional changes are not yet in sight. *Externally,* the increasing need to cooperate with the rest of the world renders the traditional Swiss conception of neutrality and international abstentionism obsolete. Although the government has understood the signs of the times, given the popular attachment to neutrality – especially in the German-speaking part of the country – the authorities have discovered that it is difficult to steer away from the traditional strategy of armed neutrality.

4   Politics of identity and politics of interest

In Switzerland today, the reform of federalism as well as the reorientation of foreign policy are first and foremost a *politics of nationhood.* And as such, to use Rogers Brubaker's (1992: 182) apt phrase, they refer more to a politics of identity, and less to a politics of interest (in the restricted materialist sense). They pivot more on self-understanding than on self-interest. But, of course, interests are not entirely separable from identity, since people interpret their interests in terms of their own identities. This is another way of saying that the national myths become all too real in their consequences. We have, for example, noticed this to be true in the popular vote on the adherence of Switzerland to the European Economic Space (EES) in December 1992 (Kriesi et al. 1993): those who voted against the treaty were afraid not only that they would lose their venerated political institutions, i.e. the basis of their national identity, but also that the level of unemployment would rise, if Switzerland joined the EES. By contrast, those who voted in favor of the treaty did not have any apprehensions with respect to their national identity, but they were afraid of rising unemployment in the event that Switzerland did *not* join the EES.

However, the relationship between interest politics and identity politics is even more intricate than that. Above all, structurally induced interests may constitute a potential to be exploited by identity politics. Thus, the increasing global interdependence certainly creates losers, in the restricted materialist sense. For some, the liberalization of economic exchange and the increasing mobility of people, goods, services and capital imply a loss of traditional privileges. We find the losers among the unskilled in general, among declining old middle classes, among people involved in the economic sectors oriented towards the internal market – in short, among members of society whose resources are not convertible and whose geographical and occupational mobility is limited (Kriesi 1999). Traditionally, small European countries have developed neo-corporatist arrangements which provided the weaker groups of their societies with compensations for the hardships resulting from their country's openness to the world markets. This was, of course, Katzenstein's (1985) well-known and amply documented thesis[3]. Now, the more recent push towards increasing economic integration on a global scale has not only increased the need for such compensations, it has also given rise to a neo-liberal challenge: the welfare state and economic protectionism in certain sectors (e.g. agriculture) have come under heavy attack (see also Richard Münch in this volume)[4].

Those who stand to lose from this attack constitute a structural potential for the mobilization of defensive movements – from either the socialist left or the conservative right. I would like to suggest that the relative success of these defensive political forces depends crucially on identity politics. More specifically, the «national populism» of the conservative movements succeeds precisely to the extent that it is able to establish a link between the material predicament of the losers and their insecurity about their national identity. The mobilization of the conservative right today may be interpreted as a response to a crisis of national identity in the context of (real or imagined) economic hardship. The conservatives' mobilization today is not of a bellicose, expansive kind, but rather has a defensive character, resembling more closely a movement of self-defense that mobilizes citizens frightened by today's increasingly interdependent world (Taguieff 1992: 9; Gentile 1996: 75). More than anything else, theirs is a mobilization in defense of a threatened national identity.

In the Swiss case, the conservative, nationalist mobilization articulates *a new political cleavage* – a cleavage between the traditional, rustic and inward-looking (parochial, internal market-oriented) Switzerland, on the one hand, and

---

3   Katzenstein was mainly concerned with compensations to the social partners in tripartite arrangements. As is pointed out by Sciarini (1992) and Mach (1999), he paid less attention to the other crucial mechanism of compensation, which concerns the economic sectors producing mainly for the national market.
4   For the Swiss case, see Leutwiler et al. (1991), and de Pury et al. (1996).

the modern, urban and outward-looking (cosmopolitan, export-oriented) Switzerland, on the other hand (Sardi and Widmer 1993). This is a cleavage between those who believe in the myth of the «special case» («Sonderfall») and who wish to continue the «solitary route» («Alleingang») in foreign policy, and those who believe that Switzerland is a country resembling its neighbors ever more closely and that the increasing need to cooperate requires its integration into the European Union. Given the depth of the identity crisis in the Swiss case, the nationalist mobilization in favor of the «solitary route» has proven to be very impressive in the course of the 1990s – in terms of electoral results and in terms of direct-democratic votes. It has been *the* political game in the country, which has left both opposing camps – the neo-liberals and the social-democrats – somewhat perplexed.

5 The increasing salience of language

With the increasing secularization of modern society, the traditionally dominant religious conflict has lost much of its force and no longer threatens the unity of the country. But given the divergent sensibilities of the major language communities with respect to the new cleavage that I have just described, language has become more important: while the French-speaking minority massively approves of Swiss participation in the process of European integration, the Swiss-German majority (and the Italian-speaking minority) have so far been opposed to it. A minority in the Swiss confederation, the French-speaking population has always been less identified with the Swiss nation as a whole and has kept a more communal, cantonal or regional identity than the Swiss-German majority (Kriesi et al 1996: 55; Widmer and Buri 1992: 385). At the same time, relationships with larger neighbors have always been better among the French-speaking Swiss, who feel much closer to France than the Swiss-Germans feel towards neighboring Germany. Finally, the national myths of the heroic past seem to resonate more in the Swiss-German part of the country, given that, until the early 19th century, the Swiss confederation was essentially Swiss-German-speaking. Except for bilingual Fribourg, the future French- and Italian-speaking parts of the country were, until the Vienna Congress, either allied or occupied territories (bailliages) of the Confederates (Froidevaux 1997: 31).

Language has also become more important because *the public space is segmented by language:* the members of the major language communities only use television, radio, and the press of their own respective communities (Kriesi et al. 1996). Moreover, rather than following the TV programs of the other Swiss language communities, the members of the several Swiss language groups pay considerably more attention to the programs of the respective foreign neighbors which speak the same language. In other words, French-speaking Swiss watch Francophone Swiss television and French stations, while the Swiss-German-speaking Swiss watch Germanophone Swiss television and German and Austrian programs.

Although linguistically segmented, the public space need not lack unity. It may still be a national space, if the issues debated are the same in all the different language segments and if the lines of political conflict are not segmentally specific. To the extent that all language groups debate the same national issues (e.g. within the framework of a direct-democratic campaign), and to the extent that the political camps opposing each other on the various issues are the same in all language groups, politics can still result in national closure (see Ernst 1998: 230). However, we should keep in mind the fact that, in the Swiss case, such closure has never been completely achieved, because cantonal politics has remained so important down to the present day. The political parties still have their roots in cantonal politics, and their national organizations are still exceptionally weak (Kriesi 1998: 143ff.). As a result equally of the lack of national closure of the public space and of the diverging sensibilities with regard to the politics of identity, the political debates about foreign policy have developed in different directions among each of the major language groups. The accompanying tensions between the respective communities have not yet reached Belgian proportions (see Deprez in this volume), but they are not to be taken lightly, given that the issues involved touch upon fundamental questions of Swiss nationhood.

6   Switzerland – a model for Europe?

Switzerland has often been represented as *an ideal model* of «unity in diversity» for European integration. In spite of the difficulties which I have just described, I believe that there is something to this observation. The development over a period of one and a half centuries of an ambiguous combination of a mainly cultural or communitarian nationhood at the regional level with a civic or political nationhood at the central level holds out some promise for European integration.

In her contribution to this volume, Liah Greenfeld claims that the nation as the defining cultural system of the modern age appears to be unavoidable today – for lack of viable alternatives: «No other image of the social order, no other cultural system that forms a framework for identity, seems to be able to perform the role that nationalism performs for us and to deliver the goods to

which it made us accustomed.» Similarly, Anthony Smith (1991: 171) has pointed out that «serious attempts to move beyond the nation have to start from
its principles and use them to go further». And since the principles of the nation are those of nationalism, he continued, «it may only be possible to transcend the nation through a form of nationalism, one that is paradoxically broa-
der than the compact nation that has usually been the object of its endea-
vour».

The Swiss example of *a federation of nations* may indicate the way forward.
There is no guarantee that this recipe will work, of course, as the failure of the
Yugoslavian attempt to create a similar federation of nations amply illustrates.
Like Switzerland, Yugoslavia was built around a federation of nations, and a
common cultural-historical experience (Smith 1991: 146). Unfortunately, the
history of Yugoslavia has not fulfilled the hopes which were placed in it (see
Vjeran Katunaric in this volume). But the Swiss example holds out the promise
that it might work.

In many ways, today's Europe resembles the Swiss confederation as it was in
the early 19th century, on the eve of the creation of the federal state. In the
Swiss case, the federal state together with a universal (male) suffrage was imposed by a liberal elite which subsequently created a national myth of the civic, republican type to shape the national identity of the populations of all of
the cantons. In the European case, the elite created a political structure, which
so far lacks the political institutions for the appropriate integration of the
European populations, and which also still lacks a civic myth which would as-
sist in the creation of an appropriate common, federal identity for the different populations at the united European level. As Klaus Armingeon suggests
in his introduction to the third part of this volume, the first step in the direction of a European nation is the creation of a democratic polity. Provided that
there is a more thorough democratization of the European political institutions, however, the creation of a civic myth of a common European past which
would allow the promotion of a «constitutional patriotism» does not seem an
unlikely possibility. Such a civic identity could be added, at the European level, to the more heavily cultural or ethnic elements of the national identities at
the level of the member-states. Europe could follow the Swiss example and
create a multilayered identity (see Robert Hettlage in this volume). As the data
presented by Max Haller in the final chapter of this volume indicate, such a
multiple identity is not at all utopian: Europeans presently feel close to multiple levels of governance and, except for the British and the Swedes, majorities in all the countries surveyed appear to feel close (or very close) to the
European level in particular. The Swiss experience suggest that, in order to be
successful, the construction of a common European myth must employ ancient

materials in order to create a new type of tradition that resonates well with the past experiences of the different European nations. Suffice it to say that the history of Europe offers many possibilities from which to add the required «historical depth» to the invention of a common European tradition.

The Swiss precedent also suggests some limits to the common European experience. Just as in the Swiss case, unity may come at the price of external political abstentionism and far-reaching internal decentralization of political authority. Again following the Swiss example, state formation at the European level may stop far short of the traditional model of the European nation-state. Neutrality in foreign affairs, and multi-level governance with a relatively weak center may be the recipe for European state formation. There are plenty of indications that this is exactly the direction in which the European polity is heading.

In many ways, however, the Swiss model may *not be sufficiently complex*. This can be illustrated with the question of *language*. It is true that Switzerland has been capable of integrating different language communities based on the principle of territoriality. This principle implied that only one language was to be spoken on a given territory, but that the language could vary from one territory to the other. In order to communicate with each other, the members of the different language communities were supposed to understand (if not to speak) both of the two major languages (French and German). But of course the European Union embraces many more languages than Switzerland. The Swiss solution therefore, will not do. Even in Switzerland, given the increasing prominence of English in an ever more interdependent world, the Swiss solution is becoming less and less feasible.

In fact, *India* may constitute a more adequate point of reference in this respect. As Laitin (1997) points out, India is a multilingual state where citizens who wish to have a broad range of mobility opportunities must learn 3+/-1 languages: English and Hindi are necessary for communicating with the central state; the language of the member-state is necessary for communication with the corresponding administration; and minorities in a member-state may continue to use their native language. The resulting *language constellation* is generally accepted throughout India. In Europe, a similar language constellation is taking shape: English is becoming the true European language; the languages of the member-states are here to stay; and regional languages are reasserting themselves to an extent unknown for centuries. The resulting constellation might include 2+/-1 languages.

To conclude, the point Laitin (1997) is trying to make is worth emphasizing: the citizens of a future European state will have a cultural or national identity that involves a far more complex language repertoire than was required of citizens of early-developing European states. European citizens in the future are likely to have *multiple languages* and *multiple cultural identities,* just as they are likely to have a *multi-layered national identity.* As such, they will resemble the citizens of a latecomer to the scene of state formation, like India. My point is that, in the European context, they will most closely resemble the citizens of a European state that has never really achieved political and cultural closure – the citizens of Switzerland.

References

Bartolini, Stefano (1998). *Exit Options, Boundary Building, Political Structuring. Sketches of a theory of large-scale territorial and membership «retrenchment/differentiation» versus «expansion/integration» (with reference to the European Union).* Working Paper. Florence: European University Institute.

Birnbaum, Pierre (1997). «Introduction: Dimensions du nationalisme», pp. 1–33 in Pierre Birnbaum (ed.). *Sociologie des nationalismes.* Paris: PUF.

Brubaker, Rogers (1992). *Citizenship and Nationhood in France and Germany.* Cambridge, Mass.: Harvard University Press.

Calhoun, Craig (1993). Nationalism and Ethnicity. *Annual Review of Sociology* 19: 211–39.

Centlivres, Pierre and Dominique Schnapper (1991). «Nation et droit de la nationalité suisse», *Pouvoirs* 56: 149–161.

De Pury, David, Heinz Hauser, Beat Schmid et al. (1996). *Ayons le courage d'un nouveau départ. Un programme pour la relance de la politique économique de la Suisse.* Zürich: Orell Füssli.

Ernst, Andreas (1998). «Vielsprachigkeit, Öffentlichkeit und politische Integration: schweizerische Erfahrungen und europäische Perspektiven», *Revue suisse de science politique* 4, 4: 225–240.

Flora, Peter et al. (1993). *State, Economy and Society in Western Europe. 1815–1975. A Data Handbook in two Volumes.* Volume 1. Frankfurt: Campus.

Froidevaux, Didier (1997). «Construction de la nation et pluralisme suisses: idéologie et pratiques», *Revue suisse de science politique* 3, 4: 29–58.

Gentile, Pierre (1996). Les trajectoires de la droite radicale. 1984–1993. *Etudes et recherches* No. 33. Université de Genève: Département de science politique.

Hobsbawm, Eric (1992). «Introduction: Inventing Traditions», pp. 1–14 in Eric Hobsbawm and Terence Ranger (eds.). *The Invention of Tradition.* Cambridge University Press.

Im Hof, Ulrich (1991). *Mythos Schweiz. Identität – Nation – Geschichte. 1291–1991.* Zürich: Verlag NZZ.

Jost, Hans Ulrich (1998). «Der helvetische Nationalismus. Nationale Identität, Patriotismus, Rassismus und Ausgrenzungen in der Schweiz des 20. Jahrhunderts», pp. 65–78 in Hans-Rudolf Wicker (ed.). *Nationalismus, Multikulturalismus und Ethnizität.* Bern: Haupt.

Katzenstein, Peter (1985). *Small States in World Markets.* Ithaca: Cornell University Press.

Kleger, Heinz and Gianni D'Amato (1995). «Staatsbürgerschaft und Einbürgerung – oder: Wer ist ein Bürger? Ein Vergleich zwischen Deutschland, Frankreich und der Schweiz». *Journal für Sozialforschung* 35, 3/4: 259–81.

Klöti, Ulrich (1997). «Kommentar – Föderalismusreform: die Grenzen des ökonoimischen Ansatzes», *Revue suisse de science politique* 3, 3: 153–60.

Kriesi, Hanspeter (1999). «Movements of the Left, Movements of the Right: Putting the Mobilization of Two New Types of Social Movements into Political Context», pp. 398–425 in Herbert Kitschelt, Peter Lange, Gary Marks, John D. Stephens (eds.). *Continuity and Change in Contemporary Capitalism.* Cambridge University Press.

Kriesi, Hanspeter (1998). *Le système politique suisse.* 2e édition. Paris: Economica.

Kriesi, Hanspeter and Dominique Wisler (1999). «The Impact of Social Movements on Political Institutions: a Comparison of the Introduction of Direct Legislation in Switzerland and the United States», in Marco Giugni, Doug McAdam, and Charles Tilly (eds.). *How Movements Matter: Theoretical and Comparative Studies on the Consequences of Social Movements.* Minneapolis: Minnesota University Press.

Kriesi, Hanspeter, Boris Wernli, Pascal Sciarini and Matteo Gianni (1996). *Le clivage linguistique: problèmes de compréhension entre les communautés linguistiques en Suisse.* Bern: Office fédéral de la statistique.

Kriesi, Hanspeter, Claude Longchamp, Florence Passy, Pascal Sciarini (1993). Analyse der eidgenössischen Abstimmung vom 6. Dezember 1992. *Vox* Nr. 47. Bern: Schweiz. Gesellschaft für Sozialforschung.

Laitin, David D. (1997). «The Cultural Identities of a European State», *Politics and Society* 25, 3: 277–302.

Leutwiler, Fritz et al. (1991). *Schweizerische Wirtschaftspolitik im internationalen Wettbewerb. Ein ordnungspolitisches Programm.* Zürich: Orell Füssli.

Lüthy, Herbert (1971). *Vom Geist und Ungeist des Föderalismus.* Zürich: Arche.

Mach, André (ed.) (1999). *Globalisation, néo-libéralisme et politiques publiques dans la Suisse des années 1990.* Zürich: Seismo.

Meier, Alfred (1997). «Unrealistische Theorie oder theorielose Realität?», *Revue suisse de science politique* 3, 3: 161–64.

Mottu, Eric (1997). «Réforme de la épréquation financière et principe de subsidiarité», *Revue suisse de science politique* 3, 3: 133–151.

Renan, Ernest (1991[1882]). *Qu'est-ce qu'une nation?* Texte intégral de la Conférence. Paris: Bordas.

Rougement, Denis de (1965). *La Suisse ou l'histoire d'une peuple heureux.* Lausanne: Ed. L'âge d'homme.

Sardi, Massimo and Eric Widmer (1993). «L'orientation du vote», pp. 191–212 in Hanspeter Kriesi (ed.). *Citoyenneté et démocratie directe.* Zürich: Seismo.

Sciarini, Pascal (1992). «La Suisse dans la négociation sur l'Espace économique européen: de la rupture à l'apprentissage», *Annuaire suisse de science politique* 32: 297–322.

Siegenthaler, Hansjörg (1993). «Supranationalität, Nationalismus und regionale Autonomie; Erfahrungen des schweizerischen Bundesstaates – Perspektiven der Europäischen Gemeinschaft», pp. 309–333 in Heinrich A. Winkler and Hartmut Kaelble. *Nationalismus – Nationalitäten – Supranationalität,* Stuttgart: Klett-Cotta.

Smith, Anthony D. (1991). *National Identity.* London: Penguin.

Smith, Anthony D. (1986). *The Ethnic Origins of Nations.* Oxford: Basil Blackwell.

Taguieff, Pierre-André (1992). «Réactions identitaires et communauté imaginée. Sur la production contemporaine de nationalisme», *Sexe et Race,* no VI: 3–38.

Widmer, Thomas and Christof Buri (1992). «Brüssel oder Bern: schlägt das Herz der ‹Romands› eher für Europa?», *Annuaire suisse de science politique* 32: 363–88.

Part I

Perspectives and Concepts

Introduction

Andreas Wimmer

Nationalism and national states form the dominant ideology and the prevalent political organization of the modern age, which has, after all, been characterized by conflicts between groups considering themselves as nations rather then by fights between classes, contrary to Marx's vision of the future. This book does not seek to explain this salience of nationalism and national states in modern societies, it does not discuss in a systematic way the various theoretical approaches that have been developed in the last two decades of renewed interest in the subject. Its aim is rather more modest: to map the different forms that nationalism and national identity have taken at different times and in different places, and to seek to understand the mechanism of their reproduction and transformation. The first part of this volume consists of a series of chapters that approach these issues at the level of typological and conceptual analysis. Three develop, build on, and critique different forms of specific nationalist discourse and politics; two discuss some of the symbolic and institutional processes that help to sustain and uphold nationalist images of the social world.

Liah Greenfeld's chapter builds on her impressive and brilliant book (1991), in which she compares the evolution of British, French, German, Russian, and American nationalism. In her book she describes the transformations that the notion of nation has undergone since the Middle Ages – from referring to a group of students of the same regional origin, to denoting a political elite and finally, «the people», as in our current understanding of the term. It is this last transformation which explains, according to Greenfeld, the historical force of nationalism: the previously dispossessed lower classes are elevated to the status of an elite group with privileged access to state power, equal treatment before the law and, most importantly, the dignity of belonging to a «chosen people» valued for the richness and depth of its culture and history.

In this way, Greenfeld subsumes under the term «nationalism» two processes of political modernization that unfolded independently of nationalism and which, for analytical purposes, should be kept separate, although they finally fused with nationalist thinking into the dominant discourse of the nation-state: the rise of equality, and representational justice, as central values of modern societies which found formal expression in the institutions of citizenship and democratic politics respectively. However, nationalism, citizenship, and democracy, are intertwined in different ways in different nation-states.

Greenfeld goes on to show that the rise of national identities and politics did not everywhere follow the same paths. While in cases of early nationalisms, notably in the Anglo-Saxon world, the emphasis lay on democracy and citizenship rights as core institutions defining the nation and expressing its historical achievements, in those regions that adopted nationalist ideologies at a later time and against the hegemony of British or French nationalisms, more collectivist forms of imagining the nation tended to emerge, based on ideas of shared cultural features and historical experience. Correspondingly, the political role of the individual is conceived of differently in many instances, giving rise to authoritarian and collectivist forms of nationalism opposing individualistic, libertarian models. Cross-tabulating the binary oppositions between civic and ethnic on the one hand, individualistic and collectivist on the other, Greenfeld arrives at a four-fold typology of national identities.

It is against this well-established method of typological reasoning that Rogers Brubaker's chapter is directed. Modifying some of his own arguments presented in his widely praised book on «Citizenship and nationhood in France and Germany» (1992), Brubaker shows that the dualistic opposition between civic, inclusive, liberal nationalism (good) on the one hand, and ethnic, exclusive, and collectivist nationalism (bad) on the other hand, does not help us to understand the many variations under which nationalist thinking has appeared in the modern world. His argument is three-pronged and contains a pragmatic, an analytical, and a political/moral point.

First, he shows that depending on how widely or narrowly we define the terms «civic» and «ethnic», we end up with a typology that contains heavily underpopulated and overpopulated boxes as soon as we start filling them with concrete examples. More challenging than this argument of practicability – which can be raised against almost every typology – is his analytical critique. According to Brubaker, the dichotomy is misconstrued because we cannot define civic nationalism without referring to ethno-cultural elements, such as notions of a «people» united by common language and by a specific political culture, which enable the political process holding the civic nation together to unfold. The French and American examples illustrate the fact that notions of civic nationhood build on implicit meanings of cultural (not only linguistic) homogeneity and identity. On the other hand, ethnic nationalism contains elements of choice and free association, mainly through processes of cultural assimilation that logically should be the exclusive characteristic of civic nationalism.

The third argument is of a moral/political nature. Brubaker firmly opposes the moral implications of the civic-ethnic distinction by showing that civic nationalism is just as exclusive as its ethnic counterpart – albeit in different ways.

Those who are excluded are not ethnic others, but opponents of what is considered to be the nation's political project (e.g. anti-democratic communists, catholic conservatives, aristocrats, groups for whom cultural identity counts more then republican integration, etc.). Nationalism – and its institutional «realization», the modern nation-state – can be seen as a form of political and social closure that, even in its ideologically most acceptable (i.e. civic) form, nourishes a powerful machinery of inclusion and exclusion that splits up the modern world into its many national segments.

Building on this insight, one could try to go a step further in explaining the enormous success of nationalist ways of organising politics. It is due to the fusion of three different notions of «peoplehood», which had developed independently from each other, that this form of social closure became attractive to large sections of society and led ultimately to its hegemonic dominance over all other, competing claims of political solidarity: the notion of people as an ethnic community held together by historical experience and shared culture; the notion of citizens enjoying equal rights and duties towards the state; and the notion of a political sovereign in whose name the government has to act. All were fused into one People writ large, the ideological and institutional base of modern nation-states. In this way, the limits of democratic inclusion and of guaranteed civil rights came to coincide with the boundaries of ethno-national groups, even in the case of the most civic nation-states (cf. Wimmer, forthcoming).

Jürg Altermatt's article reminds us that this mode of political organization and ideology has not always been the dominant one. Rather, there is a wide variety of ways in which ethnicity, polity, and citizenship can be related to each other. Of special interest are the historical examples from Eastern Europe, which he draws upon in order to show how, under the umbrella of pre-nationalist empires such as the Austrian-Hungarian monarchy, various ethno-religious groups lived side by side without distinguishing between (the politically dominant) nation and «minority». Altermatt's main aim is similar to that pursued by Rogers Brubaker: to overcome the normatively attractive, but analytically unsatisfactory dichotomy between civic and ethnic nationalisms. To this end, Altermatt presents his own two typologies, one based on the relative importance attributed to the territorial separation of ethnic groups, and a second one based on the different degrees to which the central state tries to enforce the cultural hegemony of a particular ethnic group.

The remaining two papers by Joane Nagel and Richard Münch leave the field of typological analysis behind. Both focus on forces of cohesion that once held nationally framed societies and polities together but which have become seriously weakened, giving rise to new challenges for nationalist representations of the world and established institutions of social integration.

Joane Nagel introduces her paper by reminding us that nationalist discourse and political practice are just one possible way of representing the world and of constructing political solidarity. Building on her earlier work on ethnic competition and conflict (most recently Nagel 1996), she maintains that national identity and political solidarity have to compete with other, cross-cutting ways of creating boundaries, whose political salience and visibility have to be limited and controlled if nationalism is to triumph. Three such competing ways of dividing the social world are discussed.

First, waves of immigration lead to the formation of ethnic minorities and thus threaten the ideal of ethnic homogeneity and exclusive political solidarity towards the state, of which every nationalism dreams. Secondly, nationalists have to control the potentially conflicting gender divide by enforcing a patriarchal vision of society and by controlling women's sexual and reproductive behaviour. In this most interesting and innovative section of her chapter, Joane Nagel shows how images of the nation as mother, the enforcement of group endogamy for women but not for men, the linkage between the nation's honour and female sexual virtue, between the nation's future and women's fertility, and the generalization of military bravery as a standard for national manliness, all contribute to a specifically nationalist discourse of male dominance. Finally, similar processes of discursive control and exclusion help to police another potentially disruptive borderline: that which separates groups with different sexual orientations.

Nagel's analysis of the gendered nature of nationalism goes far beyond tracing women's forgotten or unacknowledged contributions to nationalist movements, and beyond depicting women as mere victims of male nationalist chauvinism, as is the case with some feminist writings on the subject. She shows that nationalist discourse is linked not only with the ideal of democracy and citizenship, as well as with a romantic notion of culture and personality, but also with patriarchal forms of thought and social organization. However, whether this relation is historically contingent (male dominance in public life developing concurrently with nationalist movements), or whether, on the contrary, this linkage is «functionally necessary» – as one would have said some decades ago – in order for nationalism to succeed, remains a question for further research.

Like Joane Nagel, Richard Münch starts from the basic insight that nations are a contested and reversible way of organising political and social cohesion, in competion with other possible models. His focus lies on the notions and practices of solidarity provided through nationally framed welfare institutions. By introducing the issue of social solidarity, he makes an extremely valuable point in showing that nationalism, most importantly but not exclusively in the West, is related not only to the ideals of cultural dignity and male heroism, of political sovereignty, and citizenship, but also to both notions and actual institutions of solidarity. If patriarchal images of manliness helped to overpaint differences of interest between men and women, welfare institutions bridged the divide between social classes within the national social space by making the risks of unemployment, illness, and age an object of state intervention. The nation was thus transformed into a quasi-family bound together by obligations of solidarity and support.

According to Münch's analysis, this model of national solidarity is nowadays under severe pressure from global market forces. Welfare state integration and inclusion into a labour market restructured according to the logic of international competition seem to contradict each other. When low qualified immigrant workers are the main victims of these developments, as their high rate of unemployment in all European societies shows, a mismatch between obligations of support and actual feelings of solidarity results, because the welfare state is regarded as an institution of *national* solidarity designed for members of the *national* community. This provides a breeding ground for ultra-nationalist, xenophobic movements.

How can these problems be overcome? Münch foresees and at the same time recommends two remedies. On the one hand, new forms of institutions should/will develop in order to ensure social solidarity on a sub- or transnational level. Welfare state functions will thus be taken over by organizations of civil society. On the other hand, more flexible labour markets will provide new opportunities for immigrant workers and their children. Flexible labour markets and new institutions of social solidarity will in turn produce trans-ethnic forms of socio-political inclusion and thus overcome the divide between «nationals» and «minorities», «immigrants» and «autochthonous», thus leading us into a truly post-national world of freely chosen, cosmopolitan associations of interest.

Münch's chain of arguments links fields of research not usually associated with each other (ranging from nationalism, welfare state, and immigration, to issues of labour market transformation and globalization). In this way, he prepares the ground for a new understanding of nationalism and national identities (see also Bommes and Halfmann 1998). However, some of the arguments might need further elaboration and empirical testing. For example, one may ask under what conditions the combination of flexible labour markets and downsizing national welfare states will lead to a weakening, rather then a resurgence of ethnic ties of solidarity, since trade unions might, under certain circumstances, be replaced by ethnic networks of support, welfare payments by mutual aid between members of extended families and ethnic neighbourhoods.

Taken together, the different chapters of this first part of the book make it clear that nationalism and national identity cannot be studied as a topic of political history or the history of popular consciousness alone. Intertwined as nationalist representations have become with modern institutions of citizenship, democracy, the welfare state, and certain gender roles, we should analyse variations between nationalisms and national identities as emerging out of different constellations in this quadripolar field of forces. This book may provide a good starting point from which to pursue this line of enquiry.

Making sense of the different forms and appearances of nationalist identities should not, however, allow us to forget the considerable common aspects: everywhere in the modern world where the nation-state has appeared, it has done so according to nationalist principles that defined the boundaries of the citizenry, of the political sovereign, and of those worthy of support in times of need. In this way, nationalism helped to limit the modern promises of equality, participation, and solidarity to a group, within which they were more possible of achievement than they would have been as part of a truly universalist project. Thus, nationalism has enabled modern society to unfold, while at the same time it continues to be its main obstacle.

References

Bommes, Michael and Jost Halfmann (eds.) (1998). *Migration in nationalen Wohlfahrtsstaaten. Theoretische und vergleichende Untersuchungen*. Osnabrück: Universitätsverlag.

Brubaker, Rogers (1992). *Citizenship and Nationhood in France and Germany*. Cambridge MA: Harvard University Press.

Greenfeld, Liah (1991). *Nationalism: Five Roads to Modernity*. New Jersey: Harvard University Press.

Nagel, Joane (1996). *American Indian Revival: Red Power and the Resurgence of Identity and Culture*. New York: Oxford University Press.

Wimmer, Andreas (Forthcoming). *Shadows of Modernity. The Anthropology of State Formation, Nationalism, and Ethnic Conflict*.

Is Nation Unavoidable? Is Nation Unavoidable Today?

Liah Greenfeld

The division of mankind into nations today appears to be the fundamental element of geo-political reality. Every person is believed to belong to one or another nation and, therefore, to have a national identity, whether or not he or
she is aware of this. Nations which achieve a certain level of development acquire national consciousness; the nation takes the form of a perverse and violent nationalism. In some cases, patriotism takes the perverse and violent form
of nationalism. The nation is unavoidable. This, I believe, is the dominant lay
view of the matter, and it is not much different from the established expert
opinion.

Today, when the grip of nationalism on people's minds and its effect on their
lives is demonstrated daily, it is hard to question this view and to remember
that nationalism is a fairly recent phenomenon. Yet, for most of recorded history human groups and individuals, who obviously had some form of identity
and consciousness, did not have national identity or consciousness, and did not
belong to nations, because nations did not exist. The division of mankind, and
of the political universe, into nations is, to borrow a word from Benedict
Anderson (1991), a matter of a specific «imagination.» 500 years ago nations
did not exist, because human collectivities were not imagined as nations.
Nationalism, as a general phenomenon (rather than as a perverse form of national sentiment), thus is a particular way of seeing – a modern perspective or
a style of thought.[1] It is a cultural construction, an historically contingent phenomenon, and thus, in a certain sense, an accident. For millennia, humanity
was able to do without it, and this represents a good reason for presuming that
it can be avoided again.

1 The principles of nationalism

The nationalist «imagination» rests on two principles – the principle of popular sovereignty and the principle of fundamental equality of membership in
the community – which reflect the idea of the nation as it emerged in the course
of a complex semantic, and more generally socio-cultural, evolution.[2] The presence of these principles allows us to define as nationalisms otherwise quite

---

1   The concept «style of thought» was coined by Karl Mannheim in his essay «Conservative Thought» (1953).
2   See Introduction to my *Nationalism: Five Roads to Modernity* (1992).

dissimilar systems of ideas and sentiments. The differences among them correspond to the often dramatic differences in the interpretation and institutional realization of the two principles and, as a result, in their effects on human experience.

A largely unquestioned assumption in the field – at least since Hans Kohn's (1961) pioneering work, *The Idea of Nationalism* – has been that nationalism is just an expression (though the fullest expression) «of the oldest and most primitive feelings of man» and that national identity is but another name for (a fully developed) identity as such. This is a misconception. No human group of any duration, and no individual, unless severely handicapped or (as an infant) mentally undeveloped, can live without an identity. Having an identity appears to be a psychological imperative, and therefore, a sociological constant. But there is nothing imperative in the development of any specific identity. None of the many identities human beings and groups can have and in the course of history have had (not even gender identity, as we now know) is objectively necessary: they are all a matter of social – cultural – construction. None of them – not the tribal, not the religious, not the national identity – is determined by the immutable logic of social forces. They result from historical contingency, the unpredictable ramble of history, rather than the orderly march of directed social evolution.

An identity defines the position of its bearer (which may be an individual or a group) in, and serves as a map or blueprint for, a certain, more or less extensive, sphere of the social world, with the help of which this world, in fact, is constantly reconstructed. An identity, every identity, in other words, represents a means of constructing and defining the social reality of the bearer. The social importance of an identity increases with the importance and size of a group that shares it, but even more so with the extent of its applicability.[3] The modern national identity has been the most generally applicable identity for those who have acquired it from the moment of its acquisition – and today this is so for the majority of the world population.

Whatever its kind, a generally applicable or «fundamental» identity, which is believed to define the bearer's very essence, shapes behavior in a wide variety of contexts. It also reflects – in effect, contains in a microcosm – the image of the social order or the *social consciousness* of the given society. This makes na-

---

3   For example, the «national identities» of foreign communities in Rome, of students in medieval universities
    or merchants in the trading centers of Flanders and Brabant, and of parties of the church councils provided
    guidelines for relatively narrow spheres of the actors' social lives (in addition to applying to very small
    groups of actors); they were at most as important as other partial – for example, gender, family, local – identities of these actors, and certainly less important than their religious identities.

tionalism the framework of the fundamental identity in the modern world, and also the framework of the modern social consciousness. It implies nothing less than that in the modern world social consciousness takes the form of national consciousness. Nationalism is the cultural framework of modernity; it is its main cultural mechanism of social integration, and therefore, construction. It is the order-creating cognitive system which invests with meaning, and as a result shapes, our social reality, or the cognitive medium, the prism through which modern society sees this reality.

The difference between nationalism and national identity, on the one hand, and other order-creating cultural systems, for instance, religion, and identities reflecting them, on the other, is at least as great as the difference between modern society, which represents the implementation of the principles of nationalism, and other types of societies. Few principles are capable of immediate and unproblematic translation into reality. Nevertheless, one can clearly see the two principles of nationalism, the principle of popular sovereignty and the principle of the fundamental equality of membership, reflected in the modern political and social structure, specifically in the institution of the state and the class system of social stratification.

All polities that define themselves as nations, as well as those which claim membership in the community of nations without being defined as nations themselves (such as modern empires: for example, the Russian and Austro-Hungarian empires in the beginning of this century, and the Soviet Union in the end of it) adopt an impersonal, legal-rational, or *state,* form of government which, in principle, has a representative character. The state is an implication of the principle of popular sovereignty. The authority it exercises emanates neither from itself, nor from the transcendental sources beyond the nation, but from the nation. This principle applies equally to polities which are representative democracies in actual fact and to modern dictatorships which dispense with representative institutions. What allows for such differences in the implementation of the same principle are differences in the definition of the nation, which this essay addresses below. The principle itself, however, materially affects the general experience of politics and life, in modern societies, bestowing previously unknown dignity upon those who, *in principle,* did and could not see themselves as represented in and by the power wielded over them and even, theoretically speaking, had no share in it. It is this in-principle-impersonal and representative character of political authority in nations, which permits openly authoritarian modern regimes to insist on their democratic character.

The principle of equality of membership and the inclusive character of national identity is responsible for the most important structural implication of nationalism: the change in the nature of social stratification. In distinction to prenational social formations, nations – or modern societies – develop the open, *class,* system of stratification. The class system is based on achievement, rather than ascription, and has the individual, rather than the family, as the unit, and transferable properties, such as money and education, rather than birth, as the basis of status distinctions. Though achievement may be variously defined and education and wealth ascribed different relative importance, all societies defined as nations accept social mobility as legitimate in principle and allow considerable, though different, rates of mobility in practice. This, ideally open form of stratification also, obviously, has a tremendous effect on the experience of life in modern societies. On the one hand, it makes each and every one of us the maker of our own destiny, increasing our sense of control and empowerment and adding excitement to life, which, by definition, becomes less predictable. On the other hand, by making life less predictable, it creates an inherently anomic, and thus stressful, environment, oppressing us with choices which must be made and the responsibility for our success or failure, and depriving us of the sense of security and peace of mind which come with predictability and limited possibilities.

Every modern society experiences dignity and empowerment to a degree unknown to any society before it, and every modern society to a degree heretofore unknown suffers under conditions of pervasive anomie and disorientation. This is what the experience of modernity is, and it is directly related to the structures of the state and class stratification, in turn directly related to the twin principles of nationalism, which provide the cognitive framework of modernity – popular sovereignty and fundamental equality of membership.

2   Nationalism, patriotism and ethnicity

The failure to realize the specificity of nationalism not only forces one to lose sight of its historical social context – namely, the empirical context in which it must, and apart from which it cannot, be understood – and leads to vague and futile theorizing. In addition, it diverts attention from the issues central to nationalism and focuses it on marginally related phenomena and side-effects, contributing to further conceptual confusion. This confusion is most widespread in regard to the relations between nationalism, patriotism, and ethnicity.

Patriotism is often seen as a reflection of underlying national consciousness, and sometimes as the positive side or expression of nationalism which can also have negative expressions – «good nationalism» so to speak. In fact, however, patriotism is not necessarily connected to nationalism; the concept denotes «love of country,» *patria* – the land of one's fathers, and is a natural sentiment that is likely to exist whether or not one's community is defined as a nation. The civic sentiment of classical antiquity – attachment and dedication to the city – is the paradigmatic example of patriotism, but the image of the social order it reflected was very different from the one contained in nationalism, and the institutional, structural reality constructed on the basis of this image was different too. Different from both – the classical and the modern, national patriotism – was the idea of patriotism prevalent during the Middle Ages in Europe: Christian patriotism. The Heavenly Kingdom – *la patrie celeste* – was the true *patria* of a Christian, and it is there, rather than in any earthly domain, that his supreme loyalty was due. Patriots were those who, like the Crusaders, loved and fought for God above all.

National patriotism, in distinction to the classical attachment to the city and Christian attachment to the *patrie celeste,* is the love of the nation. Of course, it may take the form of love of a particular plot of land, as in classical patriotism. But this is not always so; more importantly, it is not such love of land which is definitive of national patriotism. National patriotism, in fact, is more akin to Christian patriotism, for it is, too, primarily a dedication to an ideal. It is the love of principles of social organization – first and foremost, the two constitutive principles of nationalism, and also additional principles selected by a particular nation. American patriotism, perhaps, reveals this idealistic nature of modern, national patriotism most clearly. «Give the American his institutions, and he cares little where you place him,» wrote Charles Mackay in 1837. But patriotisms associated with other nationalisms, particularly of the civic variety (see below) share this idealistic character.

As the American example demonstrates, the identification of nationalism with territorial particularism is misleading. Possession of a particular territory was the clinching element in Stalin's classic definition of the nation, still very much in use among the students of nationalism. But there is no reason to defer to Stalin's opinions in this area of study: they are as unwarranted as in linguistics, medicine, or any other academic discipline in which this «coryphaeus of scholarship» dabbled in his spare time. Most nationalisms indeed become attached to a certain territory, if not from the moment of emergence (which happens very often), then eventually. But territory does not breed nationalism. In the American case, as a matter of fact, it was nationalism that bred territory. In general, nationalism is not a particular case of territorialism; it belongs to a different class of phenomena. It is a cultural system, an order-shaping socio-political perspective. As such, in principle, it can be equally well applied to the entire world, as to any territorial unit within it. A world polity with a sovereign populace in which all the members were considered fundamentally equal would be a perfect nation within the framework of nationalism.

Patriotism always reflects some identity; in many cases it had reflected the development of a unique identity whose geo-political framework and/or name were at a later point inherited by the nation that was constructed in the place of the earlier social order. However, such a unique identity, the consciousness of being French or Chinese, for example, can no more than territory serve as a proxy for national identity and an evidence of nationalism. Both uniquely French and Chinese identities existed for centuries before the development of the French and Chinese national identities. The French national identity, indeed, was the third in line of unique French identities. The first one of these, which existed between the 12th and 16th centuries, was a religious one, with France defined as a church and Frenchness as a particular kind of (Catholic) Christianity. The second was a political identity whose constitutive element was the authority of the French kings – France was the king's domain, Frenchness was coterminous with the status of a subject; this identity existed between the 16th and the later 18th centuries. Though the name of France and, by and large, its borders remained, each time the nature of the French identity changed, the society that existed under this name and within these borders was transformed. France was imagined differently and thus was no longer the same France.

The view that a unique identity is evidence of nascent or even mature nationalism reflects an equally unwarranted notion, shared by many nationalists as well as students of nationalism, that the world is naturally, or primordially, divided into objectively different *ethnic* units, and that it is this objective difference between them, or their *ethnicity,* which underlies national divisions and gives rise to national identities. Among the recent theorists of nationalism, this view is common to the so called modernists, who insist on the modernity of nationalism, as well as to the primordialists who consider modern nationalism an outgrowth, or recent expression, of ubiquitous ethnic divisions between human collectivities. The differences between these two positions are differences in emphasis, rather than in fundamental conception. Representatives of both regard nationalism as a modern phenomenon and assume a link between nationalism and ethnicity, which they implicitly define as identity naturally resulting from various ascriptive characteristics. The reason for this affinity is that primordialists as well as modernists work within the long dominant (sociological) structuralist paradigm. In their discussions of nationalism, they attempt to provide a structural explanation of the activation of ethnic characteristics in the conditions of modernization, and their effectiveness as a basis of political mobilization in the service, or oriented towards the establishment, of a separate state. However, theories representative of the modernist position emphasize the structural conditions of modernization as the chief determinant of the emergence and character of nationalism and nations. Theories representative of the primordialist position, in distinction, place the emphasis on what they consider to be the raw matter out of which nationalism and nations are fashioned by modernization – ethnicity.[4]

Ascriptive characteristics, covered by the term «ethnicity» fall into cultural and physical categories and minimally include «language, religion, and race» (Ghai 1994), but also physical type more generally, as well as common territory, common history, and secular traditions. It is obvious that, in this sense, ethnicity is in fact ubiquitous. All of us inherit certain physical and cultural characteristics: unless we wear colored lenses, our eyes are a certain color we have not chosen; we have certain, genetically determined, complexion; our families, neighborhoods, and cities into which we are born often have their specific traditions, accents, and even dialects. But the ubiquity of ethnicity does not translate into the ubiquity of ethnic identities and does not automatically divide people into ethnic groups. Indeed, there is nothing natural or primordial in such ethnic division; much of it results from cultural construction along national principles.

Anyone's ascriptive characteristics – ethnicity – necessarily differ from those of many others within one's society; it follows that all societies are ethnically diverse. Nevertheless, in some societies we do not notice this diversity and consider them «homogeneous», while in others such diversity is distinctly and often painfully visible. This is so not because there is less diversity among individual members of one society, in-so-far as their ascriptive, cultural and physical, characteristics are concerned, than of another, but because the same measure of ethnic diversity is *perceived* differently. This is to say that not every society attaches cultural significance to ethnicity or makes it an element of its members' general identity. Very few societies before the modern age, if any, did so. In the framework of nationalism – the defining cultural system of the modern age – ethnic characteristics are often assigned cultural significance and are incorporated in people's national identities. But this is not because ethnicity is in any way conducive to nationality. «Ethnic» characteristics form a certain category of raw material which can be organized and rendered meaningful in various ways, thus becoming elements of any number of identities. National identity, in distinction, provides an organizing principle applicable to different materials (among which ethnic material may or may not be included)

---

4   The most notable proponent of the primordialist position, despite himself, is Anthony D. Smith (1986).

to which it then grants meaning, transforming them thereby into elements of a specific identity. Moreover, when ethnicity is utilized in the process of nationalist cultural construction, it is not the actual existence of certain ethnic characteristics which determines the ethnic profile of a group. Of the available ethnic characteristics only some are selected, not the same ones in every case, and the choice, in addition to the availability or even salience of the selected qualities, is determined by many other factors. In addition, no clear line separates selection from artificial construction. A language of a part may be imposed on an entire population and declared native to the latter (or it may be outright invented, as was the case with Russian). An «ancestral» territory may be acquired in conquest, «common» history fabricated, traditions imagined and projected onto the past.

Similarly, cultural significance attached to ethnic differences between populations is rarely proportionate to their «objective» magnitude. Very often these differences are minimal or virtually non-existent, but, when perceived as culturally significant, they are magnified – often to the point of being turned into a cultural rift that cannot be bridged. The vast majority of cases of ethnic violence are rooted in such nationalist construction of ethnicity. The former Yugoslavia, and in particular Bosnia, serves as a striking example of minimal differences being magnified and turned murderous by the cultural significance attached to them in the context of nationalism. The differences between Serbs, Croats and the so-called «Bosnian Muslims» are mostly in the imagination. These three groups of Southern Slavs belong to the same race and look the same; they speak Serbo-Croatian – the same language; their religion, which has been made so much of recently, cannot, in practice, be used to distinguish between them, because overwhelming majorities in each of them are (or were until the eruption of the recent conflict) non-believers. These facts are overlooked because the identities of Serbs and Croats have been traditionally defined as ethnic identities (and since these identities reflect the way these groups envision the world, they necessarily define as ethnic the identities of members of the third group, the descendants of Slavic Muslims in Bosnia). The definition of a «fundamental» identity as ethnic presupposes a belief that a person's inclinations, attitudes, and behavior are determined ascriptively, by the group to which one is born, which, in effect, means genetically – that they are given, so to speak, in the blood, and though they can be hidden or suppressed, cannot, under any circumstances, really be changed. One is a Serb, a Croat, or a Bosnian Muslim, in other words, every moment of one's life and in everything one does, whether one is aware of this or not. Such attitudes may create a conflict situation where none existed before and render any conflict irresolvable. They are quite independent of the ethnic realities – real differences in ascriptive characteristics – that obtain in any particular case, and, instead, represent cultural perceptions of ethnicity which give rise to a new reality.

3   Problems with definitions

It is futile to look for the sources, and understanding, of nationalism in any of the «objective» characteristics of nations. Nationalism is a kind of imagination and it reflects the autonomy of its parent faculty. The focus on «objective» characteristics, the assumption that nationalism, like any cultural system, must be an emanation of tangible, material realities, is the main source of the conceptual problems that have plagued its study. It is a reflection of these problems that most recent theories leave nations and nationalism essentially undefined. Aware of the persistent failure of the earlier scholarship to come up with an adequate definition, many students of nationalism today approach it as undefinable in principle. Some authors openly declare that since before them «nobody has been able to provide precise definitions» of the phenomena in question, one «must settle for composites of characterization» or, in other words, limit one's aspirations to description (Nielsson 1985: 27). The lack of a definition, however, severely encumbers the possibilities of analysis. It prevents effective operationalization of hypothetical relationships and makes it impossible to locate the origins of nationalism in time with any degree of precision. As a result, while the argument of many recent theories hinges on the assumption that nationalism was antedated by other modern developments, there is no possibility of testing, and therefore either substantiating or refuting this assumption. Unable to muster the evidence required by the logic of their propositions, these theories have to rely on the conclusions of older historical scholarship, which have been persistently called into question.

Sometimes, definitions are proposed, but end in circular statements or are abandoned midway. An example of the former problem is Ernst Gellner's influential 1983 contribution, *Nations and Nationalism*. The book, appropriately, opens with a definition of nationalism, postulating that it is «a political principle, which holds that the political and national unit should be congruent.» Defining «nationalism» by reference to an undefined «national unit» is obviously circular, but occurring as the definition does in the opening paragraph of the text, this does not, as such, present a problem. Several lines later the statement is reiterated in a slightly modified form. The reader is told that «nationalism is a theory of political legitimacy, which requires that ethnic boundaries should not cut across political ones.» The conclusion one must draw from the juxtaposition of the two statements is that «national unit» means an «ethnically bounded unit,» or that nationality equals ethnicity. Since ethnic boundaries are treated as unproblematic, which presupposes the ubiquity of ethnic identity, thus the equation of ethnic identity with generalized identity as such, one is further led to conclude that what Gellner means by «nationalism» is the accentuation of ethnic identity, any identity, that is, in the final analysis, politicization of an identity.

Perhaps unwilling to draw such conclusions, Gellner insists that his definition of nationalism was «parasitic» on the «as yet undefined» term «nation» and proceeds to explicitly define, or rather «pinpoint,» «this elusive concept» with the help of «two very makeshift, temporary definitions». The first one suggests that «two men are of the same nation if and only if they share the same culture, where culture in turn means a system of ideas and signs and associations and ways of behaving and communicating». The second definition proposes that «two men are of the same nation if and only if they *recognize* each other as belonging to the same nation». «A mere category of persons (say, occupants of a given territory, or speakers of a given language, for example)», explains Gellner in this context, «becomes a nation if and when the members of the category firmly recognize certain mutual rights and duties to each other in virtue of their shared membership in it. It is their recognition of each other as fellows of this kind which turns them into a nation, and not the other shared attributes, whatever they might be, which separate that category from non-members.» (Gellner 1983: 17).

The implications of the first definition are empirically untenable. According to it, two people sharing the same culture, for instance two dedicated professors of Russian literature, one in St. Petersburg, another at Yale, would necessarily be of the same nation. On the other hand, two Russians, for instance the St. Petersburg professor of literature and an illiterate peasant from a Siberian village, who obviously don't share the same culture in Gellner's sense, would not be fellow-nationals. Such implications make this definition quite unhelpful.

The second definition represents a reformulation of Renan's classical statement «une nation est un plebiscite de tous les jours». Whether one interprets it in the strongly subjectivist sense and regards a nation as a community *willed* into being by its members, which was, probably, Renan's intention, or moderates this subjectivism by transforming a will into a recognition, as does Gellner, its meaning remains essentially the same. It means that a nation is a community which is regarded as a nation, whether because its members so decide or because, as sentient beings, they recognize it as such. Either way, being a circular definition *par excellence,* it begs the question. The question is why do people decide to see, or recognize, their community as a nation, rather than as a class, as a Church, as a dynastic realm, or what not; in other words, the question with which we began: what is a nation? That is, this is the question unless a nation is simply a politicized identity, as the opening definitions of the book suggest. In that latter case, the issue is no longer that of the nature, and specificity, of the nation. It is, rather, what makes an identity politicized. It should be pointed out that this interpretation turns Gellner's definition into a reiteration of Kohn's (1961: 4) 1944 statement that «the growth of nationalism is the process of integration of the masses of the people into a common political form», which suggests a prior existence of, and focuses attention on, a modern, bureaucratic and centralized government over a large territory.

Benedict Anderson, the author of perhaps the most famous book on the subject in recent decades, proposed a novel definition, already intimated in the title: his book of «reflections on the origin and spread of nationalism» was called *Imagined Communities* (Anderson 1991). Anderson (1992: 6) proposed to define the nation as «an imagined political community – and imagined as both inherently limited and sovereign». This definition did point to the nature of nationalism. Unfortunately, it stopped short of in fact defining it, namely of distinguishing it from other, similar phenomena. The reason for this, paradoxically, is again the belief in the essential materialism of social reality and the epiphenomenal, not really real, character of everything that is not material, such as imagination.

To start with, even if we leave aside the question of the alleged inherent limitation of the nation (which, as was indicated above, is an occasional, rather than necessary element), the nation is not the only entity to which Anderson's definition applies. For example, a class such as the proletariat, in the Marxian scheme of things, would also be an imagined, political, limited, and sovereign community. It would be some other things too, but, of course, Anderson does not imply that the nation is nothing but the complex of features included in the definition. A Church, certainly for the periods in which the political sphere was subsumed under, or confounded with, the religious, would also be such a community, if we assume that anyone under God could be sovereign (which, as it happens was the assumption behind discussions of sovereignty in the Middle Ages). If we place an emphasis where, presumably, Anderson places it, given the title – namely on «imagined», the definition opens up completely. Every large-scale human community – a city, a neighborhood, a university, a professional association – is imagined, and for the same reason that Anderson (1991) mentions: «because the members ... will never know most of their fellow-members, meet them, or even hear of them, yet in the minds of each lives the image of their communion».

Moreover, defining the nation as imagined, Anderson clearly stresses the act of imagining in the sense of mental representation, rather than the content of imagination or the nature of the image. This leads to the focus on the conditions of this act (what makes this imagining possible) and thus on the limits of the community (it is easier to visualize a limited community, than a limitless one). In fact, taking up Gellner's proposition that nations are «invented», therefore artificial, communities, Anderson (1991) says: «Communities are to be distinguished, not by their falsity/genuineness, but by the style in which they are imagined.» But he does not develop this idea, and instead of the style of imagination, namely characteristics that make a society imagined as a nation different from a society imagined as a dynastic realm, or as a class, or as a Church, he focuses on the conditions – such as print capitalism – which make it possible to visualize a certain large, but nevertheless delimited, territory as a community, or, rather, as a category of belonging and a source of one's identity.

4   Three types of nationalisms

Though by and large nationalism is treated as a uniform phenomenon, most scholars recognize the existence of two types of nationalism. This typology is conceptualized in different sources as «political vs cultural» nationalisms, «Western vs Eastern» nationalisms, and, more recently, «civic vs ethnic» nationalisms. Like many other elements in the scholarship on nationalism, this conventional dichotomy is also derived from the seminal work of Hans Kohn; it reflects, and was originally intended to capture, certain conspicuous differences in the historical record of the nations whose development Kohn described.

The three pairs of categories focus attention on the same dividing line, but with a slightly different emphasis. While it is generally agreed that all nationalisms are in some sense cultural and political, the dichotomy «political vs cultural» stresses the relative salience and historical priority of principles of political organization vs preoccupations with language, literature, history and folklore in various nationalisms. The «Western/Eastern» dichotomy reflects the fact that while the archetypal example of «political» nationalism in Kohn's and other historical scholarship was France – a «Western» nation *par excellence,* most examples of «cultural» nationalism were drawn from Eastern Europe, specifically Slavic countries. Of course, the archetypal case of «cultural» nationalism – Germany – could not be easily placed in either the «East» or the «West» – geographically, it belongs in Central Europe, and some other examples of «cultural» nationalism, such as Italy, simply do not fit the dichotomy at all. Using it would incongruously define Germany and Italy as Eastern nations.

But, in fact, «East» and «West», in this context, and as categories in the social sciences generally, are cultural, rather than geographical markers. A «Western» nation is implicitly defined as a «civic» nation, and an «Eastern» nation as an «ethnic» one, therefore, these concepts contribute little to the use of that latter dichotomy. The categories «civic» and «ethnic» closely correspond to the «political» and «cultural» types, with a greater emphasis, perhaps, in the case of «civic» on the concept and institution of citizenship, and an implicit under-standing, in the case of «ethnic», that preoccupations with language, history, and folklore reflect a belief in deeper, «natural», that is, in effect, biological, forces behind them, such as race or «blood and soil», which form the ultimate reality underneath nationhood and national identity. The concepts «civic» and «ethnic» are useful, but they do not capture all of the significant differences (i.e., differences which are translated into differences in political and social in-stitutions and behavioral patterns) between historical nationalisms. Moreover, when taken as descriptive categories, intended to briefly characterize these na-tionalisms – which is indeed the inspiration behind them – they cannot explain any of these differences and thus lack explanatory value.

Empirically, one can distinguish three types of nationalism, each one of which has distinctive implications for the ways of thinking and behavior within socie-ties they help define, which are significantly different from the implications of other types. These types can be identified as an «individualistic-civic» type, a «collectivistic-civic» type, and a «collectivistic-ethnic» type of nationalism. This typology is analytical, rather than descriptive. At its basis lie not the differen-ces which the three types of nationalism produce, but the differences in the initial conceptions of the nation, which produce them.

The initial conception of the nation – the new, nationalist, image of society – must include two elements: the nature of the nation as a whole, and the nature of the human parts that compose the nation. The nation as a whole can be seen either as a composite entity, a collectivity formed by the association of in-dividuals, or in unitary terms, as a collective individual. The former conception results in the *individualistic* nationalism – the individualistic vision of the new social order, the latter – in a collectivistic vision, *collectivistic* nationalism. (It is important to keep in mind that both categories, «individualistic» and «collec-tivistic», are markers of social consciousness and of collective, namely shared, representations. To borrow Durkheim's phrasing, both concepts refer to the ways in which society – the nation – is represented to its members: i. e., as a composite or a unitary entity, not to the motivations of the members or the firmness of their commitment. Historically, individualistic nations have com-manded national patriotism as intense as, and more widespread than, that of collectivistic nations. Both the rates of desertion, in times of war, and of emigration, in times of peace, in individualistic nations have been lower than in others.).

The definition of the nation as a composite entity, as was the case with the original nationalism in England, and the other societies that adopted the English model, assumes the moral, political, and logical primacy of the human individual, who is seen not simply as a physical unit of society, but as its constitutive element, in the sense that all the qualities of the latter have their source in the nature of the former. The nation – which, in the framework of nationalism in general, is seen as a sovereign (fully independent and self-governing) community of fundamentally equal members – in the framework of this composite definition derives its freedom from the essential liberty of the individuals who compose it; while its dignity, and the dignity of national identity, reflects the natural dignity of each human being. Such dignity and liberty (which are, of course, inherently linked) make the members of the nation equal, and this equality is realized in the social and political arrangements that set individualistic nations apart from others. The principles at the foundation of individualistic nationalisms are none other than the principles of liberal democracy, which individualistic national consciousness fosters and sustains.

The definition of the nation in unitary terms, by contrast, promotes collectivist forms of social and political organization, which are conceptualized as «communism,» «socialism» of one kind or another, or «socialist» and/or «popular» democracy. Collectivistic nations share in common a predilection for authoritarian politics and, as a result, pronounced inequality in social life, at least in the relationship between the rulers and the ruled. This authoritarianism is a logical implication of perceiving the community as an individual in its own right – and one morally superior to human individuals – with a will, interests, and purpose of its own, which have priority over and are independent of the wishes and aspirations of its human members. The will, interests, and purpose of the nation are not directly known to the members and have to be deciphered and interpreted for their benefit by a specially qualified elite. This all-important service gives new meaning to the concept of representation: the elite, in such cases, represents the nation to the people, rather than representing the people. This service also establishes those who provide it in a position of vast superiority to the rest. The equality of membership that is implied in nationalism is contradicted by this superiority and is, therefore, reinterpreted and limited, becoming in the political sphere a matter of make-believe.

The other implication of nationalism, popular sovereignty, is also reinterpreted, becoming the attribute of the nation as separate from the people who compose it, and, as such, lying not in political arrangements that ensure individual liberties, but in collective freedom from foreign domination. Finally, the dignity of the nation, and of national identity is, in the framework of collectivistic nationalisms, no longer a reflection of the dignity of individuals, but is instead inherent in the nation as such and is only communicated to individuals by virtue of their membership in it.

The second element of the definition of the nation – the nature of the human parts that compose it – is in fact the definition of the criteria of membership in the nation, or nationality. It is here that one can usefully utilize the conventional distinction between civic and ethnic nationalisms. Indeed, membership in the nation can be conceived of either in civic or in ethnic terms. In the former case, nationality is equated with citizenship and is seen as an essentially political and even legal category, implying a commitment to certain rights and duties, which is, in principle, embraced voluntarily. Being, at least theoretically, a matter of choice, nationality can be acquired and lost. Though it is presumed that every person at any point in time has a nationality, and that one's choice is limited to selecting among various national identities, it is conceivable, in the framework of civic nationalism, that one could be without a nationality altogether. When nationality is defined in ethnic terms, by contrast, it is no longer conceived of as a matter of choice, but, instead, as an ineluctable, biological necessity. It is believed that one cannot be without a nationality as one cannot be without an essential bodily organ; one is born with a particular nationality and can never lose it; at best (or at worst) one's national identity can be concealed. In some mystical, but essentially biological, natural process, completely independent of human volition, nationality, in this framework, is thought to be transmitted by blood, as an inherent, genetic characteristic. It is also thought to determine one's interests and sentiments and is expected to project itself naturally and unreflectively in one's sense of attachment and commitment to the nation. It should be noted that ethnic homogeneity of a population (whether linguistic, racial, or other), even when seen as a characteristic of a nation, does not necessarily result in ethnic nationalism. France, perceived as ethnically homogeneous, for instance, is a civic nation.

The two dimensions of the definition of the nation result in the three types of nationalism mentioned above, because the composite definition of the nation as a whole, with its emphasis on the logical and moral priority of the individual, implies a civic concept of nationality. Consequently, individualistic nationalism is necessarily civic. The definition of the nation in unitary terms, however, is commensurate with both civic and ethnic criteria of membership, allowing for the existence of civic and ethnic varieties of collectivistic nationalism. The components of individualistic-civic nationalism, on the one hand, and of collectivistic-ethnic nationalism, on the other, mutually reinforce each other, and bolster the liberal tendencies of the former and the authoritarian proclivities of the latter. But the combination of a collectivistic definition of the nation as a whole with civic criteria of nationality unites these contradictory propensities and creates an ambivalent and inherently problematic type. The first historical nationalism, which appeared in 16th century England, belonged to the individualistic-civic type. The second type to emerge – with France as its first case – was collectivistic-civic. The third type was that of collectivistic-ethnic nationalism. It first developed in Russia, but its paradigmatic case became German nationalism. This third type of nationalism was destined to become the most widespread; most nationalisms developing in the late nineteenth and the twentieth centuries belong to it.

These categories should be regarded as models which can be approximated, but are unlikely to be realized fully. They serve to pinpoint certain characteristic tendencies within different, specific nationalisms. In reality, the most common type is the mixed one. But the compositions of the existing mixtures vary significantly enough to justify their classification in the above terms and render these terms analytically useful.

5 Conclusion

What makes the nation – culturally constructed and successfully avoided (to use the terms of the assignment) throughout most of history – appear unavoidable today, that is, in the present and the foreseeable future, is above all the lack of alternatives. No other image of the social order, no other cultural system that forms a framework for identity, seems to be able to perform the role that nationalism performs for us and to deliver the goods to which it made us accustomed. The remarkable quality of national identity which distinguishes it from other identities – and also its essential quality – is that it guarantees status with dignity to every member of whatever is defined as a polity or society.[5] It is this quality that recommended nationalism to European (and later other) elites whose status was threatened or who were prevented from achieving the status they aspired to; that ensured the spread of nationalism throughout the world in the last two centuries; and that explains its staying power in the face of the economic interests that ostensibly pull in the other direction.

The great majority of human beings had not known dignity before the age of nationalism, but its experience proved addictive, and it is safe to assume that in modern society people will never agree to be deprived of the dignity which

---

5   On this point see «Transcending the Nation's Worth», *Daedalus*, 22/3: 47–62 (Summer 1993).

they acquired with nationality. The possibility of the transcendence of nationalism, therefore, depends on the availability of alternative guarantees of dignity, on finding (or inventing) a functional equivalent of nationality in this respect. The only significant challenge to nationalism in the past two centuries was Marxism, which offered a dignified identity to members of nations which were regarded – by their own elites – as inferior, such as Russia, or, for a brief period of time, Italy. Its hold on their attachments, however, has proven, on the whole, rather weak (see Talmon 1991).The collapse of communism and the Soviet Union, eliminated Marxism as a basis of an alternative identity (although its rhetoric is still used to promote certain nationalist interests).

Fluctuations in the appeal of nationalism were invariably related to the ability of a particular nation to guarantee and safeguard the dignified status of its members (whether of all, or of a specific group) and to the existence of (or belief in) other possibilities for status-enhancement. They have been quite independent of economic trends and changes in technology and communications (the «material infrastructure» of society), to which nationalism has so often been attributed. On the whole, such fluctuations, and attempts to transcend nationalism, have been very rare, both because nationalism usually has been able to satisfy people's need for dignity, and because for the great majority there were no alternative ways to satisfy this need. Economic globalization is unlikely to weaken the grip of nationalism on humanity; it is largely irrelevant to the problem of nationalism. It remains appealing even when economically (and otherwise) irrational, and if the nation is going to be replaced by a community imagined differently, it is most improbable that this will be on the account of economic development.

The most we can do about the nation – in principle avoidable, but one we cannot now avoid – is to understand it. This is what we must do as scholars. Knowledge, as this case clearly demonstrates, is not always power, but this is not a reason to persist in our mistakes.

References

Anderson, Benedict (1991). *Imagined Communities: Reflections on the Origin and Spread of Nationalism.* New York: Verso (2nd Edition).

Gellner, Ernest (1983). *Nations and Nationalism.* Ithaca: Cornell University Press.

Ghai, Dharam (1994). *Opening Statement for the International Seminar on Ethnic Diversity and Public Policy.* New York: United Nations.

Greenfeld, Liah (1992). *Nationalism: Five Roads to Modernity.* Cambridge (Ma): Harvard University Press.

Kohn, Hans (1961). *The Idea of Nationalism: A Study in its Origins and Backgroud.* New York: Macmillan.

Mannheim, Karl (1953). «Conservative Thought», pp. 74–165. *Essays on Sociology and Social Psychology.* New York: Oxford University Press.

Nielsson, G. (1985). States and «Nation-Groups»: a Global Taxonomy, pp. 27–56 in E. A. Tiryakian and R. Rogowski (eds.). *New Nationalisms of the Developed West.* Boston: Allen and Unwin.

Smith, Anthony D. (1986). *The Ethnic Origins of Nationalism.* Oxford: Basil Blackwell.

Talmon, Jacob (1991). *Myth of the Nation and Vision of Revolution.* New Brunswick (USA): Transaction Publishers.

The Manichean Myth: Rethinking the Distinction between «Civic» and «Ethnic» Nationalism

Rogers Brubaker

From its late nineteenth century beginnings to the present, the study of nationhood and nationalism has been marked by deep ambivalence and intractable ambiguity. On the one side, nationalism has been associated with milita-
rism, war, irrationalism, chauvinism, intolerance, homogenization, forced assimilation, authoritarianism, parochialism, xenophobia, ethnocentrism, ethnic
cleansing, even genocide; it has been characterized as the «starkest political
shame of the twentieth century» (Dunn 1979: 55). On the other side, nationhood and nationalism have been linked to democracy, self-determination, political legitimacy, social integration, civil religion, solidarity, dignity, identity, cultural survival, citizenship, patriotism, and liberation from alien rule.

One reason for the ambivalence, of course, is that «nation» and «nationalism»
designate a whole world of different things. To a great extent, the ambivalence
reflects not so much competing understandings and evaluations of the same
thing, as alternative uses of the same term. Much of the ambivalence, that is,
has been rooted in ambiguity. How people have evaluated nationalism has de-
pended on what they have understood it to be.

Recognition of the protean quality of «nation» and «nationalism» – and of the
normative ambivalence and conceptual ambiguity surrounding the subject –
has engendered innumerable attempts at classification. Some typologies have
been elaborate. In his early book *Theories of Nationalism,* for example, Anthony Smith classified national movements by the «formal» criteria of «intensity» and «achievement» and by the «substantive» criteria of «independence»
and «distinctiveness.» The former yielded 6 types, the latter 12; cross-classify-
ing them, with some simplification, yielded no fewer than 39 types for which
Smith found corresponding historical or contemporary instances (Smith 1983:
211–229). Most classifications, however, have been quite simple, often founded
on a single dichotomous distinction. And such distinctions have often been intended to do both normative and analytical work.

The most well known distinctions – between voluntaristic and organic, political and cultural, subjective and objective, liberal and illiberal, and civic and
ethnic forms of nationalism – overlap to a great extent. They have an illustrious
pedigree, going back to Friedrich Meinecke's distinction between *Staatsnation*
and *Kulturnation* at the beginning of the century (Meinecke 1919) and, more

immediately, to Hans Kohn's influential midcentury work (Kohn 1944), usually glossed as distinguishing between «Western» and «Eastern» forms of nationalism.[1]

Of these overlapping distinctions, the one with the greatest resonance today, especially outside the narrow circle of researchers working primarily on nationalism, is the distinction between civic and ethnic understandings of nationhood and forms of nationalism. On this view there are, at bottom, only two kinds of nationalism: civic nationalism, characterized as liberal, voluntarist, universalist, and inclusive; and ethnic nationalism, glossed as illiberal, ascriptive, particularist, and exclusive. These are seen as resting on two corresponding understandings of nationhood, based on common citizenship in the first case, common ethnicity in the second.

Sometimes, as in Kohn's work, this distinction is projected in space, and used to contrast the civic nationalism of Western Europe, or of «the West» in general, with the ethnic nationalism of Eastern Europe or other world regions. Such grand contrasts of world regions easily acquire a neo-orientalist flavor and lend themselves to the invocation of a dubious series of linked oppositions – between universalism and particularism, inclusion and exclusion, civility and violence, reason and passion, modern tolerance and ancient hatreds, transnational integration and nationalist disintegration, civic nationhood and ethnic nationalism.[2]

But this is not the typical way the distinction is used. The triumphalist – or, at best, complacent – account of Western civic nationalism is too obviously problematic for this view to be seriously entertained. The unexpected (and partly nationalist) resistance to the Maastricht treaty; the longstanding violent conflicts in northern Ireland and the Basque country; the intensifying ethnopolitical conflict in Belgium; and the electoral successes of xenophobic parties in many countries – all these have made it impossible to hold such an uncritical view of the essentially «civic» quality of West European nationalism.

More common is the use of the civic-ethnic opposition to make distinctions between states – or between national movements – rather than between whole

---

1   Actually Kohn himself did not speak of «Eastern nationalism»; but his principal distinction was indeed between «the West» and «the rest,» between the original forms of nationalism that developed in the «Western world» – in England, France, the Netherlands, Switzerland, and the United States – and those that later developed elsewhere, in the first instance in Germany and Central Europe, later in Eastern Europe and Asia.

2   While Kohn has been justly criticized for overgeneralizing about Western and non-Western forms of nationalism, and for downplaying differences among Western European and among Central and Eastern European forms of nationalism, it is important to underscore that *The Idea of Nationalism* is a vastly more nuanced and sophisticated book than most contemporary critics acknowledge.

world regions. This is often done in an ideological mode, to distinguish one's own good, legitimate civic nationalism from the illegitimate ethnic nationalism of one's neighbors or of other polities or movements, specified or implied. The leaders of post-independence Ukraine and Kazakhstan, for example, have self-consciously used the language of civic nationhood to present their states – especially to international audiences – as paragons of civic inclusiveness and tolerance, as the states of and for all their citizens, rather than as states of and for a single ethnocultural group. They – and scholars sympathetic to their cause – have pointed to their inclusive citizenship legislation, liberal language laws, and rhetoric of civic inclusiveness to mark a contrast with Estonia and Latvia, with their restrictive citizenship legislation, tough language laws, and rhetorical emphasis on ethnocultural survival.

Many separatist movements, too, use this self-legitimating language of civic nationalism. The general election manifesto of the Welsh nationalist party Plaid Cymru, for example, proclaims its commitment to a «civic nationalism [that] welcomes all those living in Wales to join us in finding the solutions to [social and environmental] challenges and in restoring the equilibrium of social justice and environmental sustainablity in Wales and Europe.»[3] Scottish National Party leaders emphasize even more strongly the party's civic nationalism, especially its inclusive, residentially based definition of Scottishness. So pronounced is this emphasis that a fringe nationalist group opposed to the SNP's rhetoric of civic nationalism has caustically criticized the «hogwash about being Scottish just because you happen to live in Scotland ... it is to be hoped that Scottishness will, through means of education and restored ethnic consciousness, cease to be the sad joke which in many cases it has become.»[4]

Scottish nationalist leaders generally like to align themselves with the Catalan, Québécois and other regional nationalisms. Yet they are willing to distance themselves from these movements to underscore their own commitment to civic nationalism. For example, after the narrow defeat of the Quebec sovereignty referendum in 1995, notoriously blamed by Québécois separatist leader Jacques Parizeau on the «ethnic vote,» SNP leader Alex Salmond said that «Quebec is not Scotland and Scotland is not Quebec ...The linguistic and ethnic basis of their nationalism is a two-edged sword. ... we follow the path of civic nationalism».[5] For their part, Quebec nationalists have sought in recent years to project a more «modern,» unifying image of civic nationalism. But Parizeau's gaffe, together with a remark a few weeks earlier by separatist lea-

---

3   (General Election Manifesto, cited from http://plaid-cymru.wales.com/policy/ manifesto.htm).
4   Siol nan Gaidheal, Scottish Cultural and Fraternal Organization, Statement on «Race, Ethnicity, and Nationality» (http://www.siol-nan-gaidheal.com/raetna.htm).
5   The Scotsman, November 1, 1995.

der Lucien Bouchard about the low birth rate of Québécois, allowed critics of Québécois nationalism to turn the civic-ethnic distinction back against their opponents. To cite but one of many examples, the *Toronto Globe and Mail,* Canada's leading Anglophone newspaper, characterized Québécois separatism as «rooted in ethnic rather than civic nationalism. Blood is more important than citizenship».[6]

Paralleling this frankly political use of the civic-ethnic distinction to legitimate or discredit particular state policies or nationalist movements is its use in a scholarly mode to draw distinctions between different instances of nationalism and different modes of national self-understanding. Often this scholarly accounting of nationalism – bestowing the imprimatur of the civic on some states or movements, denying it to others – itself belongs to the sphere of nationalist politics in a broad sense. There is nothing new about this; for a century and a half, scholars have been participants in, and not mere observers of, nationalist politics. But the work done by the notion «civic,» with its normative prestige, in such accounts may be more political than analytical: it may speak more to the putative international respectability and legitimacy of the state or movement in question than to its empirical characteristics.

In recent years, many scholars of nationalism have grown uncomfortable with the unequivocal sorting of cases into «civic» and «ethnic» categories. From a detached, analytical point of view, as numerous commentators have pointed out, it is often impossible, or at best problematic, to characterize an entire state, or an entire national movement, simply as civic or ethnic. As a result, efforts have been made to use the distinction in a more abstract manner. Instead of being used to characterize concrete cases, it is now most often used to characterize opposed analytical «elements» or tendencies and to show how they are mixed in different manners and proportions in concrete cases. Indeed so prevalent in the literature is this notion that individual states or national movements display a mixture of civic and ethnic elements or tendencies that it can be said to constitute a kind of theoretical «common sense.»

In the hands of sophisticated observers such as Anthony Smith, whose *Ethnic Origins of Nations* was particularly influential in promoting it, this use of the civic-ethnic distinction to designate analytical elements that are found in concrete cases «in varying proportions at particular moments of their history» (Smith 1986: 149) is certainly an improvement over the unequivocal sorting of states and nationalist movements as a whole – to say nothing of entire regions

---

6   Reported in Washington Post, October 18,1995. On media over-reaction to Parizeau's gaffe, see Seymour et
     al. (1998: 29).

– into «civic» or «ethnic» categories. Yet even in this more abstract and analytical mode, I want to argue, the civic-ethnic distinction remains both analytically and normatively problematic. It is to this argument that I now turn.[7]

1   Analytical ambiguities

Let me begin with what I see as the analytical weakness of the civic-ethnic distinction. Both terms are deeply ambiguous. Their ambiguity can be highlighted by asking how culture fits in to the civic-ethnic scheme. There are in fact two very different ways of mapping culture onto the civic-ethnic distinction, but I will argue that neither is satisfactory.

What is «ethnic» about ethnic nationalism? Advocates of the civic-ethnic distinction have a ready answer: nation-membership is understood to be based on ethnicity. But this simply pushes the question one step back. What is «ethnicity»? As analysts going back to Max Weber have emphasized, «ethnicity» is an exceedingly ambiguous notion.[8] Consider here just one aspect of that ambiguity, involving the relation between «ethnicity» and culture.

On the one hand, ethnic nationalism may be interpreted narrowly, as involving an emphasis on descent, and, ultimately, on biology. «Strictly speaking,» as Anthony Smith noted in his first book on nationalism, «ethnicity refers to common descent» (Smith 1983: 180). Yet construing ethnicity narrowly in this manner severely constricts the domain of ethnic nationalism. For as Smith himself went on to observe, many «commonly accepted «nations» ... do not invoke a common ancestor,» and even when nationalist argumentation does in-

---

7   The core of the argument that follows was presented in «Myths and Misconceptions in the Study of Nationalism,» presented first as a paper to the Center for European and Russian Studies, UCLA, in March 1996, and published in Brubaker (1998). Since that paper was written, three other critiques of the ethnic-civic dichotomy have appeared: Yack (1996), Seymour et al. (1998) and Schnapper (1998). Although there are convergences between parts of Yack's and Seymour et al's arguments and my own, they examine the civic-ethnic distinction primarily from the point of view of normative political philosophy. (For related arguments in political theory, see also Fine (1994), Nielsen (1996), and Xenos (1996).) Schnapper, on the other hand, is a sociologist, but her argument is quite different from mine. As Seymour et al. point out (p. 25), Schnapper claims to be problematizing the civic-ethnic distinction, but in effect does so by endorsing and re-stating the civic account.

8   As Max Weber observed, «the collective term ‹ethnic› ... is unsuitable for a really rigorous analysis,» for it «subsumes phenomena that a rigorous sociological analysis ... would have to distinguish carefully: the actual subjective effect of those customs conditioned by heredity and those determined by tradition; the differential impact of the varying content of custom; the influence of common language, religion and political action, past and present , on the formation of customs; the extent to which such factors create attraction and repulsion, and especially the belief in affinity or disaffinity of blood; the consequences of this belief for social action in general, and specific for action on the basis of shared custom or blood relationship, for diverse sexual relations, etc. ... Thus the concept of the «ethnic» group ... dissolves if we define our terms exactly.» (Weber 1968: 94f.).

volve «imputed common descent,» this is «usually a minor claim» (p. 180f.).[9] On the strict understanding of ethnicity, nationalist rhetoric emphasizing common culture, but not common descent,[10] has to be coded as a kind of civic nationalism.[11] But then the category of civic nationalism becomes too heterogeneous to be useful, while that of ethnic nationalism is severely underpopulated.

On the other hand, «ethnic» may be construed broadly, as ethno*cultural.* This is the path Smith chose in *Theories of Nationalism,* treating «‹ethnic› [as] identical with the term ‹cultural›, without further specification» (1983: 180). In this case, the problem is just the opposite: virtually all nationalisms would have to be coded as ethnic. Thus for Eric Hobsbawm, «Every separatist movement in Europe ... bases itself on ‹ethnicity›, linguistic or not, that is to say on the assumption that ‹we› – the Basques, Catalans, Scots, Croats, or Georgians are a different people from the Spaniards, the English, the Serbs or the Russians.» (Hobsbawm 1996: 256). By defining «ethnicity» so expansively that it is coextensive with a sense of separate «peoplehood», however that sense of peoplehood is grounded, Hobsbawm codes as «ethnic» what others often classify as «civic» – Catalan and Scottish nationalism, for example. Civic nationalism is thereby defined out of existence or, as on Hobsbawm's account, relegated to an earlier phase of historical development.

---

9   In later work, Smith revised this view, and came to attribute greater importance to imputed common descent. In *The Ethnic Revival,* Smith argues – implausibly, in my view – that a «myth of common and unique origin in time and place» is «essential for the sense of ethnic community», and notes that «cultural dimensions remain secondary ... to the sense of common origins and history of the group. This constitutes the core of the group's identity, and of its sense of uniqueness.» (Smith 1981: 66f.). *The Ethnic Origins of Nations,* in turn, qualifies this view: «if one cannot point to alleged filiation and imputed common ancestry for all citizens, one can at least trace one's cultural pedigree back to some antique exemplars which, allegedly, embodied the same qualities, values and ideals that are being sought by the «nation-to-be» today» (Smith 1986: 147).

10   A further difficulty is that the notion of «common descent» is itself ambiguous. It too can be interpreted strictly or loosely. Strictly speaking, common descent implies descent from a single common ancestor. Loosely interpreted, common descent involves some rhetoric emphasis on common ancestry or common «blood,» without the implausible specification of a single common ancestor. (Still more loosely interpreted, as in Anthony Smith's recent work, it shades over into a rhetorical emphasis on common «ideological» rather than «genealogical» descent; see Smith (1986: 147f.) How do we know whether there is a signficant emphasis on common descent? Germany, for example, is often treated as a paradigmatic case of ethnic nationalism. Yet can one seriously maintain that there was a strong emphasis on common descent at Bismarck's time? Surely it is not enough to quote Bismarck's urging Germans to «think with your blood», as Walker Connor (1994: 93, 198) does, especially when Bismarck's consistently statist orientation, and his distance from all manifestations of voelkisch nationalism, is well documented in the literature. Nor is it enough to point to the exclusive reliance on *jus sanguinis* in German citizenship law. *Jus sanguinis* is a legal technique that is the foundation of citizenship law throughout continental Europe, France included. The distinctive consistency with which the principle has been carried though in German law indeed requires explanation, and I have tried in *Citizenship and Nationhood in France and Germany* to provide such an explanation (Brubaker 1992), but I do not think one take a legal principle for regulating membership of the state as a direct indicator of widely shared social understandings of what constitutes membership of the nation.

11   This assumes, of course, that the civic-ethnic distinction is understood to be exhaustive, which is how it is usually treated: understandings of nationhood are said to be *either* civic *or* ethnic.

Nor is ambiguity limited to the term «ethnic.» The category «civic» is equally ambiguous. On the one hand, civic nationalism may be interpreted strictly, as involving an acultural, ahistorical, universalist, voluntarist, rationalist understanding of nationhood. «The nation» is then construed as a voluntary association of culturally unmarked individuals. Nation-membership is understood as chosen rather than given, as a «daily plebiscite,» in Renan's celebrated metaphor.

Yet construing civic nationalism strictly in this fashion risks defining the phenomenon out of existence. Even the cases most often cited as paradigmatic of civic nationalism – France and America – involve a crucial cultural component or, in Hobsbawm's terms, a strong sense of separate peoplehood.[12] A purely acultural understanding of nationhood has never been widely held. It is a model of nationhood that has never been instantiated, existing only as a conceptual ideal type. Even as an ideal type, it is problematic. Although Ernest Renan is often cited as the locus classicus for this model, this reflects a one-sided reading of his famous lecture. The «daily plebiscite» remark – a self-conscious rhetorical flourish which Renan prefaced by asking his audience to «pardon the metaphor» – does indeed underscore the importance, for Renan, of the importance of subjective self-understanding in constituting nationhood (Renan 1996: 53). But Renan's understanding of nationhood is far from acultural or purely voluntaristic. It is a «thick,» not a «thin» understanding. Renan stresses the constitutive significance of the «possession in common of a rich legacy of memories»; he characterizes the nation as «the culmination of a long past of endeavors, sacrifice, and devotion» (p. 52). In this sense, the nation is «given» as well as «chosen».[13]

On the other hand, civic nationalism may be defined broadly. The definition offered by Michael Keating, a sympathetic yet sophisticated analyst of Scottish, Catalan, and Quebecois nationalisms, is worth quoting at length. Keating defines civic nationalism as a collective enterprise

> «rooted in individual assent rather than ascriptive identity. It is based on common values and institutions, and patterns of social interaction. The bearers of national identity are institutions, customs, historical memories and rational secular values. Anyone can join the nation irrespective of birth or ethnic origins, though the cost of adaptation varies.

---

12 Two recent books argue for the existence of an American cultural nationality. Against the «exceptionalist» view that sees American nationhood as uniquely and purely political, as founded on an idea, they see America is a nation-state founded on a common, and distinctive, American culture (Hollinger 1995, Lind 1995).

13 The argument here parallels Yack (1996: 197f.).

There is no myth of common ancestry ... [Nationhood is] based on territorially defined community, not upon a social boundary among groups within a territory. This is not to say that any piece of real estate can form the basis for a nationalism. There need to be a structured set of political and social interactions guided by common values and a sense of common identity.» (Keating 1996: 5–6).

Keating wants to have it both ways. He retains the rationalist, universalist emphasis on choice characteristic of «thin» understandings of civic nationalism. At the same time his more sociologically realistic understanding of nationhood pushes him to acknowledge the importance of «common values,» «customs,» «historical memories» and a «sense of common identity.» Yet these are just the sort of particularist, thick, given factors highlighted by broad, culturalist understandings of ethnicity. The factors highlighted by Keating are not all that different, for example, from the quartet of «myths, memories, values, and symbols» emphasized by Anthony Smith in *The Ethnic Origins of Nations.*

To sum up the argument so far: A narrow understanding of ethnicity severely constricts the domain of ethnic nationalism and leaves the residually defined civic category too large and heterogeneous to be useful. Conversely, a narrow understanding of the civic severely constricts the domain of civic nationalism and leaves the residually defined ethnic category too large and heterogeneous to be useful. If one combines a strict understanding of civic and a strict understanding of ethnic nationalism, then one is left with few instances of either one and a large middle ground that counts as neither, and one can no longer think of the civic-ethnic distinction as *exhaustive* way of classifying types or manifestations of nationalism. If one combines, finally, a broad understanding of civic and a broad understanding of ethnic nationalism, one confronts a large middle ground that could be classified either way, and one can no longer thing of the civic-ethnic distinction as *mutually exclusive.*

Advocates of the civic-ethnic distinction would argue that this large middle group consists of cases that combine civic and ethnic elements. But the problem is not that it is difficult to know, on balance, how to classify a «case.» The problem is rather that the deep ambiguity of the terms «civic» and «ethnic,» and in particular the uncertain place of culture in the civic-ethnic scheme, calls into question the usefulness of the distinction itself. It can be just as difficult to classify an «element» as it is to classify an entire «case.»

How, for example, are we to classify policies designed to promote a particular language at the state or provincial level? From the point of view lyrically articulated by Benedict Anderson, for whom the nation is «conceived in language, not in blood,» and is therefore «joinable in time» (Anderson 1991: 145), there can be nothing «ethnic» about such policies, even if they might be judged re-strictive, illiberal, or even chauvinistic. Indeed, from another point of view one could go further and characterize such policies as positively civic, that is, as in-dispensable for the promotion of republican citizenship. The assimilationist language politics of the French Revolution was justified in just such a civic idiom in Abbé Grégoire's report «On the necessity and means of abolishing the patois and universalizing the use of the French language.» Only when all citizens speak the same language, the report argued, can all citizens «commu-nicate their thoughts without hindrance» and enjoy equal access to state of-fices (de Certeau et al. 1975: 302) And as John Stuart Mill put it 65 years later: «Among a people without fellow-feeling, especially if they speak different lan-guages, the united public opinion, necessary to the working of representative government, cannot exist» (Mill 1975: 382).

From another point of view, however, linguistic nationalism is simply a particu-lar expression of ethnic nationalism. When «ethnic» is understood broadly as ethnocultural, or simply as cultural without qualification, then to conceptua-lize the nation as a community of language, to demand autonomy or independ-ence in the name of such a community, to limit access to citizenship to per-sons knowing the language, and to promote or require teaching, publishing, broadcasting, administering, or advertising in that language count as central, indeed paradigmatic manifestations of ethnic nationalism.

2 Normative ambiguities

The distinction between civic and ethnic understandings of nationhood and forms of nationalism is not only, or even primarily, an analytical distinction. It is also, at the same time, a normative one. This fusion of analytical and norma-tive criteria was characteristic already of Hans Kohn's work. Kohn's portrayal of pioneering Western nationalisms joined neutral analytical observations about their «predominantly political» character, reflecting the fact that national con-sciousness developed within the framework of existing states, to a normative celebration of the spirit of «individual liberty and rational cosmopolitanism» that he saw as informing such nationalisms. Similarly, his portrayal of the later nationalisms of Germany and central and Eastern Europe joined neutral ana-lytical observations about their initially cultural character, reflecting the fact that national consciousness developed outside of and in opposition to the frame-work of existing states, to a normatively charged evocation of the illiberal ten-dencies that he saw as inherent in those nationalisms (Kohn 1944: 329–331).

Even as the distinction has been stripped, in most uses, of the concrete spatial reference given to it by Kohn, it has retained the same normative valence. Civic nationalism is generally glossed as liberal, voluntarist, universalist, and inclusive, ethnic nationalism as illiberal, ascriptive, particularist, and exclusive. Except for the opposition between universalism and particularism, which finds contemporary partisans on both sides, it is hard to imagine a more normatively loaded, one-sided characterization. Who could have a good word for a form of nationalism routinely glossed as illiberal, ascriptive, and exclusive? How could one criticize a form of nationalism understood to be liberal, voluntarist, and inclusive? When civic and ethnic nationalism are paired, the former is invariably a term of praise, the latter a term of abuse.

Yet although the normative opposition seems unambiguous, matters are in fact more complicated. Take for example the characterization of civic nationalism as inclusive and of ethnic nationalism as exclusive.[14] In fact all understandings of nationhood and all forms of nationalism are simultaneously inclusive and exclusive. What varies is not the fact or even the degree of inclusiveness or exclusiveness, but the bases or criteria of inclusion and exclusion.[15]

Civic understandings of nationhood are glossed as inclusive for one of two reasons. The most common is that the civic nation is based on citizenship, and therefore includes all citizens, regardless of their particularistic traits. But citizenship itself, by its very nature, is an exclusive as well as an inclusive status. On a global scale, citizenship is an immensely powerful instrument of social closure (Brubaker 1992). It shields prosperous and peaceful states from the great majority of those who – in a world without borders and exclusive citizenries – would seek to flee war, civil strife, famine, joblessness, or environmental degradation, or who would move in the hope of securing greater opportunities for their children. Access to citizenship is everywhere limited; and even if it is open, in principle, to persons regardless of ethnicity, this is small consolation to those excluded from citizenship, and even from the possibility of applying for citizenship, by being excluded from the territory of the state. This «civic» mode of exclusion is exceptionally powerful. On a global scale, it is probably far more important, in shaping life chances and sustaining massive and morally arbitrary inequalities, than is any kind of exclusion based on putative ethnicity. But it is largely invisible, because we take it for granted. Only among philosophers and political theorists, in recent years, has there been some attention to issues such as open borders, or some moves to recast Rawlsian accounts of jus-

---

14   For recent exampes, see Ignatieff (1993), Kupchan (1995), and Khazanov (1997).
15   For a treatment of the civic/ethnic distinction that recognizes this point, see Breton (1988).

tice on a global scale[16]. In wider spheres of public debate, this kind of closure and exclusion is simply never questioned.

Civic understandings of nationhood have also been characterized as inclusive because they comprise «all those – regardless of race, color, creed, gender, language, or ethnicity – who subscribe to the nation's political creed» (Ignatieff 1993: 6). The emphasis on a constitutive political creed echoes an older literature on American nationalism, according to which American national identity was essentially ideological and therefore uniquely open.[17] That view has been much criticized in the last two decades, notably by Rogers Smith, who sees American understandings of nationhood as pervasive informed, for much of the country's history, by an ethnocultural or «inegalitarian ascriptive» strand of thinking as well as by liberal and republican strands (R. Smith 1997: 2ff, 14ff). But even apart from its historical accuracy in the American context, the creedal model of membership has its own logic of exclusion. The French Revolution provides the paradigmatic examples of such exclusions – of emigrés, refractory priests, noblemen, rebels, and other presumed political opponents. At the opposite end of the political spectrum, McCarthyism provides the paradigmatic example in the American context. But it is worth remembering that even in Germany – often treated as the key exemplar of ethnic nationalism – Catholics and Social Democrats were excluded from the moral community of the nation in Bismarck's time and characterized as internal «enemies of the Reich» not by virtue of ethnicity, but by virtue of their imputed lack of loyalty to the national state.

Understandings of nationhood as based on citizenship or political creed, then, are not *more* inclusive, but *differently* inclusive – and exclusive – than understandings of nationhood as based on cultural community or common descent. And not only are the *exclusions* on which they are premised normatively problematic, but so too, in certain contexts, is their very *inclusiveness.* Transylvanian Hungarians, for example, resent and resist the putatively inclusive, citizenship-based rhetoric of nationhood which construes them as members of the Roma-

---

16 On open borders, Carens (1987) is a pioneering statement. For the more general argument that the Rawlsian «original position» should be interpreted on a global scale, see Beitz (1979).

17 Drawing on Hans Kohn's influential account (Kohn 1957), Philip Gleason argues that «To be or become an American, a person did not have to be of any particular national, linguistic, religious, or ethnic background. All he had to do was to commit himself to the political ideology centered on the abstract ideals of liberty, equality, and rpeulbicanism. Thus the universalist ideolgoical character of American nationality meant that it was open to anyone who willed to become an American» (Gleason 1980: 32). To be sure, the overwhelming British stock of white American settlers at the end of the eighteenth century meant there was a «latent predisposition toward an ethnically defined concept of nationality ... [But] such exclusiveness ran contrary to the logic of the defining principles, and the offiical commitment to those principles has worked historically to overcome exclusions and to make the practical boundaries of American identity more congruent with its theoretical universalism» (p. 33).

nian nation. On their own self-understanding, they are citizens of the Romanian state, but members of a Hungarian cultural nation that cuts across the boundaries of state and citizenship.

In the early 1980s – to take another example – some second-generation Algerian immigrants protested against the French nationality that had been attributed to them automatically at birth. For reasons having to do with a technicality of French citizenship law, they had been unaware of this attribution until, upon reaching age 16 and applying for residence permits as foreigners, they were stupefied to be told by officials that they were French. While some welcomed this news – French nationality, after all, would protect them against expulsion – others «experienced the attribution of French nationality as a violation of their personality, their familial attachments, and their membership of a newly emancipated [Algerian] nation» (GISTI 1983: 6), and several thousand formally requested – in vain – to be released from the nationality that had been attributed to them without their knowledge, against their will, and in violation of their self-understanding as Algerians. The Algerian government too objected to the unilateral imposition of citizenship on «its» emigrants; after «the years of murderous conflict aimed precisely at giving them their own nationality,» [142] this was regarded as a neocolonial affront to Algerian sovereignty.

The conventional gloss of civic and ethnic understandings of nationhood as voluntaristic and ascriptive, respectively, is also problematic. In the first place, it is greatly overdrawn. Only on implausibly acultural and ahistorical construals of civic nationalism can nation-membership be understood as entirely voluntary; on richer and more realistic accounts, including Renan's own account, as we have already seen, the nation is understood as given as well as chosen. On the other hand, choice is far from irrelevant in settings where nationhood is understood to be based on ethnocultural commonality such as Central and Eastern Europe, usually considered the *locus classicus* of ethnic nationalism. As Hobsbawm observed, commenting on the «paradoxes of primordial ethnicity,» «early twentieth century Europe was full of men and women who, as their very names indicate, had *chosen* to be Germans or Magyars or French or Finns» (Hobsbawm 1996: 260–259, emphasis in the original).

Moreover, the normative valence of the opposition between chosenness and givenness is more complex than the loaded contrast between voluntary and ascriptive suggests. Liberal moral and political theory have indeed celebrated voluntary engagements, commitments, and affiliations over ascribed statuses. But the communitarian critique of liberalism (Sandel 1982), and the development of a variant of liberalism more sensitive to the cultural contexts of choice (Kymlicka 1989) have led to an enhanced appreciation of the ways in which choices are meaningful only against the horizon of unchosen cultural contexts. And this in turn has led to a tempering and relativization of the opposition between chosenness and givenness.

I have mentioned Kymlicka in connection with newly «culturalist» accounts of liberalism. But he has also, of course, been a central figure in recent discussions of multiculturalism (Kymlicka 1995). These discussions, too, have problematized the normative opposition between civic and ethnic nationalism. By valorizing particular cultural attachments and identities – including ethnic or ethnocultural attachments and identities – and by seeing the public recognition of such particularistic attachments as central to and supportive of rather than antithetical to citizenship (even to *liberal* citizenship, on Kymlicka's account), multiculturalism destabilizes and relativizes the normative contrast between civic and ethnic nationalism.

3   A modest alternative

From an analytical point of view, a less ambiguous distinction than that between civic and ethnic nationalism can be drawn between *state-framed* and *counter-state* understandings of nationhood and forms of nationalism. In the former, «nation» is conceived as congruent with the state, and as institutionally and territorially framed by it. In the latter, «nation» is imagined as distinct from, and often in opposition to, the territorial and institutional frame of an existing state or states. The former is equivalent to Meinecke's notion of the *Staatsnation;* the latter, however, is a wider category than Meinecke's *Kulturnation.*

There is not necessarily anything «civic» – in the normatively robust sense of that term – about state-framed nationhood or nationalism. It is the state – not citizenship – that is the cardinal point of reference; and the state that frames the nation need not be democratic, let alone robustly so.[18] The sense of «nation» that developed gradually in *ancien régime* France was framed by the state from the beginning, but it became linked to ideas of citizenship only during the Revolution. To take another example, when Prussian reformers sought to transform Prussia into a «nation» in the early nineteenth century, to «do from

---

18   In the notion of civic nationalism, the reference to citizenship is ambiguous. What does it mean for nation-membership to be based on citizenship? In a thin sense, it means only that nationhood is framed by the state, and that the nation is understood to comprise all citizens – or subjects – of the state. In a thicker sense, it implies some connection to active citizenship, to civic participation, to democracy. It is these latter connotations that give the notion of civic nationalism its normative prestige. Once again, the conflation of analytical and normative criteria engenders ambiguity, which the normatively neutral notion of state-framed nationalism permits us to escape this ambiguity.

above what the French had done from below,» as one of the leading reformers put it, the «nation» they envisaged – Prussian, not German! – was conceived as framed by the state, yet one could not characterize it as based on citizenship. The same is true of the nationalisms of many authoritarian contemporary states.

Moreover, the notion of state-framed nationhood or nationalism enables us to talk about the way in which linguistic, cultural and even (narrowly) ethnic aspects of nationhood and nationalism may be framed, mediated, and shaped by the state. For while there is a definitional antithesis between *civic* nationhood and ethnicity – and on some interpretations between civic nationhood and culture – there is no such antithesis between *state-framed* nationhood and ethnicity or culture. State-framed nationalisms are often imbued with a strong cultural content.[19] France, for example, is a paradigmatic instance of state-framed nationhood. At the same time, culture is understood as constitutive of French nationhood.[20] There is no contradiction here. The culture that is understood to be constitutive of nationhood is a pervasively state-framed, and, in modern times, state-propagated culture; it is not conceived as prior to and independent of the territorial and institutional frame of the state.

Counter-state nationalisms, on the other hand, need not be specifically ethnic; nationhood conceived as distinct from or in opposition to an existing state need not be conceived in ethnic terms, or even, more loosely, in ethnocultural terms. Quite apart from the difference, discussed above, between narrowly ethnic and broadly ethnocultural under-standings of nationhood, counter-state definitions of nation may be based on territory, on historic provincial privileges, or on the possession of a distinct political history prior to incorporation into a larger state. Early anti-Habsburg Hungarian nationalism, for example, was couched in the idiom of historic constitutional privileges until the end of the eighteenth century, when increasing emphasis began to be placed on protecting and developing the Magyar language. An intriguing contemporary example is furnished by Northern Italian regional nationalism, in which «Padania» (the term is from the Po river valley) is conceptualized not simply as a «region» but as a north Italian «nation» entitled to national self-determination.

---

19 As Anthony Smith (1986:136) puts it, albeit in language too functionalist for my taste, «territorial nations must also be cultural communities. The solidarity of citizenship required a common «civil religion» formed out of shared myths and memories and symbols, and communicated in a standard language through educational institutions. So the territorial nation becomes a mass educational enterprise. [Its] aim is cultural homogeneity. Men and women must be socialized into a uniform and shared way of life and belief-system, one that ... marks them off from outsiders.» (*Ethnic Origins of Nations*, 136).

20 I believe now that I was mistaken when I argued in earlier work that «political unity has been understood as constitutive, cultural unity as expressive of nationhood.» (Brubaker 1992:10).

Moreover, even when the nation in question is defined in cultural or ethnic terms, counter-state nationalisms may partake of «civic» qualities. This is most evident in cases such as Catalonia, Scotland, or Quebec where there is an institutionally defined sphere within which a substantial degree of self-government is possible (Keating 1996). But even counter-state nationalist movements without a formally secured sphere of institutionalized autonomy within the larger state can provide settings for the cultivation and exercise of «civic» virtues – for example by organizing and running schools, credit associations, cooperative enterprises, and welfare organizations.

4 Conclusion

The civic-ethnic distinction addresses important analytical and normative issues, but it does not do so in a satisfactory fashion. It can be seen as a routinization and codification of the various efforts scholars have made to come to terms with the normative ambivalence and empirical ambiguity surrounding the protean phenomena grouped under the umbrella term «nationalism.» It represents an effort to domesticate these normatively and empirically unruly phenomena, to impose conceptual and moral order on them, to subsume them under a convenient formula, to render them suitable grist for academic mills.

Yet nationalism resists neat parsing into types with clearly contrasting empirical and moral profiles. Distinctions are of course unavoidable in analytical and normative inquiry alike, but we should not expect too much of a single distinction. The civic-ethnic distinction is overburdened; it is expected to do too much work. We would do better to disentangle the work of analytical ordering from that of normative appraisal. The distinction between state-framed and counter-state understandings of nationhood is offered as one very modest way of doing some of the analytical work done by the civic-ethnic distinction without the attendant confusion. The inexhaustible moral and political ambiguities and dilemmas generated by nationalism can then be addressed on their own terms.

References

Anderson, Benedict (1991). *Imagined Communities: Reflections on the Origin and Spread of Nationalism*. London: Verso Press.

Beitz, Charles (1979). *Political Theory and International Relations*. Princeton: Princeton University Press.

Breton, Raymond (1988). «From Ethnic to Civic Nationalism: English Canada and Quebec», *Ethnic and Racial Studies* 11(1): 85–102.

Brubaker, Rogers (1992). *Citizenship and Nationhood in France and Germany*. Cambridge (Mass.): Harvard University Press.

Brubaker, Rogers (1998). «Myths and Misconceptions in the Study of Nationalism», pp. 272–305 in John Hall (ed.). *The State of the Nation: Ernest Gellner and the Theory of Nationalism*. Cambridge: Cambridge University Press.

Carens, Joseph (spring 1987). «Aliens and Citizens: The Case for Open Borders», *The Review of Politics* 49: 251–273.

Connor, Walker (1994). *Ethnonationalism: The Quest for Understanding*. Princeton (NJ): Princeton University Press.

De Certeau, Michel, Dominique Julia and Jacques Revel (1975). *Une politique de la langue: La Révolution française et les patois*. Paris: Gallimard.

Dunn, John (1979). *Western Political Theory in the Face of the Future*. Cambridge: Cambridge University Press.

Fine, Robert (1994). «The ‹New Nationalism› and Democracy: A Critique of *Pro Patria*», *Democratization* 1(3): 423–43.

GISTI (Groupe d'information et de soutien des travailleurs immigrés) (January 1983). «Note sur les jeunes Algériens en France». Paris.

Gleason, Philip (1980). «American Identity and Americanization», pp. 31–58 in Stephan Thernstrom, Ann Orlov, and Oscar Handlin (eds). *Harvard Encyclopedia of American Ethnic Groups. Cambridge* (MA): Belknap Press of Harvard University.

Hobsbawm, Eric J. (1996). «Ethnicity and Nationalism in Europe Today», pp. 255–66 in Gopal Balakrishnan (ed.). *Mapping the Nation*. London: Verso.

Ignatieff, Michael (1993). Blood and Belonging: Journeys into the New Nationalism. New York: Farrar, Straus and Giroux.

Keating, Michael (1996). *Nations Against the State: The New Politics of Nationalism in Quebec, Catalonia and Scotland*. New York: St. Martins Press.

Khazanov, Anatoly M. (1997). «Ethnic Nationalism in the Russian Federation», *Daedalus* 126(3): 121–42.

Kymlicka, Will (1989). *Liberalism, Community And Culture*. Oxford: Oxford University Press.

Kymlicka, Will (1995). *Multicultural Citizenship*. Oxford: Oxford University Press.

Kohn, Hans (1957). *American Nationalism: An Interpretative Essay.* New York: MacMillan Company.

Kohn, Hans (1944). *The Ideal of Nationalism: A Study In Its Origins and Background.* New York: Collier Books.

Kupchan, Charles A. (1995). «Introduction: Nationalism Resurgent», in Charles A. Kupchan (ed.). *Nationalism and Nationalities in the New Europe.* Ithaca and London: Cornell University Press.

Lind, Michael (1995). *The Next American Nation.* New York: Free Press.

Meinecke, Friedrich (1919). *Weltbürgertum und Nationalstaat: Studien zur Genesis des Deutschen Nationalstaates.* München and Berlin: R. Oldenburg.

Mill, John Stuart (1975). *Considerations on Representative Government,* reprinted in John Stuart Mill, Three Essays. Oxford: Oxford University Press.

Nielsen, Kai (1996). «Cultural Nationalism, Neither Ethnic Nor Civic», *The Philosophical Forum* 28(1–2): 42–52.

Renan, Ernest (1996). «What is a Nation?», in Geoff Eley and Ronald Grigor Suny (eds.). *Becoming National: A Reader.* New York: Oxford University Press.

Sandel, Michael J (1982). *Liberalism and Limits of Justice.* Cambridge: Cambridge University Press.

Schnapper, Dominique (1998). «Beyond the Opposition: Civic Nation Versus Ethnic Nation», pp. 219–34 in. Jocelyne Couture, Kai Nielsen, and Michel Seymour (eds.). *Rethinking Nationalism.* Calgary, Alberta, Canada: University of Calgary Press.

Seymour, Michel, Jocelyne Couture and Kai Nielsen (1998). «Introduction: Questioning the Ethnic/Civic Dichotomy», pp. 1–61, in Jocelyne Couture, Kai Nielsen, and Michel Seymour (eds.). *Rethinking Nationalism.* Calgary, Alberta, Canada: University of Calgary Press.

Smith, Anthony D. (1986). *The Ethnic Origins of Nations.* Oxford: Basil Blackwell.

Smith, Anthony D. (1981). *The Ethnic Revival.* Cambridge: Cambridge University Press.

Smith, Anthony D. (1983). *Theories of Nationalism.* Second edition. London: Duckworth.

Smith, Rogers (1997). *Civic Ideals: Conflicting Visions of Citizenship in U.S. History.* New Haven and London: Yale University Press.

Weber, Max (1968). *Economy and Society.* Berkeley: University of California Press.

Xenos, Nicholas (1996). «Civic Nationalism: Oxymoron?», *Critical Review* 10(2): 213–31.

Yack, Bernard (1996). «The Myth of the Civic Nation», *Critical Review* 10(2): 193–211.

Multiculturalism, Nation-State and Ethnicity: Political Models for Multi-Ethnic States

Urs Altermatt

In this contribution, I will first discuss various models which show how, in both the past and the present, different multi-ethnic political communities have handled their ethnic diversity. To demonstrate the various approaches to ethnic diversity, I outline four different historical models. I will then examine three policy strategies that can be applied in order to deal with ethnic minorities. Finally, I will argue on a normative level for a multicultural strategy that distinguishes between *demos* and *ethnos,* between political and cultural spheres in multicultural societies and states.

The course of European and American history, as Michael Walzer (1992) pointed out, has given rise to a number of types of multi-ethnic states which had different ways of dealing with cultural diversity. First, there is the multi-nation empire, examples of which include the Roman empire (…) and the Habsburg empire. Here, the basis for co-existence is provided by a legal framework which gives different religious and national groups a certain amount of collective autonomy. In traditional societies, it was the group rather than the individual that was tolerated, especially where the groups lived in homogeneous communities and occupied their own administrative region. Ethnic and religious groups generally respected the cultural and geographical borders, so for most of the time they co-existed peacefully.

A second type consists of states composed of two or three ethnic nations, like Switzerland, Belgium, Cyprus, Lebanon, and former Bosnia-Herzegovina. Provided that there is tolerance between the different religious and ethnic groups, accepted rules can be negotiated according to which the groups can live together, and as long as there is no fear that one group will dominate, the multi-ethnic state can continue to function without breaking up.

A third type is the classic Western nation-state, in which one dominant ethnic group controls public life, organising the state according to its own ideas and making its culture a characteristic feature of the entire nation-state. Generally, nation-states do not grant minority groups the right to be different, although this right is granted to individuals, since cultural difference is viewed as a private, rather than a collective matter.

Finally, there is a fourth type, exemplified by states like the USA, which have come about as the result of immigration. Here, the state provides a political and legal framework, outside of which cultural pluralism is publicly endorsed. This arrangement allows for the integration of groups like the Chinese, who can consider themselves as Americans when in the public sphere, despite the fact that they may maintain a Chinese identity in their private lives.

Historically, ethnic relations have varied greatly, involving considerable discrepancies in access to power, wealth, and social position. The twin concepts of state and territory play a key role in determining inter-ethnic relationships. Our modern notion of the state denotes sovereignty over a precisely delineated territory. The concept supplies a geographical frame within which human society and political power over that society are brought into alignment.

1   Territoriality, state and ethnicity

Territoriality, therefore, plays a decisive role. We will now consider four basic models of the relationships between ethnicity, state, and territory *(Figure 1)*. First, the integration model. The nineteenth and twentieth centuries saw the influx of hundreds of thousands of immigrants into North and South America, Australia, and New Zealand. With a variety of cultures, languages, and religions they moved into vast areas which had previously been thinly populated, sometimes by indigenous groups living a nomadic existence. They spread out and settled together across these large lands.

This ethnic and cultural variety produced an American society, for example, which saw itself as a «melting pot». Most of the immigrants came from Europe, but it is interesting that in North America, the different linguistic groups among the immigrants did not seek to establish any ethnoculturally exclusive territory or «homeland» which might have been given legitimate form as an independent state. Even where there were large concentrations of immigrants from a common background, like the Germans in Wisconsin or the Irish in parts of New England, these groups did not attempt to claim the territories for their own groups. English became the *lingua franca* for the new society, and the different ethnic groups demanded only equal rights with the initially dominant Anglo-Saxon group, focussing mainly on civil liberties and political rights, while the idea of territory as such did not play any significant role.

However, the native Americans were a group apart who were driven from their lands by the society founded by white immigrants, and they remained for many decades peoples without rights. They were even denied their own history, as the pre-colonial history of America had no place in the idea of society which was established by the immigrants.

The immigrants in America intermingled, the different ethnic groups were dispersed and remain so today. But in Europe, the experience has been different. Newcomers have found established ethnic groups which vigorously defended their ancestral territory. In Europe, most peoples have historic lands. Wars may have repeatedly driven hundreds of thousands from their homes, displacing or exterminating large ethnic groups, but people cling to the memory of the homeland. Poland, for example, lived on in the consciousness of its people during more than 125 years of partition. In the nineteenth century, although there was no Polish state and the Poles lived under foreign domination, governments acknowledged the existence of the Polish nation. This contrasts with what happened in America, where the white immigrants were able to partially erradicate the Indian communities and their traditional way of life, while, at the same time, for white immigrants, the American «melting pot» became a powerful force for social integration (Daniel Cohn-Bendit and Thomas Schmid 1992).

Secondly, the co-existence model: Central and Eastern Europe experienced a massive wave of immigration by a variety of ethnic groups in the 17th, 18th and 19th centuries comparable to that which America experienced in the 19th and 20th centuries. Towards the end of the medieval period, many Jews moved east to Poland, where the Polish kings gave them shelter from persecution in Western Europe. In the late 18th and early 19th centuries, there was a wave of German emigration from Germany to Hungary, Poland and, to a lesser degree, Russia. By 1900 Vienna, Budapest, Prague and other central European cities had become prototypes of the multicultural societies which now exist at the end of the twentieth century in cities like London, New York, Paris, Berlin and Zurich. More than any others, these central European cities were the multicultural laboratories of the modern age. With increasing industrialization, these cities grew at a tremendous rate, with hundreds of thousands of people leaving the countryside to look for employment.

In everyday life, the various ethnic communities in these cities were largely socially segregated, living peacefully side by side, rather than together. Elias Canetti, Joseph Roth, and other central and eastern European writers have left us vivid accounts of life in these cities.

Prague may be considered as an example. Until the nineteenth century, Prague was very much a German town.[1] The Charles University had switched from Latin to German as its language of instruction in 1783. In the first half of the nineteenth century, German was the language of the political and cultural elite, with the majority of the working population and the servant classes speaking Czech. In the last decades of the nineteenth century, the situation changed radically. The number of German speakers declined. In 1880, there were 42 000 of them, representing 15% of the city's population. By 1900, only twenty years later, the number had fallen to 34 000 or seven and a half per cent. 40% of the German speakers were now Jews, whose nationality might change from one census to the next. Although German might have been their mother tongue, the census classified them according to the language they used in everyday life. A majority of Jews spoke Czech in their daily interaction with the world, even though German was claimed to be their mother tongue: by 1900, the figure was 55%.

The shift from the dominance of German to that of the Czech language has to been seen against the background of industrialization. The social and economic cause of the increasing importance of Czech in Prague was the migration of many ethnic Czechs from the countryside into the capital, which altered the language balance there. In everyday life, German rapidly became marginalized. In 1882, the Charles University opened a separate section in which Czech was the language of instruction. By the eve of the First World War, Czech had come to dominate cultural milieus as well. There were Czech language schools, theatres, and literary and other clubs and associations.

People with different languages and cultures now sharpened their sense of ethnic or national identity and began to segregate themselves from each other. A harmonious co-existence between the two language communities was no longer possible. According to one historian of the Czech capital, Czechs and German-speakers, living side by side, kept contact between the two groups to a minimum. In 1892, thanks to pressure from Czech nationalists, bilingual street signs went up. *Karpfengasse* became *Kaprova*. While German speakers would go to the *kasino*, Czechs had their own clubs and theatres. For Czechs, Prague's main promenade was the former *Ferdinandova trída* (now called *Národní*), while the Germans frequented *Na Príkopech* off the opposite side of Wenceslas Square.

---

1   For the social and cultural history of linguistic and ethnic groups in Prague, I have relied principally on Le Rider's study of central Europe: Jacques Le Rider, *Mitteleuropa. Auf den Spuren eines Begriffs.* Vienna 1994. Le Rider himself refers to Jean-Pierre Danès' work: *De Kafka à Schweik. Etudes.* Versailles 1989. Otto Urban's monumental study of the second half of the nineteenth century is essential reading (see Otto Urban, *Die tschechische Gesellschaft 1848–1918.* Vol. 1, Vienna/Cologne/Weimar 1994).

In their private lives, people spoke the two languages, but for official purposes they insisted on being either German or Czech. It was thus in people's minds that the link between language and territory began to take shape, that territoriality became concrete. Public space in Prague was divided into German and Czech areas, although clear and extensive territorial divisions could not be established while people from different ethnic groups were living alongside one another in these central and eastern European cities. And indeed, as long as the two groups remained mutually dependent within a single society, there were relatively few problems. The development of modern society has permanently transformed this social system of co-existence with its division of tasks.

Similar tendencies can be observed in the 1980s and '90s in Western Europe. Immigrant workers or asylum seekers do not formally occupy territory, but they tend nevertheless to concentrate in certain areas of large cities, as the Turks do in Berlin or the North Africans in Paris, making integration more difficult.

Third, the autonomy model: The majority of Western European states organized themselves in the nineteenth century according to the following programme: one state, one people, one nation, one culture, one language, and one school system. This left regional linguistic and cultural groups no part in the public arena of the nation-state, so that they either disappeared or were repressed (Gellner 1983; Hobsbawm 1990).

After the Second World War, resistance began to appear in some regions which challenged the cultural hegemony of national cultures dominated by capital cities. Movements for regional autonomy demanded cultural and political independence. Generally, they aimed at cultural autonomy, increased political representation in the central government, and economic support. These movements did not seriously challenge the nation-state as such. The centre and the periphery had already become so intertwined that any separation would inevitably bring great disadvantages for both groups (Altermatt 1996).

One example of significant success is the movement for autonomy in South Tyrol, a German-speaking territory forming part of Italy. We may also mention the process of decentralization in Spain after the end of the Franco era, which led to the creation of *comunidades autónomas:* regional governments with varying degrees of autonomy[2].

---

2   Catalonia published an advertisement in TIME magazine in 1995 in which it introduced itself as «a country in Spain».

Closer examination of the debate about ethnicity and nationality within western European movements for autonomy reveals that territoriality plays a greater role here than in the immigration model or the co-existence model. Cultural regions form more or less closed territories within established nation states. For language communities like the Catalans or Basques, the territories have immense practical and symbolic value. These linguistic and cultural communities are much more firmly anchored in an identification with their territory than are their counterparts in Eastern Europe, even though today's social mobility is tending increasingly to break down the homogeneity of the populations in these territories. Like a number of Swiss cantons, these regions are taking on the role of pseudo-states, which see it as their task to preserve and protect the indigenous culture. In such cases, if one speaks of an ethno-national community, what is meant is a territorially defined community rather than a community of persons. Most old nation-states seem to fear federalization, but in Europe, history shows that the fullest possible degree of political autonomy generally promotes political stability in multicultural nation-states.

Fourth, the separation model. If the dominant group imposes itself too strongly on the minorities, these may lose confidence in the state and revoke its legitimacy. This constellation represents a strong potential risk of separatist attempts. The collapse of the Soviet Empire brought the break up of what was the last multi-nation empire on European soil, an empire that had grouped together many different races, religions, ethnic and language communities. The Russians had been the dominant group in the population, dominating not only politically, but also more or less imposing their language and way of life on the other groups. Like the Czechs and Slovaks after the fall of the Habsburg Empire, in 1989 the Baltic nations, the Belo-Russians, Ukranians, Georgians and others took advantage of the favourable international situation to break away from the former Soviet Union and set up new nation-states. But in these cases, the right to self-determination has proved extremely ambivalent. In many cases, the new political masters mobilized ethno-nationalistic emotions, but defended existing territorial state borders which did not coincide with ethnic, linguistic and cultural boundaries.

Figure 1 shows the importance of various factors for each political model. These factors include territorial, structural, and ethno-political aspects, which are respected or neglected according to the specific conditions of each model.

Figure 1:   Relationships between territory, state and ethnicity

model factor	Integration model	Co-existence model	Autonomy model	Separation model
Importance of territory	weak	weak/ medium/	medium strong	strong
Assimilative power of dominant group	strong	weak	weak	non-existent
Importance of a federalist structure	weak	weak/non- existent	strong	weak
Existence of parallel institutions	weak	weak/ medium	strong	potentially strong but not permitted

2   Strategies of multi-ethnic states toward ethnic minorities

In examining the policies of multi-ethnic states toward ethnic minorities, Inglis (1996) distinguishes three ideal types of strategy. Admittedly, though, concrete political actions do not always coincide with normative positions, and often within a society or a state we will find a lack of congruence between the two levels.

First, we must mention the assimilationist strategy. This model assumes that individuals within ethnic groups renounce their various cultural, linguistic and social characteristics and conform to those of the dominant group. Various cultural, linguistic and social practices are discouraged. The state assumes that through the process of integration, potential or actual ethnic conflicts will be eliminated. If assimilation is achieved, it is because individuals adapt; the state remains in the background.

Second, the differentialist strategy: This model stands in opposition to the first and assumes that potential for conflict is reduced if contacts between different ethnic groups are prevented. Efforts are often made to stop members of ethnic groups from participating in mainstream society. The state may support parallel institutions to meet the cultural and social needs of ethnic minorities, as in Belgium. In extreme cases, however, policies may lead to the expulsion of ethnic groups, as in the Balkans.

Third, the multicultural strategy: This strategy allows ethnic groups to participate fully despite cultural differences. This means that the state has an important part to play in guaranteeing political participation for everybody. Ready
accessibility to citizenship is one of the main prerequisites of this model, and
mainstream political institutions may need to be modified in order to make
this possible.

Figure 2:   Strategies of multi-ethnic states toward ethnic minorities

aspects: / strategies:	assimilationist strategy	differentialist strategy	multicultural strategy
emphasis on the individual	X		X
emphasis on the collective		X	X
willingness to integrate foreigners	X		X
state plays important part		X	X
civic nation	X		X
ethnic/cultural nation		X	

These are abstract models which tell us little about the concrete policies of a
particular state. They represent normative ideological points of reference.
Historically based beliefs about origins of the nation-state and national identity play an important role. Policy is also influenced by the way in which the
state views itself: is it the embodiment of an ethnic nation, as in Germany, or
the product of a daily plebiscite as in France and Switzerland? And in a world
of increasing mobility, does the state see itself as a country which welcomes
new members – immigrants – into its society? *Figure 2* summarizes the characteristics of each one of the three strategies.

Figure 3 below attempts to link the historical types, the political models, and
the strategies employed with regard to ethnic minorities. The first column contains historical types of multi-ethnic communities. The second column shows
the political model applied in each historical case. The third column shows the
strategy that is most likely to be adopted in each political model towards ethnic minorities.

Figure 3: Links between the various models and strategies

Historical models	Political models	Strategies toward ethnic minorities
Multi-nation empire	Co-existence model	Multicultural strategy
Multi-ethnic state	Co-existence model/ Autonomy model	Multicultural strategy/ Differentialist strategy
Classical nation-state	Separation model/ Integration model	Differentialist strategy/ Assimilationist strategy
Immigration state	Integration model	Assimilationist strategy/ Multicultural strategy

As Brubaker (1992) has pointed out, in many cases, more than one model may apply at the same time. Switzerland is a particularly appropriate case in point (Altermatt 1996, 1996a, 1997). For the four different language communities, there is full political recognition at the national level. This is in accordance with the multicultural strategy. However, when individuals living in Switzerland move from one language area to another, they are obliged to use the language of the new area of residence at least for public business, and this is more in line with the differentialist strategy. When we look at the naturalization rules governing the acquisition of Swiss citizenship by immigrants, we find that Switzerland adheres to the principles of *ius sanguinis* and has erected procedural hurdles in order to make the acquisition of citizenship more difficult for immigrants. While countries like Sweden and the Netherlands are making it easier for their foreign population to gain citizenship, Switzerland is making it hard. The effect of this is that the official figures for numbers of foreign residents remain artificially high. If Switzerland changed its policy in order to make citizenship easier to obtain, the percentage of the population classified as foreign residents would fall considerably.

Another example is Australia, where the Aboriginal population did not obtain full citizenship rights until 1967. For many decades, Australia applied the differentialist strategy in its treatment of the Aborigines, while at the same time it had an assimilationist policy towards immigrants.

In a number of countries, policy responses to diversity have been changing. If we look at countries where citizenship is based on principles of *ius sanguinis,* Germany granted citizenship to ethnic Germans from the diaspora in eastern Europe, while individuals born in Germany of parents from ethnic minorities, like the Turks, were excluded under *ius sanguinis* citizenship provisions. Germany is beginning to abandon its differentialist position. Naturalization procedures existed in many countries, but were fraught with so many difficulties that even permanent residents and locally born children found it difficult to obtain citizenship. France, on the other hand, has officially accepted the assimilationist position. Although French citizenship was based on *ius sanguinis*, it also had strong elements of *ius soli*. The rules in France provided that citizenship could be granted to children born in France where one parent had French nationality or where the child declared between the age of 16 and 21 that it wished to be French. Restrictions that were imposed in this area have now been revoked under the socialist government. In France, ethnic groups can form associations to promote their cultural identity. However, the reality is that institutional measures often remain inadequate for the meeting of the cultural needs of ethnic groups.

3   Conclusions

First of all, it seems clear that civic society in Europe must be built primarily on the rights of individual citizens and not on collective rights for groups. It is the great achievement of the European Enlightenment that human rights guaranteeing legal rights for individuals were set down which superseded the primacy of collective rights, and led to the disappearance of class privileges. Additionally, of course, minority rights, such as freedom of religion, for instance, should be granted to the collective.

Second, we must argue for the primacy of the state. Regardless of the model of integration applied in dealing with those who are different or of foreign origin, one thing is clear: the international world order is based on states and not on ethnicity. As long as this remains the case, all attempts at resolving conflicts must be based on the state as an organising principle.

Third, we plead for the principle of multiple identities: it is only when citizens have multiple identities that political and cultural loyalties can be combined. (Walzer 1992; Altermatt 1996).

These three points form the main prerequisites of a multicultural strategy as mentioned above. Collective and national identity and citizenship are key issues. With European integration, controls over citizenship in the face of the pressure of immigration have become the last bastion of national sovereignty. The question of citizenship remains a central problem. State citizenship is the gatekeeper that grants access to the territory, the labour market, and the social welfare system. The majority of immigrants have a legal basis for residence, access to the labour market, apart from certain public services, and also enjoy the basic advantages of the social and welfare state. But they are not protected from possible expulsion: they do not have the security of knowing that they can remain in the territory. In addition, foreign residents do not have the political rights which are the basis of the nation-state (Brubaker 1992).

At the end of the twentieth century, immigration remains the one issue that, more than any other, right across Europe, has the power to emotionally involve and politically mobilize the masses. To explain this fact, we need to look beyond the actual material interests involved, to the symbolic value of the question. The question of state citizenship is directly linked to national identity. It is therefore all the more necessary that there should be public debate about the varying concepts of national and European identity. Nation, ethnicity, and citizenship are three key issues that both Eastern and Western Europe will increasingly need to confront.

When discussing European integration, it is helpful to refer to the Greek terms *ethnos* and *demos* (Francis 1976; Lepsius 1990). If by «nation» we mean a political *demos*, then political sovereignty is central. The notion of «demos» allows states to demand political loyalty from their citizens and to regard cultural identity as a matter of individual choice (Altermatt 1996). Such a development is possible in Europe, as the history of modern Switzerland shows. Switzerland has provided differing cultural and linguistic communities with a shared collective consciousness and a common political culture.

If Europe is not to be a community based on ethnic communities, i.e. *ethnos*, then entry to the community, the gaining of citizenship, becomes the most important issue. It also becomes easier to bring particular interpretations of an individual cultural view into line with universal principles of human rights. As the German philosopher Jürgen Habermas (1994) has pointed out, the identity of a political community depends primarily on the legal principles anchored in the political culture, and not on any general ethnocultural way of life. Immigrants must, however, be willing to accept the rules which have developed within a polity, adapting to the political culture of the receiving country but without abandoning their own religious or cultural practices. This means that a working knowledge of the language of a region is essential, otherwise mutual intercultural communication is impossible. At the same time, the established population must refrain from defensive mechanisms, which are often simply the expression of a chauvinism based on prosperity. As Marko (1995) has pointed out, it is the combination of autonomy and integration that allows an ethnically pluralist social and political system. These two factors are prerequisites for the institutional organization of equality based on the recognition of difference.

Strict division of *ethnos* and *demos* makes it possible for many cultural worlds to co-exist in the Europe of the future. Both on the national level and within the new Europe, the doors to citizenship must be kept open if we wish to consider ourselves citizens of the world.

References

Altermatt, Urs (1996). *Das Fanal von Sarajevo. Ethnonationalismus in Europa.* Zürich: Verlag Neue Zürcher Zeitung.

Altermatt, Urs (Ed.) (1996a). *Nation, Ethnizität und Staat in Mitteleuropa.* Vienna: Böhlau.

Altermatt, Urs (1997). *Sprache und Nation.* Freiburg (CH): Universitätsverlag.

Anderson, Benedict (1983). *Imagined Communities. Reflections on the Origin and Spread of Nationalism.* London: Verso.

Brubaker, Rogers (1992). *Citizenship and Nationhood in France and Germany.* Cambridge MA: Harvard University Press.

Cohn-Bendit, Daniel and Thomas Schmid (1992). *Heimat Babylon. Das Wagnis der multikulturellen Demokratie.* Hamburg: Hoffmann und Campe.

Francis, Emerich K. (1976). *Interethnic Relations. An Essay in Sociological Theory.* New York: Elsevier.

Gellner, Ernest (1983). *Nations and Nationalism.* Oxford: Blackwell.

Habermas, Jürgen (1994). «Staatsbürgerschaft und nationale Identität. Überlegungen zur europäischen Zukunft», pp. 11–29 in Nicole Dewandre und Jacques Leonble (eds.). *Projekt Europa. Postnationale Identität: Grundlage für eine europäische Demokratie?* Berlin: Schelzky und Jeep.

Hobsbawm, Eric J. (1990). *Nations and nationalism since 1780. Programme, myth, reality.* Cambridge: Cambridge University Press.

Inglis, Christine (1996). *Multiculturalism: New Policy Responses to Diversity.* Paris: Unesco.

Lepsius, Rainer (1990). *Interessen, Ideen und Institutionen.* Opladen: Westdeutscher Verlag.

Marko, Joseph (1995). *Autonomie und Integration. Rechtsinstitute des Nationalitätenrechts im funktionalen Vergleich.* Vienna: Böhlau.

Smith, Anthony D. (1991). *National Identity.* Reno: University of Nevada Press.

Taylor, Charles (1992). *Multiculturalism and «The Politics of Recognition»: an essay.* Princeton (NJ): Princeton University Press.

Walzer, Michael (1992). *Zivile Gesellschaft und amerikanische Demokratie.* Berlin: Rotbuch-Verlag.

Ethnic Troubles: Gender, Sexuality and the Construction of National Identity

Joane Nagel

1 Ethnicity and nationalism

Ethnicity is both a building block and a stumbling block to national identity and national unity. Common ethnic ancestry – shared language, religion, or culture – is often the foundation upon which national identity is constructed. However, few states today can convincingly argue that those living inside their borders are ethnically homogenous. In fact, most modern states are ethnically diverse and getting more diverse every day. One reason for this is immigration. Immigration is the engine that creates new ethnic groups. When populations migrate across state borders, particularly when they settle in ethnic neighborhoods or enclaves in host societies, they often quickly change from «foreign migrants» to become «ethnic groups».[1]

This is not to say that all differences in language, religion, or culture *automatically* become «ethnic» differences or always produce well-defined and strongly defended ethnic boundaries dividing various historical ethnic communities or separating host from migrant populations. If we view ethnicity as a series of crisscrossing boundaries dividing populations into multiple groups differentiated by religion, color, language, or culture, and if we note that these boundaries are changeable and permeable (with some boundaries weakening and other boundaries strengthening and with people crossing over from one group into another), then we can begin to move away from essentialist understandings of ethnicity as biological or cultural. According to this boundary model, color, language, religion, or culture become *potential* bases for ethnic identity, community, or conflict, not inevitable grounds for ethnic differentiation. As international and historical examples easily demonstrate, people are not always mobilizing or constantly conflicting along ethnic lines, only sometimes. This

---

1   Ethnicity can also be created by the same processes *inside* states, when religiously, culturally, or linguistically distinct populations migrate from one region to another; see Cohen (1974), Horowitz (1985), McGarry (1998).

leads to questions of *when* will ethnic boundaries become sites of conflict, movements, or revitalization.[2]

Researchers suggest several conditions under which ethnic conflict or mobilization erupts on ethnic boundaries: during times of ethnic competition for land, resources, jobs, or access to political decisionmaking, during periods of international tension when diaspora populations become scapegoats or targets of hate crimes, during periods of high migration when large numbers of visibly or culturally distinct ethnic migrant populations appear to host residents as «invading» or «overrunning» host societies and changing the character of neighborhoods or communities, or during periods of political upheaval when opportunistic politicians «play the ethnic card» by targeting ethnic communities as a threat in order to consolidate their own ethnic constituencies. We have seen numerous examples of all of these situations producing ethnic conflict in Europe during the past few decades. Competition for jobs is one of the reasons given for the rise of skinhead racism in Britain in recent years; international tensions between Russia and its former Baltic states (Lithuania, Latvia, Estonia) led to ethnic tensions between Baltic nationalists and newly redefined ethnic Russian «minority» populations in these republics during the early 1990s; high rates of Muslim immigration into France in the 1980s led to ethnic tensions and calls to restrict Muslim women from wearing Islamic veils or headdresses in public schools; and of course, the political vacuum that opened in the former state of Yugoslavia following the disintegration of the Soviet Union in the early 1990s, led to the programs of forced migration better known as «ethnic cleansing», as well as interethnic rapes, massacres, and war.[3]

The transformation from migrant group to ethnic group involves two processes. First, local residents view migrants as different from themselves and create an ethnic category to fit migrants into («blacks» or «Muslims» or «southerners»). Second, migrants view themselves as different from host residents, and adopt an ethnic identity to build community solidarity, often to insulate themselves from racism or discrimination. Through this ethnic dialectic of external

---

2   Boundaries are also useful devices for moving away from the focus on the *content* of ethnicity – i.e., culture, and away from the common assertion that ethnicity is simply the result of cultural differences. By focusing on boundaries that surround particular cultural systems, we are free to observe cultural change inside boundaries, cultural spread across boundaries, and cultural flux originating at boundary edges or borderlands. These observations show us that cultures are revised, reorganized, reinvented, and sometimes invented, and that these cultural renewal projects are part of the ethnic and racial boundary construction process. We can also see that since ethnic boundaries are constructed, they can be fluid and permeable. What this means is that who is inside and who is outside a particular ethnic category can change over time, can be a source of controversy, and can result in the formation of new ethnic identities for individuals, the creation of entirely new ethnic groups (e.g., out of immigrant groups), the discarding of old individual ethnic identities, and the disappearance of old ethnic groups.
3   For a discussion of these ethnic conflicts, see Cronin (1996), Denitch (1996), Sells (1996), Nielsen (1992) and Norgaard et al. (1996).

ascription and internal identification, new ethnic boundaries are created out of the demographics of population movements. Ethnic stereotypes each group holds about the other begin to fill the meaning vacuum created by these new ethnic categories. The ethnic histories and traditions each group draws on and invents provide further cultural symbolic content to fill ethnic vessels. Ethnic suspicions and fears add to the broadening ethnic boundaries separating the two groups. The result: the construction of new ethnic identities and communities on both sides of the ethnic divide. For the host residents, we refer to this cultural, linguistic, and/or religious self-awareness as «nationalism»; for the migrant groups, we refer to this cultural, linguistic, and/or religious self-awareness as «ethnicity». Thus, ethnicity serves both as a source of nationalist (albeit reactionary) unity and as a source of national division, separating hosts from migrants, «us» from «them», residents from strangers, «nationals» from «ethnics».[4]

Immigration fosters the creation of new ethnic groups around the world. Wherever populations move into host settings, the nationalist/ethnic dialectic gets underway with more or less intensity depending on local conditions. Old resident groups become more aware of themselves as national majorities; new immigrant groups become aware of themselves as ethnic minorities. This ethnic construction process has been a familiar script for settler societies like the United States, Canada, Australia, Brazil, or South Africa. Although each of these states has a unique history of relations with indigenous populations, immigrant groups, and the emergence of national and ethnic identities, all have consistently seen the production of new ethnic categories and identities as waves of settlement and immigration have occurred at various points throughout their histories. All of these societies have had to face the legacy of unfair, often brutal treatment of indigenous populations, and the challenge of integrating settler, indigenous, and later immigrant populations into a single state and nation.[5]

European states have also struggled with issues of ethnic diversity and national unity throughout their histories. Europeans have devised various strategies for creating national unity out of religious, linguistic, or cultural diversity. Switzerland has pursued a decentralized approach to national rule by organizing government at the canton level which more closely adheres to internal ethnic boundaries than does the larger Swiss national border. Other states, France, for example, have adopted more centralized approaches to construc-

---

4   For a discussion of the role of the «other» in the construction of national identity, see Triandafyllidou (1998).

5   For a discussion of the role of immigration in the construction of ethnic communities and identities in these and other states, see Zappala (1998), Croucher (1998), Waldinger (1996), Hill (1996), Carmon (1998).

ting the nation, emphasizing integration and national homogeneity. Still other states, such as Britain or Spain, have pursued more mixed policies of devolution, falling somewhere in between decentralization and centralization.[6]

European integration has created new challenges for European states, even for those with relatively placid ethnic histories, such as Sweden or Czechoslovakia. One reason is that the consolidation and integration of Europe has opened the way to greatly increased migration across historical European state borders. Since immigration is part of the machinery that creates new ethnic groups, one unintended consequence of European integration has been disintegration, that is, the creation of new patterns of ethnic diversity and ethnic tensions including secessionist movements inside many European states. Another consequence of the increased immigration resulting from European Union migration policies has been a kind of hyperintegration in some European states in the form of heightened nationalism, sometimes taking the frightening, but familiar form of fascism.[7]

The creation of national identities often depends on ethnic history and solidarity as building blocks of national unity. History has shown us that this process of differentiation – separating «us» from «them» – often carries with it a set of tensions and contradictions that can make nationalism a costly basis of social organization. Nationalism not only is built on the back of ethnicity, it also represents a particular gendered, sexualized vision of social and political reality. In virtually all cases, nationalist movements stress masculinized heterosexualized standards for behavior that have several consequences. Masculinist heterosexuality coupled with nationalism tends to embrace patriarchal forms of social organization that create different and unequal places for men and women in the nation. Such patriarchal systems tend to be unsympathetic to feminist efforts to eliminate gender inequality, and see women's rights as secondary and subversive to nationalist goals and struggles. Further, standards for national conduct that reflect masculinized heteronormativity tend to result in homophobia, and thus to be intolerant of sexual diversity, particularly homosexuality. The next two sections explore the role of gender and sexuality in the making and unmaking of nations.

---

6   For a discussion of the management of ethnic diversity and the construction of national identity in European states, see Spencer (1997), Mar-Molinero and Smith (1996), Weber (1976).
7   For a discussion of the resurgence of the far right in Europe see Cronin (1996) and Cheles, Ferguson, and Vaughn (1995).

2   Gender and nationalism

There are two important links in the relationship between gender and nationalism noted above, that I will explore here in more detail: the gendered and different places for men and women in the nation, and the masculinist and heterosexual assumptions underlying the ideology of nationalism. In her study of gender, race, and sexuality in colonialism, *Imperial Leather,* McClintock (1995: 356–7) notes the «gendered discourse» of nationalism, commenting that «if male theorists are typically indifferent to the gendering of nations, feminist analyses of nationalism have been lamentably few and far between. White feminists, in particular, have been slow to recognize nationalism as a feminist issue». And when feminist scholars do set about to even the gender score, Messerschmidt (1993) argues, in his analysis of *Masculinities and Crime,* the gender lens appears to focus exclusively on women. The resulting scholarship, while more gender balanced in its coverage, still fails to examine systematically what is uniquely masculine in a structural, cultural, or social sense, about such clearly gendered activities and institutions as crime, nationalism, politics, or violence, among others.

In *Bananas, Beaches, and Bases,* Enloe (1990: 45) observes that «nationalism has typically sprung from masculinized memory, masculinized humiliation and masculinized hope». She finds that women are relegated to minor, often symbolic, roles in nationalist movements and conflicts, either as icons of nationhood, to be elevated and defended, or as the booty or spoils of war, to be denigrated and disgraced. In either case, the real actors are men who are defending their freedom, their honor, their homeland, and their women.

By definition, nationalism is political and closely linked to the state and its institutions. Like the military, most state institutions have been historically and remain dominated by men. It is therefore no surprise that the culture and ideology of hegemonic masculinity go hand in hand with the culture and ideology of hegemonic nationalism.[8] Masculinity and nationalism articulate well with one another, and the modern form of Western masculinity emerged at about the same time and place as modern nationalism. Mosse (1996: 7) notes that nationalism «was a movement which began and evolved parallel to modern masculinity» in the West about a century ago. He describes modern masculinity as a centerpiece of all varieties of nationalist movements:

---

8   For a discussion of various models of masculinity, including a definition of hegemonic masculinity, see Connell (1995).

The masculine stereotype was not bound to any one of the powerful political ideologies of the previous century. It supported not only conservative movements ... but the workers' movement as well; even Bolshevik man was said to be «firm as an oak». Modern masculinity from the very first was co-opted by the new nationalist movements of the nineteenth century (Mosse 1996: 7).

Other political ideologies of that time, in particular colonialism and imperialism, also resonated with contemporary standards of masculinity.[9] Many scholars link the late nineteenth-century renaissance in manliness in Europe to the institutions and ideology of empire.[10] Springhall (1987: 52) describes the middle-class English ideal of Christian manliness, «muscular Christianity», with its emphasis on sport – the «cult of games» in the public schools; he outlines how, through organizations such as the «Boys' Brigades», these middle-class values were communicated to «less privileged, board school-educated, working-class boys in the nation's large urban centres». Boys from both classes served throughout the empire in British imperial armies.

Nationalist politics is a major venue for «accomplishing» masculinity (Connell 1987) for at least two reasons. First, as noted above, the national state is essentially a masculine institution. Feminist scholars point out its hierarchical authority structure, the male domination of decision-making positions, the male superordinate/female subordinate internal division of labor, and the male legal regulation of female rights, labor, and sexuality.[11] Second, the culture of nationalism is constructed to emphasize and resonate with masculine cultural themes. Terms like *honor, patriotism, cowardice, bravery,* and *duty* are hard to distinguish as either nationalistic or masculinist since they seem so thoroughly tied both to the nation and to manhood. My point here is that the «microculture» of masculinity in everyday life articulates very well with the demands of nationalism, particularly its militaristic side. While local masculine cultures differ from one another in terms of the class, race, ethnicity, or nation of the men involved, in all societies there are distinct gender cultures shaping the lives of boys and girls, of men and women, and it is male gender culture that tends to dominate nationalism.

Let me illustrate what I mean by gender microcultures. Over the years, I have asked my undergraduate students in the United States to write down on a piece of paper their answer to the question: «What is the worst name you can be called?» The gender difference in their responses is striking and has been con-

---

9   See Bologh (1990), MacKenzie (1987), Walvin (1987).
10 See Sinha (1995), Koven (1991), Hobsbawm (1990).
11 See Connell (1995), Franzway, Court, and Connell (1989), Grant and Tancred (1992).

sistent over the past generation of students. The vast majority of women respond: «slut» (or its equivalent, with «bitch» a rather distant second); the vaster majority of men respond: «wimp» or «coward» or «pussy». What is particularly telling about this difference between female and male student responses is that the worst insult for women (being called a «slut») has virtually no meaning, or is seen a compliment by many men; and the most insulting thing a man can be called (a «coward» or «wimp») makes most women laugh when they imagine being so named.

Like men, women occupy a distinct, though very different symbolic role in nationalist culture, discourse, and collective action. Women tend to be restricted (sometimes legally, sometimes according to social convention or political appointment) to more «private» spheres of action in nationalist arenas that reflects a gender division of nationalism that parallels the gender division of labor in the larger society. Anthias and Yuval-Davis (1989: 7–8) have identified five ways in which women have tended to participate in ethnic, national, and state processes and practices:
a) as biological producers of members of ethnic collectivities;
b) as reproducers of the [normative] boundaries of ethnic/national groups [by enacting proper feminine behavior];
c) as participating centrally in the ideological reproduction of the collectivity and as transmitters of its culture;
d) as signifiers of ethnic/national differences;
g) as participants in national, economic, political and military struggles.

While some of these roles involve action, e.g., women participating in nationalist struggles, scholars note the pressure felt by women nationalists to remain in supportive, symbolic, often suppressed and traditional roles.[12] Thus women's place as national symbols often limits their interest in or ability to assume active, public roles. There are, of course, exceptions to this, i.e., women leaders of nationalist movements, resistance movements, and states, but that list is short and the same names are repeated again and again. As Horrocks (1992: 25) notes when discussing male dominance in public life: «The exception – Margaret Thatcher – proves the rule.»

Some scholars argue that «woman nationalist» is an oxymoron that reflects the historic contradiction between the goals and needs of women and those of nationalists.[13] Feminists often find themselves attempting to negotiate the difficult, some would say, impassable terrain that separates the interests of women

---

12 See Anthias and Yuval-Davis (1989, 1992), Walby (1992), Tohidi (1991), Skurski (1994) and Jayawardena (1986).
13 See McClintock (1995), Calhoun (1994a, 1994b: 326) and Enloe (1990).

and the interests of nationalists. Discussing Hindu and Muslim nationalism in Indian politics, Hasan (1994: xv) notes the tension between feminist principles and communal religious solidarity: «Forging community identities does not imply or guarantee that women will always identify themselves with or adhere to prevailing religious doctrines which legitimize their subordination.»

The goals of feminists and nationalists, particularly «retraditionalizing» (Nagel 1996: 193) nationalists (which many are), are often at odds. This is because, Enloe (1990: 54) argues, men in many national communities have an interest in regulating the activities and appearance of women since

> they see women as 1) the community's – or the nation's – most valuable *possessions;* the principal *vehicles* for transmitting the whole nation's values from one generation to the next; 3) *bearers* of the community's future generations – crudely, nationalist wombs; 4) the members of the community most *vulnerable* to defilement and exploitation by oppressive alien rulers; and 5) most susceptible to *assimilation* and cooptation by insidious outsiders.

Sometimes women have supported male nationalist efforts, while at other times women have been involved themselves in cadres and military units.[14] Despite their bravery, sometimes taking on traditional male military roles, and despite the centrality of their contribution to many nationalist struggles, it is often the case that feminist nationalists find themselves once again under the thumb of institutionalized patriarchy once national independence is won. A nationalist movement that encourages women's participation in the name of national liberation, often balks at feminist demands for gender equality.

> Women who have called for more genuine equality between the sexes – in the [nationalist] movement, in the home – have been told that now is not the time, the nation is too fragile, the enemy is too near. Women must be patient, they must wait until the nationalist goal is achieved, *then* relations between women and men can be addressed. «Not now, later», is the advice that rings in the ears of many nationalist women (Enloe 1990: 62).

But, waiting is a dangerous strategy, Enloe (1990: 60) argues, «every time women succumb to the pressures to hold their tongues about problems they are having with men in nationalist organizations, nationalism becomes that much more masculinized». Women who press their case face challenges to

---

14 Sayigh and Peteet (1987), Helie-Lucas (1988), Jayawardena (1986), Nategh (1987), Urdang (1989).

their loyalty, their sexuality, or their ethnic or national authenticity: they are either «carrying water» for colonial oppressors, or they are lesbians, or they are unduly influenced by Western feminism. Third World feminists are quite aware of these charges and share some concerns about the need for an indigenous feminist analysis and agenda; as Delia Aguilar, a Filipina nationalist feminist comments:

> when feminist solidarity networks are today proposed and extended globally, without a firm sense of identity – national, racial and class – we are likely to yield to feminist models designed by and for white, middle-class women in the industrial West and uncritically adopt these as our own (Enloe 1990: 64).[15]

Despite efforts to build an indigenous feminism into nationalist movements, many women in these movements and states fail to achieve gender equality. Indeed, patriarchal, masculinist notions of men's and women's roles often become more entrenched during nationalist mobilizations and after independence. There are some exceptions to this. For instance, in the many socialist revolutions in the Second and Third World, women were granted constitutionally equal rights, though in practice this complete *de jure* gender equality generally fell short of the mark. Nonetheless, the legal challenges to patriarchal customary and official law brought about by socialist gender policies often represented quite a radical break with tradition, though this radicalism was sometimes short-lived.

Perhaps the most well-known case of a nationalist movement «turning» on its female supporters is that of Algeria. In 1962 Algeria finally freed itself from French colonial rule. The struggle had been a long and bitter one, and the fight for Algerian independence had been notable for the involvement of Algerian women. Daniele Djamila Amrane-Minne, who interviewed women veterans of the Algerian liberation movement in *Des Femmes dans la Guerre d'Algerie,* reports that 11 000 women were active participants in the national resistance movement, and that 2 000 women were in the armed wing of the movement (Kutschera 1996: 40–41). Despite this extensive involvement of women in a Muslim country's military movement, once independence was won, Algerian women found themselves «back in the kitchen» (Boulding 1977: 179), forced to trade their combat fatigues for Islamic dress *(hijab)* and the veil. Although the new independent Algeria embraced principles of socialism, few gender equality aspects of that doctrine were institutionalized into the formal or informal politics of independence. While women had the vote, their «place» in

---

15   See Jayawardena (1986), «Introduction», for a discussion of Third World indigenous feminism.

Algerian society was dictated more by Islamic patriarchal traditionalism than by egalitarian socialism. The place of women in post-independence Algeria reflected the Algerian saying: «Men deal with politics, women prepare couscous» (Mehdid 1996: 83). An established feminist movement in Algeria has protested unsuccessfully the creation and imposition of a traditionalist Shari'a-based «family law», and has been unable to quell the tide of resurgent Islam. Algerian women have paid a high price for their resistance in recent years. Following the suspension of the results of the 1992 elections, whose outcome would have installed a pro-Islamic government, Islamic militants have escalated their armed opposition, and women, particularly those who do not wear the *hijab*, have become targets of their violence:

> Crimes against women included abduction, torture, rape, gang rape and killing, crimes which were common by mid-1995 ... Feminist, militants, female journalists and teachers are particularly targeted, some of them forced to lead a clandestine life, having to hide from the bullets of the killers and their knives by constantly changing addresses and covering their tracks (Mehdid 1996: 93–94).[16]

Indeed, women's sexuality often turns out to be a matter of prime national interest around the world for at least two reasons. First, women as mothers are exalted icons of nationalism. In their discussion of Afrikaner nationalism in South Africa, Gaitskell and Unterhalter (1989: 60) argue that Afrikaner women appear regularly in the rhetoric and imagery of the Afrikaner «volk» (people), and that «they have figured overwhelmingly as mothers». As Theweleit (1987: 294) summarizes: «woman is an infinite untrodden territory of desire which at every stage of historical deterritorialization, men in search of material for utopias have inundated with their desires.» Placing women on nationalist pedestals, however, puts them at risk of falling off; their elevated position makes women's actions and demeanor much easier to scrutinize ... and police.

Women's sexuality is also of concern to nationalists because, as wives, sisters, mothers, and daughters, women are the bearers and incarnations of masculine honor. For instance, ethnographers report that the Afghani Muslim nationalists' conception of resource control, particularly labor, land, and women, is defined as a matter of honor; «purdah is a key element in the protection of the family's pride and honor» (Moghadam 1991: 433). El-Solh and Mabro (1994: 8) further refine the connection between men's and family honor and women's sexual respectability as a situation where honor is men's to gain and women's to lose: «honour is seen more as men's responsibility and shame as women's ...

---

16 For news accounts of these attacks, see Youssef (1994) and Steinfels (1995).

honour is seen as actively achieved while shame is seen as passively defended.»

It is not only Third World men whose honor is tied to their women's sexuality, respectability, and shame. While female fecundity is valued in the mothers of the nation, unruly female sexuality threatens to discredit the nation. Mosse (1985: 98) describes this duality in the depiction of women in European nationalist history: on the one hand, «female embodiments of the nation stood for eternal forces ... [and] suggested innocence and chastity», and most of all respectability. On the other hand, the right women needed to be sexually available to the right men: «the maiden with the shield, the spirit that awaits a masculine leader» (Mosse 1985: 101) to facilitate «the enjoyment of peace achieved by male warriors» (p. 98). These images of acceptable female sexuality stood in contrast to female «decadents» (prostitutes or lesbians) who were seen as «unpatriotic, weakening the nation» (Mosse 1985: 109) and dishonoring the nation's men ... which brings us to the next section, sexuality and nationalism.

3   Sexuality and nationalism

In her well-known song, American singer, Tina Turner asks the question: «What's love got to do with it?» Following her lead, I would like to ask the question here: «What's sex got to do with it?» With ethnicity, that is ... and with nationalism? If not everything, then quite a bit, I will argue in this section. Ethnicity and sex are strained, but not strange bedfellows. Ethnic boundaries are also sexual boundaries – erotic intersections where people make intimate connections across ethnic and national borders. The borderlands that lie at the intersections of ethnic and national boundaries are «ethnosexual frontiers» which are surveilled and supervised, patrolled and policed, regulated and restricted, but which regularly are penetrated by individuals forging sexual links with ethnic and national «others». Some of this sexual contact is by «ethnosexual settlers» who establish long-term liaisons, join and/or form families, and become members of ethnic communities «on the other side». Some of this sexual contact is by «ethnosexual sojourners» who stay for a brief or extended time, enter into sexual liaisons, but eventually return to home communities. Some of this sexual contact is by «ethnosexual adventurers» who undertake expeditions across ethnic and national boundaries for recreational, casual, or «exotic» sexual encounters, often more than once, but who return to their sexual home bases after each excursion. Some of this sexual contact is by «ethnosexual invaders» who launch sexual assaults across ethnic and national boundaries, inside alien ethnic territory, seducing, raping, and sexually enslaving ethnic «others» as a means of sexual domination and colonization.

It is the sexualized nature of things ethnic, racial, and national, that heats up discourse on the values, attributes, and moral worth of «us» and «them», that arouses passions when there are violations of sexual contact rules, that raises doubts about loyalty and respectability when breaches of sexual demeanor occur, that stirs reactions when questions of sexual purity and propriety arise, that sparks retaliations when threats to sexual boundaries are perceived. A young Frenchwoman, whose father was in the French resistance, describes the fate of French women in World War II who were identified as «Nazi collaborators» during the liberation of France in August, 1944:

> The war was not finished, but in Paris it assumed another form – more perverse, more degrading ... The «shorn woman» of rue Petit-Musc ... walked along with her wedge-soled shoes tied around her neck, stiff like those undergoing a major initiation. Her face was frozen like a Buddha, her carriage tense and superb in the midst of a shouting, screeching mob of faces contorted by hatred, groping and opportunistic hands, eyes congested by excitement, festivity, sexuality, sadism (Weitz 1995: 277).

This account reveals several interesting and important aspects about national sexual boundaries, and shows how (in this case hetero)sexual behavior on the margins can strengthen hegemonic social and sexual orders. First, we see that national and sexual boundaries are mutually reinforcing, since implicit in the meaning of national boundaries («who are we?») are certain prescriptions and proscriptions for sexual crossings. In this case, «our» women should not be having sex with «their» (particularly «enemy») men. Second, is the ubiquitous double standard that applies to many sexual boundaries: «our» men can have consensual sex, rape, or even sexually enslave «their» women and not have their heads shaved and tattooed and be paraded around the town. At least I have found no reports of this practice as retribution for male sexual misbehavior,[17] and in fact, Japan has yet to make satisfactory restitution to Korean and Filipina «comfort women» who were sexually enslaved during the Second World War.[18] Indeed, in times of war, «our» women might even want to do their patriotic duty by making themselves sexually available to «our» men while the sexual police look the other way [as long as internal racial or ethnic boundaries aren't violated.[19] Another lesson to be learned from this tale of punishing women sexual collaborators lies in the implications of the margins for the center. In this case rule breaking was seized as an opportunity to reinforce and reestablish sexual and nationalist hegemony. By disciplining women colla-

---

17 Although there are occasional prosecutions for rape during war; see Brownmiller (1975).
18 See Hicks (1995), Howard (1995), Mydans (1996).
19 See Saunders (1995), Enloe (1990), Smith (1988).

borators, «proper» sexual demeanor and approved ethnosexual partners were publicly proclaimed.[20]

At least as familiar a picture from World War II as women sexual collaborators with shaved heads, is the pink triangle forced to be worn by homosexuals in Germany and Nazi-occupied territories, and considerably more familiar than either image is the six-sided Star of David forced by the Nazis on Jews. Pink triangles and Stars of David not only served to distinguish publicly outcast non-Aryans from Aryans, these symbols communicated potent and degenerate sexual stereotypes about their wearers. In fact, discredited sexuality is an important part of anti-Semitism. For instance, Mosse (1985) reminds us that early twentieth century views of female sexuality (consistent with Freudian theory) depicted women's sexual passions as out of control (hysterical?). Male sexual deviants were often seen as «feminized», since their urges were seen as feminine failures of self-restraint.[21] Mosse (1984: 36) reports that while Jews were seldom accused of homosexuality in articulations of fascist and European racism, they were considered «sexual ‹degenerates›»:

> Blacks, and then Jews, were endowed with excessive sexuality, with a socalled female sensuousness that transformed love into lust. They lacked all manliness. Jews as a group were said to exhibit female traits, just as homosexuals were generally considered effeminate.[22]

Sexualized racism, homophobia, and misogyny were all foils against which propagandists contrasted the superior morality and sexuality of fascist nationalists across Europe. In the words of Italian fascist, E.F. Martinetti, writing in *Democrazia Futurista* (1919):

> We speak in the name of the race, which demands ardent males and inseminated females. Fecundity, for a race like ours, is its indispensable defense in times of war, and in times of peace, its wealth of working arms and genial heads ... we futurists condemn the spreading feminine idiocy and the devoted imbecility of males that together collaborate to develop feminine extravagance, prostitution, pederasty, and the sterility of the race (Spackman 1996: 12).

---

20 See Durkheim (1966) for a classical articulation of this social fact.
21 Depicting «others» as feminine often is used in other ways, to delegitimize or trivialize grievances or dissent (Brown 1996), to denigrate or dismiss opponents or colonized people (men) (Sweet 1993; Ortner 1996; Petkov 1997), or as a critical discourse act against a dominant group (Mac An Ghaill 1994).
22 For a discussion linking the effeminization of Jews to the resurgence of masculinist heteronormativity in late nineteenth-century Europe, see Boyarin (1997); for a detailed, albeit heavily psychoanalytic, discussion of the Nazi preoccupation with sexuality and homosexuality, see Theweleit (1987).

The literatures on historical and contemporary sexualities are filled with examples of sexuality in the service of racial, ethnic, and nationalist agendas of various sorts: reproducing the nation or ethnic group, controlling women and men inside ethnic boundaries, reinforcing ethnic segregation, maintaining ethnic inequalities, intimidating and subjugating ethnic «others» under colonialism or imperialism, extending and/or establishing sexual and ethnic policies and regimes in postcolonial settings. This list points to links between ethnicity and sexuality and between nationalism and sexuality in many times and places.

Just as feminism has the capacity to challenge the stability of the masculinist heterosexual order that props up ethnic and nationalist boundaries, so too does homosexuality. Both queers and feminists are problems for nationalists. This is partly because nationalists tend to be traditionalists, since nationalists like to look back to real or invented histories for their legitimation and to mark their paths to the future. History is often used by nationalists to identify authentic membership (often as assertions of racial purity), to lay claim to ancestral territory, and to celebrate their unique and valuable traditions and culture. Feminists tend to raise questions about the accuracy and justice of these usually patriarchal «golden ages», and homosexuals tend to raise questions about what often is the core nationalist project of reproducing the nation and about the strength of members' commitment to the nation as the primary unit of identification.

4   Queering nationalism

Nationalists' preoccupation with and fear of homosexuality is not confined to the Nazi targeting of homosexuals during the Second World War. The Cold War represented another period of «homosexual panic» (Butler 1993: 126) when many gay men working in Western governments, particularly in the British Foreign Office and U.S. State Department, were fired or reassigned because they were considered to be «security risks». This presumption was based on the belief that they could be blackmailed because their moral character was considered questionable, or because their trustworthiness could be undermined by loyalties divided between sexual orientation and nation. Moran (1991) argues that the search for homosexual security risks in post-World War II Britain was in part a reaction to declining British global power and its increasing dependence on and replacement by the United States as a dominant economic and political superpower. In the United States, Senator Joseph McCarthy was not only interested in finding and flushing out communists in various arenas of American life, he was also interested in homosexuals, presumably because of their vulnerability to communist influence (Epstein 1994; see also Patton 1997;

Fried 1997). The fact that one of his most vicious lieutenants, Roy Cohn, was a gay man, was one of the McCarthy era's best kept and most ironic breaches of Republican security. Another irony of the focus on homosexuals as likely blackmail targets is that heterosexual misconduct was a far more common source of government employee vulnerability, since, as history has shown again and again, people frequently engage in, and frequently go to great lengths to hide, heterosexual affairs.

In recent years lesbian and gay rights groups around the world, but particularly in the West have mounted assaults on ethnosexual exclusionary policies, claiming equal rights to be members of the ethnic community or nation. In the United States, one such effort to penetrate an ethnosexual frontier involved an attempt by an Boston-based gay and lesbian group to march in the annual St. Patrick's Day parade. As we have seen routinely in Northern Ireland, parades are powerful symbolic statements that often arouse strong passions. As «spectacles of nation», parades demarcate national membership, dramatize national history, celebrate victories, and denigrate the defeated (Stychin 1998). The Boston St. Patrick's Day parade has evolved over the years from a strictly Irish ethnic celebration into a huge event with «Irish and non-Irish participants and a blend of ethnic and dominant American symbols» (Bodnar 1992: 68), with estimates of 20 000 participants and 1 million spectators (Stychin 1998: 31). When the request of the «Irish-American Gay, Lesbian and Bisexual Group of Boston» (GLIB) to march in the 1992 Boston St. Patrick's Day parade was denied by the South Boston Allied War Veterans Council, GLIB filed a lawsuit claiming their free speech was being violated. GLIB lost the suit and did not march in the parade, though they held a counter parade and have marched in many gay pride parades since then (see Van Ness 1996). The case of Boston's St. Patrick's Day parade reflects the efforts of gays and lesbians to assert membership in ethnic and national communities around the world, frequently with more success than in Boston, but sometimes not. In the Third World homosexuality is often defined as a «problem» unique to the west, either non-existent in Third World states or the result of the immoral influences of colonialism and imperialism. In the early 1990s, Zimbabwean president, Joseph Mugabe justified the exclusion of Gays and Lesbians of Zimbabwe from an international book fair, denouncing «homosexuality as a Western corruption imported to Africa through colonization» (Stychin 1998: 52). In the summer of 1998, the decennial Anglican Bishops Conference voted to continue church policy that finds homosexuality incompatible with biblical teachings; those voting to retain the policy were mainly from the ranks of Third

World bishops, one of whom claimed that homosexuality is a problem of the West and is non-existent in his country.[23]

The integration of Europe is playing an interesting, emerging role in efforts to weaken ethnosexual boundaries inside European states. For instance, in the Republic of Ireland, both feminist and lesbian and gay rights groups have appealed *outside* national boundaries, to the European Union, to claim rights within the Irish state. The notorious case of a pregnant Irish teenager denied an abortion in Ireland in 1997,[24] led feminists opposed to Ireland's restrictions on abortions to seek support in the more liberal arenas of European legal and public opinion. Irish gay and lesbian rights groups have appealed to the European Convention on Human Rights, in particular, to the right of privacy, to seek the decriminalization of same-sex acts between consenting adults (Stychin 1998: 137). In Eastern Europe, there has been pressure on states seeking admission to the Council of Europe to abandon codes outlawing homosexual relations; for instance, in 1993, Lithuania repealed its laws against same-sex acts (Sanders 1996: 82).

Just this past spring Europe was the setting for yet another ethnosexual controversy when Israeli transsexual, Dana International, won the 1998 Eurovision Song Contest in Birmingham, England in May. Dana's official representation of Israel in the contest generated death threats and heated controversy in Israel, including a comment by Israel's Deputy Minister of Health, Rabbi Shlomo Ben-Izri: «She is an abomination. Even in Sodom there was nothing like it.» (Gross 1998: 23). Ben-Izri believed that Israel was sending the world «‹a message of darkness› by having Ms. International represent it» (Horowitz 1997). The controversy extended throughout the Middle East:

> Dana has also come under harsh attack in the Arab world, where, despite attempts by the authorities to ban her, an estimated five million illegal cassettes of her music have been sold. Under the headline, «The Israeli Dana drives 20 million Arabs crazy», one Jordanian magazine labelled her work, «prostitution by singing» (Gross 1998: 23).[25]

---

23 *New York Times*, August 3, 1998.
24 The Irish Supreme Court did permit the 13 year old girl, who was raped, to travel to England to have an abortion in December, 1997 (Clarity 1997).
25 My thanks to my colleague, Robert Antonio, for bringing to my attention the case of Dana International.

5   Conclusion

This paper has examined ethnic, gender, and sexual troubles which nationalism confronts inside and across national boundaries – in Switzerland, Europe, and in states around the world. Ethnicity, gender, and sexuality have double-edged relationships with nationalism in that all three either can strengthen or weaken nationalist movements, ideologies, and agendas. Inside national borders are ethnic boundaries, gender boundaries, and sexual boundaries that can either promote or impede national unity. Securing these borders and imposing strict controls on the meanings and enactments of ethnicity, gender, or sexuality can help to reinforce national identities and movements, but debates and conflicts over ethnic, gender, or sexual relations can become the nation's undoing. Specifically, I have argued that masculinist heterosexuality is a central component of the bedrock upon which nationalist boundaries rest, and that feminism, unruly female sexuality, and homosexuality are three cracks in that foundation.

A number of recent changes in the global system have created a landscape of flux for nationalist imaginings. The spread of western feminism and the strengthening of indigenous feminisms around the world has raised questions about the proper role of women and of men in the nation. To the extent that men and women come to positions of national and/or nationalist leadership with different gendered cultures and points of view («guns versus butter»), then the struggle for control of the state and the nation can become not only a «culture war», but also a «gender war». To the extent that the gay rights movement continues to challenge the heteronormative foundations of social and political life, then we should expect to see ongoing juridical and political challenges to the exclusion of homosexuals from social, economic, and political institutions and national communities. To the extent that the post-Soviet world and the end of the Cold War leads to a gradual reduction in the prominence of military institutions in the West, then the social and political definition of effective national leadership may become increasingly detached from a requirement of militarized manliness as a prerequisite for patriotism or strong leadership. Finally, to the extent that states become increasingly interconnected to suprastate institutions and organizations (such as the European Union), then local conservatisms may have to give way to more liberal regional or global standards of national citizenship, thus economic incentives for transnational benefits and associations become engines for change within nations and states.

Contemporary states must manage and control not only the frontiers of international borders, but they must also contend with internal ethnic frontiers, gender frontiers, and sexual frontiers. Efforts to regulate activity in these «eth-nosexual frontiers» represent some of the most controversial contemporary social issues in the global system. How nations choose to deal formally and informally with these many internal and external boundaries and frontiers constitutes an important challenge for the new millennium.

References

Anthias, Floya, and Nira Yuval-Davis (1992). *Racial Boundaries: Race, Nation, Gender, Colour and Class and the Anti-Racist Struggle.* London: Routledge.

Bodnar, J. (1992). *Remaking America: Public Memory, Commemoration, and Patriotism in the Twentieth Century.* Princeton (NJ): Princeton University Press.

Bologh, Roslyn Wallach (1990). *Love or Greatness: Max Weber and Masculine Thinking – A Feminist Inquiry.* London: Unwin Hyman.

Boulding, Elise (1977). *Women in the Twentieth Century World.* Beverly Hills: Sage Publications.

Boyarin, Daniel (1997). *Unheroic Conduct: The Rise of Heterosexuality and the Invention of the Jewish Man.* Berkeley: University of California Press.

Brownmiller, Susan (1975). *Against Our Will: Men, Women, and Rape.* New York: Simon and Schuster.

Butler, Judith (1993). *Bodies that Matter.* New York: Routledge.

Calhoun, Craig (1994). «Social Theory and the Politics of Identity», pp. 9–32 in C. Calhoun (ed.). *Social Theory and the Politics of Identity.* Cambridge (MA): Blackwell.

Calhoun, Craig (1994). «Nationalism and Civil Society: Democracy, Diversity, and Self-Determination», pp. 304–335 in C. Calhoun (ed.). *Social Theory and the Politics of Identity.* Cambridge (MA): Blackwell.

Carmon, Naomi (ed.) (1998). *Immigration and Integration in Post-Industrial Societies: Theoretical Analysis and Policy-Related Research.* Basingstoke: Macmillan.

Cheles, Luciano, Ronald Ferguson and Michalina Vaughn (eds.) (1995). *The Far Right in Western and Eastern Europe.* New York: Longman.

Clarity, James E. (December 2, 1997). «Top Irish Court Lets Girl, 13, Have Abortion in England», *New York Times* A6–7.

Cohen, Abner (1974). *Urban Ethnicity.* New York: Harper and Row.

Connell, Robert W. (1987). *Gender and Power: Society, the Person and Sexual Politics.* Stanford: Stanford University Press.

Connell, Robert W. (1995). *Masculinities.* Berkeley: University of California Press.

Cronin, Mike (ed.) (1996). *The Failure of British Fascism: The Far Right and the Fight for Political Recognition.* Basingstoke: Macmillan, 1996.

Croucher, Sheila (1998). «South Africa's Illegal Aliens: Constructing National Boundaries in a Post-Apartheid State», *Ethnic and Racial Studies* 21(4): 638–60.

Denitch, Bogdan (1996). *Ethnic Nationalism: The Tragic Death of Yugoslavia.* Minneapolis (MN): University of Minnesota Press (rev. ed.).

Durkheim, Emile (1996). *The Rules of Sociological Method* (8th edition). New York: Free Press.

El-Solh, Camilla Fawzi and Judy Mabro (1994). «Introduction: Islam and Muslim Women», pp. 1–32 in C.F. El-Solh and J. Mabro (eds.). *Muslim Women's Choices: Religious Belief and Social Reality.* Providence (RI): Berg Publishers.

Enloe, Cynthia (1990). *Bananas Beaches, and Bases: Making Feminist Sense of International Politics.* Berkeley: University of California Press.

Epstein, B. (1994). «Anti-Communism, Homophobia, and the Construction of Masculinity in the Postwar U.S.», *Critical Sociology* 20(3)

Franzway, Suzanne, Dianne Court and R.W. Connell (1989). *Staking a Claim: Feminism, Bureaucracy, and the State.* Cambridge: Polity Press.

Fried, Albert (1997). *McCarthyism.* New York: Oxford University Press.

Gaitskell, Deborah and Elaine Unterhalter (1989). «Mothers of the Nation: A Comparative Analysis of Nation, Race, and Motherhood in Afrikaner Nationalism and the African National Congress», pp. 58–78 in N. Yuval-Davis and F. Anthias (eds.). *Woman-Nation-State.* New York: St. Martin's Press.

Grant, Judith and Peta Tancred (1992). «A Feminist Perspective on State Bureaucracy», pp. 112–128 in A.J. Mills and P. Tancred (eds.). *Gendering Organizational Analysis.* Newbury Park (CA): Sage Publications.

Hasan, Zoya (1994). «Introduction: Contextualising Gender and Identity in Contemporary India», pp. viii–xxiv in Z. Hasan (ed.). *Forging Identities: Gender, Communities and State in India.* Boulder (CO): Westview Press.

Helie-Lucas and Marie-Aimee (1988). «The Role of Women during the Algerian Liberation Struggle and after: Nationalism as a Concept and as a Practice towards both the Power of the Army and the Militarization of the People», pp. 171–189 in T. E. Isaksson (ed.). *Women and the Military System.* New York: St. Martin's Press.

Hicks, George L. (1995). *The Comfort Women: Japan's Brutal Regime of Enforced Prostitution in the Second World War.* New York: W.W. Norton and Company.

Hill, Jonathan (ed.) (1996). *History, Power, and Identity: Ethnogenesis in the Americas, 1492–1992.* Iowa City (IA): University of Iowa Press.

Hobsbawm, Eric (1990). *Nations and Nationalism since 1780.* Cambridge: Cambridge University Press.

Horowitz, David (November 25, 1997). «Transsexual Singer Arouses Religious Ire in Israel», *The Irish Times.*

Horowitz, Donald (1985). *Ethnic Groups in Conflict.* Berkeley: University of California Press.

Horrocks, Roger (1994). *Masculinity in Crisis: Myths, Fantasies, and Realities.* New York: St. Martin's Press.

Howard, Keith (1995). *Three Stories of the Korean Comfort Women.* London: Cassell.

Jayawardena, Kumari (1986). *Feminism and Nationalism in the Third World.* London: Zed Books.

Koven, Seth (1991). «From Rough Lads to Hooligans: Boy Life, National Culture, and Social Reform», pp. 365–391 in A. Parker, M. Russo, D. Sommer and P. Yaeger (eds.). *Nationalisms and Sexualities.* New York: Routledge.

Kutschera, Chris (April 1996). «Algeria's Fighting Women», *The Middle East* 40–41.

Gross, Tom (April 21, 1998). «She Is an Abomination. Even in Sodom there Was Nothing Like it», *London Evening Standard* 23.

Mac, An Ghaill (1994). «The Making of Black English Masculinities», pp. 183–99 in H. Brod and M. Kaufman (eds.). *Theorizing Masculinities.* Thousand Oaks (CA): Sage Publications.

MacKenzie, John M. (1987). «The Imperial Pioneer and Hunter and the British Masculine Stereotype in Late Victorian and Edwardian Times», pp. 176–198 in J.A. Mangan and J. Walvin (eds.). *Manliness and Morality: Middle-Class Masculinity in Britain and America, 1800–1940.* Manchester: Manchester University Press.

Mar-Molinaro, Clare and Angel Smith (eds.) (1996). *Nationalism and the Nation in the Iberian Peninsula: Competing and Conflicting Identities.* Washington (DC): Berg.

McClintock, Anne (1991). *Imperial Leather Race, Gender and Sexuality in the Colonial Contest.* London: Routledge.

McGarry, John (1998). «‹Demographic Engineering›: The State-Directed Movement of Ethnic Groups as a Technique of Conflict Regulation», *Ethnic and Racial Studies* 21 (4): 613–38.

Mehdid, Malika (1996). «En-Gendering the Nation-State: Woman, Patriarchy and Politics in Algeria», pp. 78–102 in S.M. Rai and G. Lievesley (eds.). *Woman and the State: International Perspectives.* London: Taylor and Francis.

Messerschmidt, James (1993). *Masculinities and Crime.* Lanham (MD): Rowman and Littlefield.

Moghadam, Valentine M. (1991). «Revolution, Islam, and Women: Sexual Politics in Iran and Afghanistan», pp. 424–446 in A. Parker, M. Russo, D. Sommer, and P. Yaeger (eds.). *Nationalisms and Sexualities.* New York: Routledge.

Moran, L.J. (1991). «The Uses of Homosexuality: Homosexuality for National Security», *International Journal of the Sociology of Law* 19.

Mosse, George L. (1985). *Nationalism and Sexuality: Middle-Class Morality and Sexual Norms in Modern Europe.* Madison (WI): University of Wisconsin Press.

Mosse, George L. (1996). *The Image of Man: The Creation of Modern Masculinity.* New York: Oxford University Press.

Mydans, Seth (November 12, 1996). «Inside a Wartime Brothel: The Avenger's Story», *New York Times,* A3.

Nagel, Joane (1996). *American Indian Ethnic Renewal: Red Power and the Resurgence of Identity and Culture.* New York: Oxford University Press.

Nategh, Homa (1987). «Women: Damned of the Iranian Revolution», pp. 45–60 in R. Ridd and H. Callaway. *Women and Political Conflict.* New York: New York University Press.

Nielsen, J. (1992). *Muslims in Western Europe.* Edinburgh: Edinburgh University Press.

Norgaard, Ole, Hans Hindsgaul, Lars Johannsen, and Helle Willumsen (1996). *The Baltic States After Independence.* Brookfield (VT): Edward Elgar.

Patton, Cindy (1997). «To Die For», pp. 330–352 in E.K. Sedgwick (ed.). *Novel Gazing: Queer Readings in Fiction.* Durham (NC): Duke University Press.

Petkov, Kiril (1997). *Infidels, Turks, and Women: The South Slavs in the German Mind, circa 1400–1600.* New York: Peter Lang.

Sanders, D. (1996). «Getting Lesbian and Gay Issues on the International Human Rights Agenda», *Human Rights Quarterly* 18.

Saunders, Kay (1995). «In a Cloud of Lust: Black Gis and Sex in World War II», pp. 178–190 in J. Damousi and M. Lake (eds.). *Gender and War: Australians at War in the Twentieth Century.* Cambridge: Cambridge University Press.

Sayigh, Rosemary and Julie Peteet (1987). «Between Two Fires: Palestinian Women in Lebanon», pp. 106–137 in R. Ridd and H. Callaway (eds.). *Women and Political Conflict.* New York: New York University Press.

Sells, Michael A. (1996). *The Bridge Betrayed: Religion and Genocide in Bosnia.* Berkeley: University of California Press.

Sinha, Mrinalini (1995). *Colonial Masculinity: The ‹Manly Englishman› and the ‹Effeminate Bengali› in the Late Nineteenth Century.* Manchester: Manchester University Press.

Skurski, Julie (1994). «The Ambiguities of Authenticity in Latin America: Dona Barbara and the Construction of National Identity», *Poetics Today* 15(4):604–42.

Smith, Graham (1988). *When Jim Crow Met John Bull: Black American Soldiers in World War II Britain.* New York: St. Martin's Press.

Spackman, Barbara (1996). *Fascist Virilities: Rhetoric, Ideology, and Social Fantasy in Italy.* Minneapolis: University of Minnesota Press.

Spencer, Ian R.G. (1997). *British Immigration Policy Since 1939: The Making of Multiracial Britain.* London: Routledge.

Springhall, John (1987). «Building Character in the British Boy: The Attempt to Extend Christian Manliness to Working-Class Adolescents, 1880–1940», pp. 52–74 in J.A. Mangan and J. Walvin (eds.). *Manliness and Morality: Middle-Class Masculinity in Britain and America, 1800–1940.* Manchester: Manchester University Press.

Steinfels, Peter (July 1, 1995). «In Algeria, Women are Caught in the Cross-Fire of Men's Religious and Ideological Wars», *New York Times,* 8, 10.

Stychin, Carl F. (1998). *A Nation by Rights: National Cultures, Sexual Identity Politics, and the Discourse of Rights.* Philadelphia: Temple University Press.

Sweet, Timothy (1993). «Masculinity and Self-Performance in the Life of Black Hawk», *American Literature* 65 (3): 475–99.

Theweleit, Klaus (1987). *Male Fantasies,* Vol. 1, Translated by Stephen Conway. Minneapolis (MN): University of Minnesota Press.

Tohidi, Neyereh (1991). «Gender and Islamic Fundamentalism: Feminist Politics in Iran», pp. 251–265 in C.T. Mohanty, A. Russo, and L. Torres (eds.). *Third World Women and the Politics of Feminism.* Bloomington: Indiana University Press.

Triandafyllidou, Anna (1998). «National Identity and the ‹Other›», *Ethnic and Racial Studies* 21 (4): 593–612.

Urdang, Stephanie (1989). *And Still They Dance: Women, War and the Struggle for Change in Mozambique.* New York: Monthly Review Press.

Van Ness, G. (1996). «Parades and Prejudice: The Incredible True Story of Boston's St. Patrick's Day Parade and the United States Supreme Court», *New England Law Review* 30.

Walby, Silvia (1989). «Woman and Nation», pp. 81–99 in A.D. Smith (ed.). *Ethnicity and Nationalism.* New York: E.J. Brill.

Waldinger, Roger (1996). *Still, the Promised City? African-Americans and New Immigrants in Postindustrial New York.* Cambridge (MA): Harvard University Press.

Walvin, James (1987). «Symbols of Moral Superiority: Slavery, Sport and the Changing World Order, 1900–1940», pp. 242–260 in J.A. Mangan and J. Walvin (eds.). *Manliness and Morality: Middle-Class Masculinity in Britain and America, 1800–1940.* Manchester: Manchester University Press.

Weber, Eugen (1976). *Peasants into Frenchmen: The Modernization of Rural France, 1870–1914.* Stanford (CA): Stanford University Press.

Weitz, Margaret Collins (1995). *Sisters in the Resistance: How Women Fought to Free France, 1940–45.* New York: J. Wiley.

Youssef, Ibrahim M. (March 31, 1997). «Bareheaded Women Slain in Algiers: Killings following Islamic Threats», *New York Times,* A3.

Zappala, Gianni (1998). «The Micro-Politics of Immigration: Service Responsiveness in an Australian ‹Ethnic Electorate›», *Ethnic and Racial Studies* 21 (4): 683–702.

The Transformation of Citizenship in the Global Age: From National to European and Global Ties

Richard Münch

1 Three wrong tracks toward global modernity

The discussion concerning the changes in our social and value systems caused by globalization is dominated by three viewpoints. Firstly, the new economic liberalism considers the fully developed welfare state to be the cause of the structural crisis which manifests itself, on the one hand, in the state's excessive debts, tax loads and social security contributions which paralyze all activities, and, on the other hand, in a high level of permanent unemployment (Berthold 1997). Secondly, those who defend the welfare state see the danger of a fragmentation, disintegration and disorganization of society resulting from the deregulation program of the new economic liberalism, which produces a growing potential for violence and political extremism. As they do not believe that the European Union possesses the power necessary to contain such problems, they plead for the maintenance of the achievements of the welfare state as far as this is possible (Afheldt 1994; Marglin and Schor 1990; Altvater and Mahnkopf 1996; Hirsch 1995). Finally, those who accept a dwindling of the nation state's power as inevitable, support the European Union's democratic and social expansion, the democratization of global institutions, and the inclusion of social standards within the agreements on free world trade (Archibugi and Held 1995; Held 1995; Habermas 1996; McGrew 1997). However, all three viewpoints are characterized by a certain naiveté with regard to the constraints resulting from the growing globalization of modern life. Contrary to these three positions outlined above, the preparation of a blueprint for a more practicable transition to global modernity must begin with a realistic analysis of the structural change affecting solidarity which goes hand in hand with globalization. In the following paper, I will develop the basic features of such an analysis in order to lay the foundations for a new model for the future.

2 Structural change in solidarity

The fully developed European welfare state is confronted by its limitations not merely due to a lack of money, but above all due to a far-reaching structural change in solidarity, which is driven by the growing European and global flows of economic exchange and communication. The European nation-state succeeded in becoming a comprehensive welfare state because it ensured a high degree of national, i.e. inter-class, inter-stratum and inter-group solidarity over a long history of external demarcation – not least of all as a result of wars – and internal homogenization due to political, bureaucratic and legal centralization and cultural unification (unified language, education for all, mass communication), as well as a balance of social tensions. As a rule, this was not achieved without considerable repression and the removal of regional variety and autonomy. Relatively uniform, homogeneous nation-states came into being in otherwise quite diverse regions (Münch 1993: 15–33). On this basis, it was possible to continually increase national affluence, thanks to external economic links and co-operation between the different states, among other things. Specific advantages of location – raw materials, capital, knowledge, organizational intelligence, productivity – embraced the entire working population and, on the basis of collective solidarity, could be used to ensure, through the mediation of the state, equal conditions of life for everybody. The increase in the state's share of GNP, recently reaching more than 50% in the Federal Republic of Germany (Statistisches Bundesamt 1997: 666) presented no problem in a state which was strengthened by collective solidarity in a world of interlinked national economies and inter-state co-operation. This situation is, however, now changing, and will continue to do so even more in the future.

The nation-states' collective solidarity is now being replaced by a more complex system of solidarities. The semi-annual Eurobarometer polls give evidence of this development. Asked about their identity in the near future, up to 15% of all those questioned saw themselves exclusively or mainly as Europeans; around 40% considered themselves first and foremost as members of their own nation and, secondly, as Europeans; the remaining 45% regarded themselves exclusively as members of their own nation. The sense of identification with Europe clearly rises proportional to income, educational level, and professional status. At the same time, regional and local identities are assuming a growing importance, since the single European market involves the regions, towns and communities in a more open competition for market opportunities and financial assistance (European Commission 1997: 55, B74–75; 1998: B28–31).

Policies designed to increase the economic attractiveness of given locations by offering incentives for investors – including the continuous retraining of the working population or the promotion of a culture of the self-employed – become the most important political tools for securing economic competitiveness (Reich 1991; Thurow 1996). This type of policy is replacing social policy. At the same time, however, it increases competition. The policy of retraining not only improves the chances of all those who gain more qualifications, but at the same time reduces the chances of those who do not obtain new qualifications or who are otherwise unable to improve their position. The demand for professional work is continually rising, while all those who are unable to compete in the race for qualifications find themselves in poorly paid and insecure jobs, or unemployed. Global competition breaks up the national welfare solidarity and widens the gap between those who are able to assert themselves, and those who seem to be a burden and must be dragged along without being able to make an active contribution. In this situation of broken solidarity, nationalistic counter-movements tend to mobilize against the trend towards a European and global society. The losers of the change in solidarity provide an ever larger pool of supporters for these counter-movements (Betz 1991).

In these changed circumstances, the nation-state now lacks the resources of collective solidarity which would help it to ensure a social balance to the same extent as it was once able to do. In the future, these resources will no longer be available in the same measure as previously, either on a European or on a global level. The necessary prerequisite for their deployment would be the creation of a European or even a global super-state. A nation-state transferred onto a European or global level would need to achieve precisely that degree of internal homogenization which was attained by the nation-states in the past, in order to achieve the same capacity to act. Such a project is neither feasible nor desirable when it becomes a question of maintaining freedom and diversity. This means, however, that we must bid farewell to the extremely high level of the production of equal conditions of life in the form of the European welfare state (Scharpf 1998).

3　A change in values: justice as fairness

Corresponding to the structural change in solidarity, a shift in values will occur, in which greater importance will be attached to the principle of achievement than to the principle of social equality, with respect to the attainment of a certain standard of living. Social inequality will then increase. It will not necessarily increase to the level of the USA, but it will clearly be higher than the current level. In the course of this shift of values, from the principle of social equality to that of achievement, the interpretation of justice will also change. The idea of justice will no longer denote the provision of equal conditions of life for all, but rather conditions of life which ensure that everybody has an equal opportunity to acquire income and reputation in fair competition. Those who cannot compete will be given the means or support to help themselves, while those who are handicapped may be promoted more strongly so as to become competitive. The ultimate goal will be to grant support to those who are permanently weak or unable to participate in competition, so that they are able to live in conditions that are generally regarded as appropriate. Justice in the sense of broadly equal conditions of life will be replaced by justice in the sense of fairness (Rawls 1971, 1993). From a moral point of view, this conception of justice is more appropriate to the varied solidarity relationships in the emerging world society than is the principle of equal conditions of life, which has combined a pervasive intra-state equality with considerable global inequality. The integration of the world community through the moral principle of justice in the sense of fairness is the other side of the coin of global capitalism, a point which is frequently overlooked by moralizing social critics. It implies that the citizens of the European welfare states will have to share their affluence with other people in the world much more than they have done.

4   The driving forces behind the structural change in solidarity and justice

We might wonder now whether this structural change in solidarity is an unstoppable process. The answer to this question is: yes, under certain, historically variable conditions. An explanation for this was supplied by Emile Durkheim in his classic study on the division of labor, published in 1893. The closer people become to each other due to a rise in population, and improvements in means of transportation and communication, the fiercer will be the struggle for scarce resources, and people will only be able to survive by specialization. In the course of this specialization, they will be forced to enter into exchange relationships with one another which reach beyond the borders of small solidarity units. The global division of labor is the final stage of this process, in which the nation-states' pervasive mechanical solidarity becomes an anachronism and is superseded by the more complex and more specific organic solidarity of worldwide networks of individuals. The nation-states' mechanical solidarity was based on a strong feeling of unity between relatively equal individuals, whereas the world society's organic solidarity will instead rely on the awareness of a mutual dependence of unequal individuals, on specific and selective socialization by common involvement in joint projects, and on more loosely established networks of allegiance (Durkheim 1893/1973).

The social crises which are emerging in this stage of transformation can only be overcome to the extent that it is possible to establish global relationships on new legal and moral foundations. A change in values is required, which replaces the concrete substantive justice of sharing between equal individuals with the application of abstract and formal justice between unequal individuals. The conception of justice in the sense of fairness accomplishes this task.

Durkheim also teaches us something about the reverse side of the law of comparative cost advantages discovered by David Ricardo (Ricardo 1922; Arndt 1996). According to this law, everyone will benefit when the global division of labor ensures that products are manufactured wherever this can be done at the lowest cost. Universal affluence increases in tandem with the global division of labor. At the same time, however, the routes and means of transport and communication are extended so that competition becomes increasingly tough and necessitates ever faster innovations and shorter product cycles. The world must be inundated more quickly with more products which themselves generate a steadily rising need. Those who have never seen a video recorder, mobile phone or multi-media station will not feel a need for them. But once these products have been invented, they quickly create and conquer ever bigger markets. The process of «creative destruction», as described by Schumpeter (1950/1993: 134–142), accelerates. It permanently alters employment patterns and life circumstances and reinforces competition. Regardless of whether the adaptation occurs slowly or quickly, we are living in a state of continuous change. This development is reflected in the chronic instability of the labor market. The counterpart of a shrinking core of secure, full-time jobs is a growing number of short-term, part-time, shared, and insecure jobs going hand in hand with short-, medium- or long-term unemployment. It is true that universal affluence is increasing and that the conditions of life will improve for the winners of the competition; yet, at the same time, a range of new inequalities, uncertain employment and conditions of life, and ecological damage resulting from consumption and traffic, are appearing where good conditions of life had once prevailed. As Durkheim has shown, the reason behind the advancing global division of labor is not the growing happiness and/or rising benefit of people, but rather the increasingly fierce competition as the world population grows, and the means of transportation and communication improve (Durkheim 1893/1973: Book II, chap. 2).

5 A new model: the active society of citizens

We cannot change these structural conditions of the increasing global division of labor in any fundamental way. To do so, the infrastructure of transportation and communication would have to be reduced, which would be contrary to the century-old trend (Ohmae 1990; Hirst and Thompson 1996; Narr and Schubert 1994). It seems unlikely that sufficient support could be mobilized for such a strategy. Contrary to all previous policies, such a strategy would have to limit liberties instead of extending them. Therefore, the only realistic alternative is the regulation of factors which must in any case be taken into account. This means, for instance, that the widening circle of precarious jobs around the diminishing core of secure, full-time jobs, and the pressure on wages for simple production and service work, would have to be absorbed by a new basic safety net, which is more flexibly adapted to the switch between work and non-work, and which would offer a collective solution to the insecurities confronted by the new self-employed. The introduction of a negative income tax and a combined wage might be one way of solving this problem.

The withdrawal of the state, which is rendered inevitable by the global change in solidarity, requires a compensating activation of private welfare and voluntary organizations. The active society of citizens could become a new model of global modernity beyond economic liberalism and the welfare state. It is true that it cannot ensure equal conditions of life as they used to be known, but it would guarantee a more complex network of solidarities adjusted to current conditions to the extent that the number of organizations involved multiplies and is interlinked by citizens who belong to more than one such organization. Certainly, the new solidarity network would not be as dense as the welfare state's social network; yet it would be more open both towards the bottom, i.e. the regions, towns and communities, and towards the top, i.e. the European and global level. However, given that the civil-societal network will always have holes and gaps, the state will always, at all levels, have the task of mending these holes and bridging these gaps. It will be able to undertake this task more efficiently when it is no longer entrusted with the comprehensive provision of equal living conditions for everybody. We should remember that the comprehensive welfare state embraced the whole of society in a homogeneous way, from child allowance through to free university education and old-age pensions. As it did so, however, its capacity for coping with urgent social problems was dangerously impaired.

The active society of citizens is definitely not a bad and therefore inferior substitute for the benefits of the welfare state, nor merely an ideological invention of the neo-liberals' assault on the welfare state. It offers, rather, a chance to shape the future beyond the fruitless struggle between the defense of the old welfare state and the neo-liberal assault on its institutions.

Here in Europe, we can learn from the USA about the functioning of an active society of citizens, but also about its weaknesses. More so than in Europe, in the USA, voluntary associations and private organizations have always met the challenge of supporting society, whether in conjunction with the state, or at the point at which the state's resources were overstretched. This was perfectly done in small, white neighborhoods among the middle and upper classes. However, this integration concept is doomed to fail in the focal zones of poverty, exclusion, unstable families, crumbling city ghettos, crime, violence, drug consumption and homelessness (Gans 1995; Donziger 1996; Moore 1996; Danziger and Gottschalk 1993; Wright 1997; Murswieck 1997). Social integration through private welfare networks is very uneven and incomplete, and tends to be overwhelmingly confined to the white middle and upper classes. If we in Europe wish to avoid the disintegration and anomie which are to be found everywhere in the USA, then state action must continue to play a major role in the integration of social problem areas and must remain available at least as an anchor for the private provision of public welfare. And since we do not have an equally strong private welfare network beyond the neo-corporatist co-operation of state and large welfare organizations in Europe, targeted state support is indispensable, e.g. the transformation of state welfare administrations into agencies that support the activities of private associations, organizations and companies, and co-ordinate their activities. The co-operation of the state with large associations has become a welfare cartel which is not sufficiently sensitive to the plethora of new social problems. It must give way to state guidance of a plurality of smaller associations, companies and initiatives so as to attain that degree of flexibility which is required by the variety of rapidly changing social problem areas. The welfare cartel itself consumes substantial amounts of money and has therefore become increasingly incapable of ensuring that the limited means available are deployed where they are most urgently needed (Berthold 1997).

The active society of citizens does not come into existence by itself, but is rather a project whose establishment requires particular incentives from and continuous support by state initiatives. Only if this project succeeds, can globalization's disintegrative effects be kept within manageable limits. The active society of citizens could then become the new «third way», beyond economic liberalism and the welfare state. It might be considered as a vision of the «Third Modernity» of the global age, which succeeds the «First Modernity» of the liberal legal state, and the «Second Modernity» of the welfare state.

6 Social integration's trends to crisis: spirals of inflation and deflation caused by the utilization of equal rights

The replacement of the welfare state by an active society of citizens would increase the integration potential of the multi-level system of world society, where the nation-state represents but one level between the European and global levels on the one hand, and the local and regional levels on the other. The place of historically evolved, deep-seated solidarities is taken by abstractly constructed, less deeply rooted but more comprehensive solidarity relationships. Particular group loyalties and cultural traditions lose their integrative power and are transplanted into a wider web of solidarities and cultures. The extraordinarily demanding structural change in solidarity is driven primarily by the global division of labor which, in turn, is necessitated by the globalizing competition for resources in short supply in the wake of population growth, the shrinking of distances resulting from improvements in transportation and communication, and of migration. The advancing division of labor is the principal means of breaking up both local and national solidarities, and of reconstructing solidarity relationships which transcend primordial group loyalties and cultures. Without an inter-group and intercultural division of labor, multi-ethnicity and multiculturalism cannot lead to a new level of social integration beyond particular groups. This means that the division of labor must penetrate the particular groups and cultures, but without reproducing them. It is only on this material base – the emergence of new solidarity relationships from real inter-group co-operation – that a practicable, legally and morally founded regulation of new social relationships can develop.

Without the material substratum of the inter-group and inter-cultural division of labor, law and morality will lose any grounding in current reality. They will either remain tied to particularism, or go too far beyond the real solidarities. In the first case, global competition will heighten the tensions between particular groups and cultures. In the second case, a claim to universality will be made which cannot be substantiated due to the lack of actual solidarity relationships. The consequence of an exaggerated claim to universality by law and morality would be the provoking of strong counter-reactions, resulting in a relapse into particularistic group loyalties. A claim to universality by law and morality will become untenable in so far as individual rights are granted, on paper, which extend far beyond real solidarity relationships which are secured by factual co-operation and by the guaranteed mutual respect of participants' rights.

The cleavage between, on the one hand, the granting of and appeal to individual rights, and, on the other hand, the reality of actual solidarity relationships, clearly underlines the fact that individual rights, like money, can be regarded as a form of communication which has a symbolic or token character which itself must be differentiated from its real counterpart, the acts of solidarity (Münch 1998: 151–162). The more the conditions of life deviate from evolved solidarities and transcend them, the less likely it is that these solidarities will guarantee social integration. Individual rights extend beyond the evolved solidarities and imply a social integration beyond their limits (Marshall 1964). Moreover, when particular solidarities are not broken up by relationships created from the division of labor, so that a new, all-encompassing co-operation is unable to emerge, then individual rights may easily develop into a form of communication which has no real value. The mere declaration of individual rights (civil and human rights) by national bodies or by internationally agreed declarations, such as the General Declaration of Human Rights of the UN General Assembly in December 1948, cannot be interpreted as evidence of real social integration. In themselves, such declarations are simply like coupons whose actual value is to be measured by the extent to which the individual can expect tolerance and support when invoking such rights.

The value of rights which are granted in principle must be proven by real acts of tolerance and support. However, crises may develop as a result of a disparity between principle and actuality, as we know from economic spirals of inflation and deflation. The more people wish to appeal to formally granted rights, while older relationships of solidarity remain stronger than those born of the growing division of labor and inclusiveness of the markets (above all, the labor market), the more the substantive granting of tolerance and support will lag behind the formal granting of individual rights. An increasing discrepancy will emerge between the volume of formally granted rights and the volume of substantive acts of tolerance and support. In this sense, individual rights are subject to an inflationary devaluation process. The greater the discrepancy between the formulation and the actual recognition of rights, the more will confidence in individual rights dwindle, so that the trend towards non-legal means of preserving interests will increase, even to a resort to violence. This violence is directed against competitors, whereas support is looked for and found exclusively within the closest circle of one's own group, a fact which strengthens group particularism. Inflation thus becomes a deflationary process through an abandonment of legal solutions and recourse to particular solidarities.

7   Cross-border division of labor and the flexibility of the labor market as tools of cross-border social integration

The decisive condition for this crisis exists when an increasing frequency of appeals to rights is not accompanied by a comparable increase in the division of labor and inclusiveness of the markets, above all the labor market. It is precisely this discrepancy which characterizes the current situation. The growth in population, the extension of the means of transport and communication, and increasing migration, aggravate global competition within which, however, adequately established inter-group solidarity relationships have not yet emerged from the growing division of labor and market inclusion. The nation-states' welfare cartel proves to be an obstacle to innovations which could otherwise stimulate the division of labor and market inclusion. The consequences of this impediment to reform are growing conflicts between the winners and the losers of globalization, nationalism and regionalism. Peaceful co-operation is replaced by a struggle for scarce resources. Two examples may illustrate this trend towards a crisis: (1) the wave of xenophobia in Germany at the beginning of the nineties; (2) the confrontation between radical multiculturalism and right-wing conservative counter-reaction in the USA since the end of the eighties.

In Germany, the challenge of raising the standard of living in the East to equal that of the West after unification, amidst the total collapse of the Eastern economy, converged with the challenge of integrating a growing wave of asylum-seekers and incoming German settlers from Russia in the early 1990s. Both asylum-seekers and settlers arrived on the basis of formally granted rights, which included support by the existing welfare system. To this extent, they were integrated in a formal legal sense. But this formal-legal integration was not accompanied by a demonstration of substantive solidarity by the German population as a whole, partly because people then experienced greater competition for jobs, income, and welfare support. «Too much demand from the East», «too much inequality between East and West» and «too little support for the East by the West» were the slogans which dominated public discussion in the media.

The framing of this situation by the media focused on questions of inequality between East and West and on the increasing burdens of unification. It was therefore not surprising that people who felt disadvantaged should regard immigration as a threat to their own position in society. A growing number of people perceived asylum-seekers less as victims of political repression and persecution, and more as people who made use of the German welfare system and who were seeking better economic opportunities. Reference to the fact that the high proportion of young immigrants could help to support the pension system of the ageing German population did not help to overcome xenophobic attitudes. On the contrary, the situation was exacerbated by changes in the labor market: technological rationalization and the high costs of labor in international competition led to a decline in the demand for unskilled labor, so that immigrants were perceived as contributing to the growing rate of unemployment, whether because they themselves did not get jobs, or because they were seen as taking jobs from the indigenous work force.

The government was unable to accompany the growing wave of immigration with policies which stimulated the labor market, so that immigration could be welcomed as meeting a demand for labor. Only under such circumstances would the reference to the immigrants' contribution to the old-age pension system have been convincing. Another failure of the government was its reluctance to grant full citizenship to immigrant families who have been living in the country for generations. Here, too, the result has been an ever widening gap between the formal-legal granting of rights to integration, and substantive integration in the division of labor and in the social and political life of society. The level of acceptance of immigrants by German citizens declined, and this opened the way to an increasing incidence of violence against foreigners. The inflationary process of formally granting rights combined with a declining ability to realise those rights as a substantive integration of the whole population – immigrants and citizens – led to a loss of confidence in the government's capacity to handle the problem on the part of the citizen population and to the latter's return to particularistic group solidarity. The restrictions on the right to asylum which were introduced by an agreement between government and opposition was the final expression of the fact that neither the government nor the people were able to honour the granting of rights by substantive integration. The deflationary return to particularistic group solidarity among parts of the citizen population was complemented by the state's application of restrictions on the granting of rights.

The peaceful co-existence of citizens and immigrants was possible in Germany as long as both groups were fully incorporated into the labor market and, in this way, were tied into various relationships of co-operation. Xenophobia grew only to the extent that an increasing number of immigrants could not be integrated into the labor market, and this in turn forced the government to restrict the right to asylum (Willems 1993; Küchler 1994). If the labor market had been less regulated and therefore more active, then xenophobia would certainly not have reached such a high level. This assumption is underlined by the fact that xenophobia emerged most markedly in social problem areas, especially in Eastern Germany. What is true of the citizen population with regard to the immigrants is also true of the immigrants with regard to the citizen population. The less immigrants are integrated into the labor market, the more likely they are to cling to their original identity and to shy away from participating in the local culture. Levels of crime and violence also tend to increase among those who are not integrated into the labor market. The eruptions of violence among the beurs (second-generation North Africans living in France) in the French suburbs, to take another example, are due much less to their cultural difference than to their meagre opportunities of being integrated into the labor market (Dubet and Lapeyronnie 1994).

Our thesis that a flexible labor market turns conflict for scarce jobs into co-operation through growing job differentiation and division of labor does not necessarily imply that xenophobic attitudes and manifestations of violence against foreigners will always be more common among jobless people than among those in employment. The thesis claims rather that a failure to integrate foreigners into the division of labor maintains an absence of social relationships (or solidarity) between foreigners and the citizen population so that, in times of crisis, foreigners are perceived as outsiders and as such, a threat to society. In this situation, xenophobia grows within the whole of society, and is not confined to the unemployed who see foreigners as direct competitors for jobs.

The regulation of the labor markets in the highly developed European welfare states is the fruit of co-operation between trade unions, employers and governments. These parties have established a system which ensures a high degree of job security, high income, and good support in cases of disability, illness, invalidity, unemployment, and old age. The other side of this coin, however, was mounting pressure to meet high labor costs with increased productivity via technological rationalization. This implied a declining demand for unskilled labor and rising barriers to employment for those seeking a job. The neo-corporatist co-operation between trade unions, employers and governments, which had been so successful in constructing the welfare system, has become more and more a welfare cartel of resistance to any transformations of the system which might in fact be able to revitalize the labor market and solve the new problems of integration. The wider scenario includes mounting burdens on the working population which is obliged to support the non-working population, old age pensions for a growing number of elderly people at the cost of support for the education of younger people, increasing costs of health care, and a shortage of funding for innovations in research and technology. The rights which were guaranteed by the welfare state are defended against any changes which might actually be able to help meet the new challenges.

The regulation of the labor market is at the center of the new demands for reform. These demands have turned from focusing on measures of inclusion, to measures which exclude people from the labor market. Reforms which would allow greater flexibility in the labor market would lower the barriers confronted by those seeking employment. This should not mean the complete abandonment of any system of social security, but rather the introduction of new forms of social security which are adapted to the needs of a more flexible job market: for example, negative income tax, obligatory basic insurance with private insurance to provide a higher level of cover, incentives for part-time work, flexible movement from non-work to work and back to non-work, and support for getting started in self-employed work. A more flexible labor market would turn the competition for a limited number of jobs into new job specializations; it would increase the differentiation of jobs and hence the division of labor. People who were competing against each other for the same job, would move into different jobs and turn their competition into an exchange of goods and services, thereby establishing social relationships of mutual commitment which transcend particularistic group allegiances.

This process whereby conflict is turned into co-operation could also be applied to inter-ethnic social integration. Whereas social relationships outside of the workplace tend to be established according to particularistic group solidarities, including ethnic ties, the dynamic forces of the division of labor are able to cut across ethnic group ties, because the market is responsive to the rational calculation of the most profitable opportunities for exchanging goods and services. The working of the market to cut across ethnic ties would be supported by policies of qualifying the work force such that people would be able to continue to find employment within a permanently changing and growing division of labor, and independently of their ethnic origin. Economic relationships which cut across ethnic ties could then become a driving force for strengthening social ties which extend beyond the market place, beginning with labor associations and their social activities, reaching beyond work-related matters, and moving on to social associations of other kinds. Furthermore, in our day and age, the individual achieves more than ever before in social standing through participation in the division of labor. One therefore acquires exactly that basic social capital which can be invested in order to accumulate further social capital through participation in social activity outside the labor market. It is a well-established fact that people who participate in the division of labor also tend to participate more than other people in all kinds of social activities. The reason for this is that their job provides not only income, but also the capacity to participate in social life.

Admittedly, there is often a concentration of particular ethnic groups in some areas of business. However, this is due less to economic forces than to the penetration of group solidarities into the economy, which in turn weakens the ethnically neutral forces of economic calculation. This observation corroborates the thesis that the possibility of achieving inter-ethnic solidarity is enhanced when the division of labor transcends ethnic allegiances.

The limits of a country's ability to accept immigrants are, therefore, first and foremost determined by the flexibility of its labor market. This is basically the secret behind social integration in the culturally pluralistic society of the USA. In fact, this country owes much of its integrative capacity to its flexible labor market. The understanding of justice as fairness offers the concomitant resource of legitimation. American society is still sufficiently open that it is able to provide opportunities to new competitors. Legions of immigrants have readily filled the lower positions of production and service work, from coal mining to baby sitting, without producing serious conflicts of displacement and distribution. If a welfare cartel similar to that of the European welfare states had emerged in the USA, the country would have experienced much more serious displacement and distribution conflicts in the wake of the various waves of immigration than have in fact occurred. Nevertheless, the USA has been hit by this phenomenon. Large waves of immigration did cause defensive reactions which led to the specification of quotas according to the countries of origin. At the time of each large wave of immigration, the question arose as to the limits of ethnic and cultural plurality and the minimum requirements for national unity. As long as the labor market and a comprehensive policy of equal opportunities afforded a sufficiently large material integration, these discussions remained largely academic. They only seriously affected political decision making when minorities felt excluded from the labor market, or old-established groups felt threatened by new immigrants or up-and-coming groups in the labor market. The radicalization of the black civil rights movement and the white counter-reaction must be interpreted primarily as just such a displacement struggle (Schlesinger 1992; Puhle et al. 1994; Rex 1996).

Radical multiculturalism requires group rights, since the inclusion of disadvantaged minorities through the assertion of individual rights stretches the legitimacy of those rights and runs up against white resistance. The whites' resistance is mobilized wherever the lower white groups of the population fear that their economic position will be threatened by the previously disadvantaged minorities. The withdrawal of both sides to their own groups entails a rejection of the program of inclusion and inevitably leads to a strengthening of the conflict. A resolution of this conflict can only be expected to the extent that it is possible to increase the labor market's inclusive potential, not only with flexible jobs, but also with better education, continuous training and technical qualification. Economic inclusion will then proceed hand in hand with cultural inclusion. The struggle for either a nationally uniform or a multicultural school curriculum, for example, will become superfluous, since competition is transformed into co-operation through the permanent extension and differentiation of the division of labor. Under these conditions, it will no longer be necessary to ask whether the curriculum will ensure better mutual understanding, because the culturally dominant English-speaking pupils will be studying at least two other languages and cultures besides their own, whilst pupils from ethnic minorities will be gaining a knowledge of English alongside their own and a third language and culture. Integration into the labor market will then be complemented by cultural integration based on fairness.

8 Conclusion

In the wake of the global growth in population, the extension of the means of transport and communication, and increased migration, the European welfare states changed, from being tools of social integration, into fortresses hindering processes of integration both within their own societies and at a global level. The welfare cartel which has emerged has become the decisive obstacle to social integration, which might otherwise have been achieved by making the labor market more flexible and through a corresponding change in the concept of justice – from being regarded as the production of equal conditions of life, justice would come to be seen as fairness and equal opportunities. The path towards a solution to the new integration problems, if prepared by such achievements, can only be followed if there is an extension and further differentiation of the division of labor, and an increased flexibility in the labor market and in new forms of social security: e.g. combined wage and negative income tax, social security financed by taxes instead of cost splitting, equal basic securities for all and differentiated additional private insurance. Contrary to a widespread but rather narrow-minded viewpoint, the national and global differentiated division of labor is not simply an invention of a socially reckless capitalism, but the bearer of a structural change in solidarity, which will overcome the particularism of more local solidarities and pave the way for universal multicultural social integration. However, this new level of social integration. will only be attained when the old national welfare fortresses are demolished and new humanitarian organizations can contribute to legal change and to innovations in social policy which complement the open and flexible labor market with a similarly open and flexible social security system based on fairness.

References

Afheldt, Horst (1994). *Wohlstand für niemand. Die Marktwirtschaft entlässt ihre Kinder.* Munich: Kunstmann.

Altvater, Elmar and Birgit Mahnkopf (1996). *Grenzen der Globalisierung. Ökonomie, Ökologie und Politik in der Weltgesellschaft.* Münster: Westfälisches Dampfboot.

Archibugi, Daniele and David Held (eds.) (1995). *Cosmopolitan Democracy.* Cambridge: Polity Press.

Arndt, Helmut (1996). *Arbeitslosigkeit und Wirtschaftsentwicklung.* Opladen: Leske + Budrich.

Berthold, Norbert (1997). *Der Sozialstaat im Zeitalter der Globalisierung.* Tübingen: Mohr Siebeck.

Betz, Hans Georg (1991). «Radikal rechtspopulistische Parteien in Westeuropa». *Aus Politik und Zeitgeschichte* B 44: 3–14.

Danziger, Sheldon und Peter Gottschalk (eds.) (1993). *Uneven Tides. Rising Inequality in America.* New York: Russel Sage Foundation.

Donziger, Steven R. (ed.) (1996). *The Real War on Crime. The Report of the National Criminal Justice Commission.* New York: Harper Perennial.

Dubet, François and Didier Lapeyronnie (1994). *Im Aus der Vorstädte. Der Zerfall der demokratischen Gesellschaft.* Stuttgart: Klett-Cotta.

Durkheim, Emile (1893, 1973). *De la division du travail social.* Paris: Presses Universitaires de France.

Esping-Andersen, Goesta (1990). The Three Worlds of Welfare Capitalism. Cambridge: Polity Press.

European Commission (1997). *Eurobarometer* N° 47. Brussels.

European Commission (1998). *Eurobarometer* N° 48. Brussels.

Gans, Herbert J. (1995). *The War against the Poor.* New York: Basic Books.

Habermas, Jurgen (1996). *Die Einbeziehung des Anderen.* Frankfurt a. M.: Suhrkamp.

Held, David (1995). *Democracy and Global Order.* Cambridge: Polity Press.

Hirsch, Joachim (1995). *Der nationale Wettbewerbsstaat. Staat, Demokratie und Politik im globalen Kapitalismus.* Berlin: Edition ID-Archiv.

Hirst, Paul and Graham Thompson (1996). *Globalization in Question. The International Economy and the Possibilities of Governance.* Cambridge: Polity Press.

Küchler, Manfred (1994). «Germans and Others: Racism, Xenophobia, or Legitimate Conservatism», *German Politics* 3: 47–74.

Marglin, Stephen and Juliet B. Schor (eds.) (1990). *The golden Age of Capitalism.* Oxford: Clarendon Press.

Marshall, Thomas H. (1964). *Class, Citizenship and Social Development.* Westport (Conn.): Greenwood Press.

McGrew, Anthony (ed.) (1997). *The Transformation of Democracy*. Cambridge: Polity Press.

Moore, Thomas S. (1996). *Disposable Work Force. Worker Displacement and Employment Instability in America*. New York: Aldine de Gruyter.

Münch, Richard (1993). *Das Projekt Europa. Zwischen Nationalstaat, regionaler Autonomie und Weltgesellschaft*. Frankfurt a. M.: Suhrkamp.

Münch, Richard (1998). *Globale Dynamik, lokale Lebenswelten*. Frankfurt a. M.: Suhrkamp.

Murswieck, Axel (1997). «Soziale Unsicherheit als Entwicklungsmotor? Die Erfahrungen der USA», in *Jahrbuch für Europa- und Nordamerikastudien 1: Standortrisiko Wohlfahrtsstaat?* Opladen: Leske + Budrich.

Narr, Wolf-Dieter and Alexander Schubert (1994). *Weltökonomie. Die Misere der Politik*. Frankfurt a. M.: Suhrkamp.

Ohmae, Kenichi (1990). *The borderless World*. London: Collins.

Puhle, Hans-Jürgen, Kurt L. Shell, Söhnke Schreyer, Ulrike Fischer and Rüdiger Wersich (1994). *Probleme der Institutionalisierung des Multikulturalismus in den USA*. ZENAF Arbeits- und Forschungsbericht. Frankfurt a. M.

Rawls, John (1971). *A Theory of Justice*. Cambridge (Mass.): Harvard University Press.

Rawls, John (1993). *Political Liberalism*. New York: Columbia University Press.

Reich, Robert (1991). *The Work of Nations*. New York: Vintage Books.

Rex, John (1996). «Multikulturalismus in Europa und Nordamerika», *Berliner Journal für Soziologie* 6: 149–161.

Ricardo, David (1922). *Grundsätze der Volkwirtschaftslehre und Besteuerung* (3rd vol. 1821). Jena: Fischer.

Scharpf, Fritz W. (1998). «Jenseits der Regime-Debatte: Oekonomische Integration, Demokratie und Wohlfahrstsstaat in Europa», pp. 321–349 in Stephan Lessenich and Ilona Ostner (eds). *Welten des Wohlfahrtskapitalismus. Der Sozialstaat in vergleichender Perspektive*. Frankfurt a. M.: Campus.

Schlesinger, Arthur M. Jr. (1992). The Disuniting of America: Reflections on a Multicultural Society. New York: Norton.

Schumpeter, Joseph A. (1950, 1993). *Kapitalismus, Sozialismus und Demokratie*. Tübingen: Francke.

Statistisches Bundesamt (1997). *Statistisches Jahrbuch 1997 für die Bundesrepublik Deutschland*. Wiesbaden: Metzler & Poeschel.

Thurow, Lester (1996). *Die Zukunft des Kapitalismus*. Düsseldorf und München: Metropolitan Verlag.

Willems, Helmut (1993). *Fremdenfeindliche Gewalt*. Opladen: Leske + Budrich.

Wright, Erik Olin (1997). *Class Counts. Comparative Studies in Class Analysis*. Cambridge: Cambridge University Press.

Part II

Case Studies: National Identity in a Historical and Comparative Perspective

Introduction

Hannes Siegrist

The following case studies analyze processes of nationalization and denationalization of society, politics, and culture in Belgium, Germany, Austria, Israel, and Croatia. They understand the nation as a symbolic and institutional, political and social reality, and ask how political elites and their rivals, intellectuals and popular movements, deal with the concept of nation. Their objective is to study how «national identities» are constructed, balanced, and changed, and with which objects and dimensions of a nation its people identify themselves.

1   Concepts and questions

The main aim of this section is to examine in detail how nation-builders, their followers and successors have imagined, shaped, institutionalized, and portrayed a nation-state, a national culture and society, in different historical contexts. The five case studies show that nations should be understood as a specific ordering of meaning *(Sinnordnung)* (Cassirer, 1985), and they indicate how both citizens and foreigners learn (and unlearn) the specific cognitive map of a single nation. They discuss the extents to which and the ways in which citizens identify with values, history and myths, symbols and rituals, and various stereotypes of «their» nation. The authors try to identify the origins, both past and present, of a sense of loyalty to the nation-state and to official national imagery. At the same time, they question the role and weight of competing loyalties with respect to socio-spatial, social and cultural units (see also Haupt et al., 1998).

The following chapters focus on the current and future problems of single nations. To a certain extent, every nation is confronted nowadays with similar problems: from within – social, economic and cultural change – and from without – pressures of globalization and europeanization. Yet some problems are home-made. That is to say, for example, that in the past, a nation may have developed certain stereotypes, programs, institutions, and symbols in order to address a specific situation, and these things then guaranteed national strength and self-consciousness; but in changed circumstances and in the face of new challenges, the same things no longer achieve the same ends. The authors therefore discuss the historical preconditions of contemporary processes of constructing and de-constructing nations. They need to analyze whether nations are still able to bind generations of the living together with the dead. What then is the contemporary meaning of classic categories and concepts like «community of fate», «ethnic nation», or «homogenized historical identity» on the one hand, and a «self-chosen» and deliberately shaped community, «civic nation», and «plural identities» on the other?

2   What can we learn from a particular national history?

Each chapter in the following section presents a well-informed and very valuable report about one particular national history, showing the context-dependence of the meaning of nation and the change of national identities. Together they show that each generation gives a new interpretation to the past in the light of contemporary questions and problems. The chapters are much more inspiring than many old-fashioned national histories. Nevertheless, one cannot overlook the fact that the authors are still to a certain degree involved in a specific tradition of national discourse and historiography and, as experts in history, politics, and sociology, they tend to emphasize the peculiarities of their case from certain points of view. They participate in a single course of history – that of their own nation – and have their preferences for future developments, even if they do not wish to extoll the virtues of their own nation. These inevitable biases shape their interpretation, reduce their distance from their subjects, and lead them into approaches which are arguably less theoretical than those of the contributions in the other two sections of our volume.

I find it difficult to compare the evidence presented in the essays in this section, stressing as they do the single case and its particularities. From a methodological point of view, one might even ask whether they are true «case studies», i.e. fulfilling the criterion of full comparability. On the one hand, there are simple organizational factors here for which the authors are not responsible. On the other hand, there is a problem here which arises from methodological preferences. Many social and political scientists understand «nation» and «national identity» as holistic units and realities. Yet so long as this understanding prevails, it is impossible to compare the «histoire totale» or «the identity» of one nation with another, because such holistic phenomena are much too complex. For comparative purposes, it is necessary to choose more limited fields, problems, and situations, and to have a well defined abstract «ideal type» or an explicit «model» as a point of reference (Haupt and Kocka, 1996; Siegrist, 1996).

Effective comparative research also presupposes a sophisticated selection of the cases to be studied. The editors regret that it was not possible to bring this project to fruition in the way in which it was originally conceived, for example, by including several more deliberately chosen cases, notably a study of France (see e.g. Francois et al., 1995). The volume can therefore only document the first steps of a discussion, which must be continued in other ways.

3 Ae and types of nations

The selection of countries discussed in these papers includes nations of different age, territorial size and political type. Belgium belongs to the small group of early liberal Western European nations founded in the period to the early 19th century. Germany, founded in 1870, became for a long time the model for a more authoritarian and ethnic type of nation building, contrasting with the French ideal of the more republican, civic and democratic nation. Austria, Israel, and Croatia represent subsequent waves of modern nation building between 1918 and the early 1990s.

The chapters suggest that nations of the same «age-cohorts» have similar problems. But it also becomes clear that, in the case of nations, «age» has many meanings. Thus, depending on the criteria we apply, Germany and Austria may appear as either young or old nations, because they have had a rather interrupted history with regard to state-formation and nationhood. With the exception of Belgium, all the nation-states included here have experienced significant territorial shifts during the 20th century, caused by lost wars (Germany, Austria), victorious wars (Israel, Croatia), and dramatic political changes (German unification, Croatia). Indeed, these nations have assumed the very shapes with which we are familiar today, as a result of these events.

Nowadays, these five nations correspond more or less to the type of a «civic nation» (Croatia as yet less so than the others), but all still show traits of ethnic nations. Vjeran Katunaric mentions that Croatia, which was traditionally multi-ethnic, has recently been following a policy of «ethnicization». Bettina Westle states that in united Germany in the 1990s, the German population shows «a mix of traditional (ethnic and cultural), democratic and postnational elements of collective identity, West Germans tending more to democratic and postnational, East Germans more to traditional elements». According to Alain Dieckhoff, in Israel the Jews form an ethno-national group with specific rights, while the Israeli Arabs remain marginalized. The «ethnic rationale is clearly rejected by the state when speaking solely about Jews», but ethnicity and the ethnic gap continues to be a reality. He adds that «the political mobilization of ethnicity is, in fact, the most significant development over the past fifteen years». Josef Langer explains how Austria has traditionally not been regarded as an ethnic nation, yet until the 1950s many Austrians regarded themselves as

Germans. Finally, Kas Deprez shows that Belgium is divided by a conflict motivated by political and economic interests, but that these interests are formulated in a language of «cultures and language» which resembles the language
of «ethnicity» used in other nations. There is no political party acting nationwide, and education, social life, and the media have been split up, especially in
Brussels itself, along the linguistic divide.

All in all, the reports about the role of ethnicity in each of these countries seem
to show that single ethnic communities or cultures may not intend to actually
split the nation-state, but that they use ethnicity and language as an instrument
for gaining status, and social, political, and economic power.

4   Identity, identities and processes of identification

What can we learn from the essays about the category «national identity»?
Alain Dieckhoff begins his chapter on the pluralization of national identity in
Israel by rejecting «primordial, static and intangible» concepts of identity
which imply «that the subject (be it individual or collective) has a sort of timeless permanence». Vjeran Katunaric, who analyzes various aspects of national
and collective identities in Croatia, concludes that «national identity acquires
different meanings, and that it may expand in various and sometimes self-contradictory directions». Josef Langer, in discussing the transformations of national identity in Austria, sees identity as a «transient» phenomenon. He is more
interested in the real social processes of identification, by which elements of
what he calls «national ideology» like flags, values, and legends «reach the
everyday existence of the people». Bettina Westle starts with an analysis of the
discourses of politicians and intellectuals about German national identities, in
the two German states after 1945 and in unified Germany in the 1990s. She
then presents empirical survey-data which make it clear that elite constructions about German identity must be confronted with findings as to what citizens in East and West really identify themselves with. Finally, she pleads for
«an open debate about the potentials and dangers of collective identity». In
her opinion, «a constructive national identity must not be equated with aggressive nationalism. Instead, collective self-consciousness can be anchored in democratic values, striving for optimal realization and peaceful relationships
within and between countries».

The essays demonstrate that the concept of «national identity» has both advantages and disadvantages. The authors observe a recent trend from a single
(«homogeneous», «official») national identity to many national identities («pluralization»). This is surely correct, but I believe that we need to go beyond this,

to investigate actual processes of identification rather than merely paraphrasing identities. It seems to me to be problematic that the essays tend to use the same «language of identity» (Katunaric) as the objects of their study. Does it really make sense to use a vague category like «identity»? In the long run, it would be useful to study the processes of identification, by examining the cultural, contextual and historical specificities of social actions and actors in greater depth.

5   The «crisis of the nation»: discourses and political processes

Do the papers prove that the idea of the nation is in crisis or decline? What does «crisis» mean? And what does it mean, when national elites – including historians and political scientists – dedicate themselves to the discourse of crisis? Is the discourse about «crisis» not an element of a modern political ritual, which aims at the stabilization of the status quo?

Kas Deprez hopes that Belgium «may eventually survive as a post-national state». His scholarly historical essay dates the origins of a «Belgian individuality» back to the 17th century, and becomes at a certain point an open political appeal for conserving Belgium as state, because Flemish and Walloons have proven themselves capable of finding procedures for organizing their life in a common territory. Josef Langer sees no profound crisis for the existence of Austria at the moment, but he observes that among young people, the «idea of nation is in trouble, particularly with the employed social classes not protected from market competition». According to Vjeran Katunaric, Croatia faces the difficulty of co-ordinating a very heterogeneous «national identity» with processes of political and social change in a period of transformation. Workers, teachers, pensioners, and other dissatisfied Croats criticize the new liberal and national elites by paraphrasing the slogan of previous gatherings which had celebrated national unity: «This is your Croatia, not ours». In Germany, the discourse of national crisis focusses more on the problems of merging East and West Germany. In Israel, the steady flow of immigrants and the tensions between the concepts of religious state, de-ethnicized civic state, and consumer society (on the relationship of nation and consumption, see Siegrist, 1997) are regarded as endangering the old image of «Israeliness».

We can conclude that the nation is confronted with new pressures and challenges, which change the content, meaning, and form of the single nations, but not their existence. Whether the nation is «in crisis» or not depends upon the criteria which one employs. The chapters of this section certainly do not prove the end of the nations – rather the contrary.

References

Cassirer, Ernst (1985). «Mythischer, ästhetischer und theoretischer Raum», pp. 93–119 in Ernst Cassirer (ed.). Symbol, Technik, Sprache. Aufsätze aus den Jahren 1927–1933, Hamburg: Meiner.

Francois, Etienne, Siegrist, Hannes und Jakob Vogel (eds.) (1995). *Nation und Emotion. Deutschland und Frankreich im Vergeich (19. und 20. Jahrhundert).* Göttingen: Vandenhoeck & Ruprecht.

Haupt, Heinz-Gerhard/Kocka, Jürgen (eds.) (1996). *Geschichte und Vergleich. Ansätze und Ergebnisse international vergleichender Geschichtsschreibung.* Frankfurt am Main: Campus.

Haupt, Heinz-Gerhard, Müller, Michael G. and Stuart Woolf (eds.) (1998). *Regional and National Identities in Europe in the 19th and 20th Centuries.* The Hague: Kluwer.

Siegrist, Hannes (1996). *Advokat, Bürger und Staat.* Frankfurt am Main: Klostermann.

Siegrist, Hannes (1997). «Konsum, Kultur und Gesellschaft im modernen Europa», in Hannes Siegrist, Hartmut Kaelble and Jürgen Kocka (eds.). *Europäische Konsumgeschichte. Zur Gesellschafts- und Kulturgeschichte des Konsums (18.–20. Jahrhundert).* Frankfurt am Main: Campus.

Belgium: A Post-National State?

Kas Deprez

1 Belgium, one of the first modern nation-states in Europe

The history of Belgium has been rewritten a number of times and it is still being rewritten. In the Flemish nationalist vision, Belgium is an artificial state which came into existence in 1830 as a compromise between the great powers. I grew up with that vision. Only after many years did I find out that, quite to the contrary, the Belgian state was a climax in the process of Belgian nation building which had already begun in the 17th century, and that Belgium was in fact one of the first modern nation-states in Europe.

In medieval times, the Low Countries formed a patchwork of feudal entities. In what is now called Belgium, the most important of these were the County of Flanders – which belonged to the French Kingdom –, and the Duchy of Brabant and the Prince Bishopric of Liège – which were possessions of the German Emperor. None of them were monolingual, and nowhere was a political border drawn along a linguistic frontier.

In the second half of the 14th century, the Burgundians made their entrance into the Low Countries. By forcing his younger brother, the Duke of Burgundy, upon the Count of Flanders, as the husband of the latter's daughter and sole heiress, the French King hoped to strengthen his grip on Flanders. Yet, history took another turn as the Burgundians built their own empire in the Low Countries, independent of – and against – France. Philip the Good, the greatest of the Burgundians, not only ruled over Flanders, but also over Brabant, Hainault, Zeeland, Namur and Luxembourg.

At the end of the 15th century, the Burgundian Netherlands passed into the hands of the Habsburgs, again through marriage. Charles V – who was born in Ghent – became the most powerful monarch in the West: he was not only sovereign of the Low Countries, but also King of Spain and Emperor of Germany. In the Low Countries, he extended his possessions to the «Seventeen Provinces». In present-day terms, the latter comprised The Netherlands, Belgium (excepting the Prince Bishopric of Liège), the Grand Duchy of Luxembourg, and a small part of the North of France.

As early as the second half of the 16th century, this process of unification came to an end. The Seventeen Provinces were torn into a northern and a southern half as a result of the revolt against Philip II, son of Charles V. This revolt was inspired both by political and religious motives. There was no North-South divide as such in those days. Indeed, Protestantism counted more followers in the southern provinces than in the northern. However, the southern provinces were reconquered by the troops of Philip II. At the end of the 16th century, the separation between the northern and the southern provinces was a fact. The independence of The Netherlands was internationally acknowledged with the Peace of Münster in 1648. The Southern Netherlands remained possessions of the Spanish Habsburgs, but at the beginning of the 18th century, they passed into the hands of the Austrian branch of the House of Habsburg.

From the 17th century onwards, a process of nation building got under way in both political entities. Several factors brought about a deep divide between them. Of course, there was the difference in religion, which acquired a dynastic dimension. The House of Orange eventually became the head of the Calvinist Dutch nation, whereas the Habsburgs continued to act as the guardians of the Roman Catholic Church. Parallel to the religious opposition, a cultural gulf developed: to the sobriety of the Reformation, the Counter Reformation reacted with an exuberant, triumphant Baroque. Political and economic interests also played a part. The Southern Netherlands were difficult for the Spanish Habsburgs to defend because of the distance separating them from Spain. Louis XIV exploited this situation and annexed several parts of the Habsburg Netherlands to France. The Dutch, on the other hand, used the Habsburg Netherlands as a buffer against France. The Dutch also forced the Habsburg Netherlands to give up their Ostend Trade Company, thereby protecting the interests of their own United East India Company.

Belgian individuality is clearly older than the Belgian state. It is the 17th and 18th centuries which gave rise to Belgium. In addition to the Counter Reformation, the cultural and political influence of France played a crucial role. The cultural prestige of the French language was enormous all over Europe, but particularly in the Habsburg Netherlands. Moreover, in 1795 the Belgian regions were annexed by revolutionary France and incorporated into the Republic. The upcoming Belgian bourgeoisie was attracted by the new republican values and, together with those values, it adopted the language through which they were expressed; thus, the cultural prestige of French was reinforced by its philosophical and political importance.

After Napoleon's defeat at Waterloo in 1815, a United Kingdom incorporating The Netherlands and the Belgian regions was created by the European powers as a buffer against France. It lasted only 15 years. A rebellion in 1830 led to the establishment of an independent Belgian state. The Belgium of 1830 was much closer to France than to The Netherlands. It came into being as the result of an alliance between Catholics and Liberals, the two major political forces in the country. As a result of the French period, liberal ideas were rooted much more deeply in Belgium than in The Netherlands. The Belgian Constitution of 1831 confirmed the union between Catholics and Liberals around a programme of «freedom in everything for everyone». Wils (1998) calls Belgium one of the first modern nations in Europe.

The Belgian national identity was emphatically affirmed after independence. In art, a new Belgian School was promoted whose programme consisted first and foremost of historical painting. Popular genre and landscape painting, too, were to make a contribution (Pil 1998). A Belgian literature also came into being. Like painting, its main aim was to give the newly formed state a proper cultural expression. This goal was pursued by both Flemish and Francophone authors. In A. Clesse's words, Belgians had one heart with which to love their fatherland and two lyres with which to sing its praise.

Some Flemish writers and philologists, however, deplored the fact that the Belgian bourgeoisie considered the country to be essentially part of the French cultural area. They regarded Belgium as a bilingual nation: it was not French, but Flemish (Nederduits/Dutch), and this made Belgium different from France. They were dedicated belgicists, but by emphasizing the important role of Flanders in the history of the Belgian regions, and by demanding language rights for the Flemings, they became the founding fathers of the Flemish Movement. H. Conscience's historical novel *De Leeuw van Vlaanderen* [The Lion of Flanders] (1838), which became the Flemish national epic, was not directed against Belgium or Wallonia, but against France. It was a grandiose evocation of the glorious past of the County of Flanders defending its liberties against the King of France (Couttenier 1998).

Francophone Belgian writers experienced greater difficulties than their Flemish colleagues in trying to respond to the Romantic demand for a national literature reflecting the Volksgeist. This necessitated the creation – in French – of a literature distinct from the literature in France. This could only be accomplished by falling back on Belgian themes which were essentially Flemish. In Ch. De Coster's *La Légende d'Ulenspiegel* (1867), the first masterpiece of Francophone Belgian literature, the hero was a Fleming but his adventures were narrated in French. De Coster also made a deliberate effort to write a Belgian kind of French. In the early 1880s, a notorious group of Francophone Belgian writers emerged. Most of them were born in the North of the country, wrote about Flemish themes, and used a language which diverged considerably from standard French. They enriched the country with both a National Bard

(E. Verhaeren) and the sole Belgian winner of the Nobel Prize in literature (M. Maeterlinck). This group made a considerable contribution to the legitimation of Belgium (Berg 1998).

2   How the Flemish nation came into existence

In 1830, Belgium was a single nation – a Belgian nation –, but gradually a Flemish sub-nation emerged. Flemish writers, academics and language activists not only detected the individuality of the Flemish people in its history, religion, art and folklore, but also in its social and economic strength. As a result, the Flemish Movement gradually transformed itself from a mere language movement into a fully-fledged national movement in which the Flemish petty bourgeoisie lined up against the French-speaking ruling classes. It transformed the basic language problem into a struggle for the social and economic emancipation of the Flemish people (Vos 1998).

Nations come into existence by acquiring power. Ethnic groups which are unable to gain power do not become a nation, but are – on the contrary – marginalized and eventually even disappear. Most (smaller) linguistic movements in Western Europe belong to the latter category. The Flemish Movement is one of the rare success stories.

The Czech historian M. Hroch (1985) distinguishes three phases in the process of revival of small nations in Europe. The first phase is that of scholarly interest. It is marked by a passionate concern on the part of some intellectuals for the study of the language, the culture and the history of the oppressed nationality. They are the «language lovers». According to Hroch (1985: 23), these individuals are usually isolated and, therefore, often remain without any widespread social influence; they do not initiate any political action because they cannot imagine that it would serve any purpose.

The second phase begins when the language lovers become «language activists» who formulate political demands. This phase is characterized by active patriotic agitation in which the nationalistic message is spread among the people; it is the fermentation phase of the national consciousness. In the third phase, the nationalist demands become the direct concern of the masses. The language movement acquires the size and the political weight of a mass movement. Most language movements only partly succeed in this, or they do not succeed at all. In order for a mass movement to develop, it is necessary that significant social groups recognize themselves in the nationalist programme. This only happens if the language movement is able to couple its linguistic and cultural demands with other factors of power in society like the church, demographic numbers, and the linguistic homogeneity of the territory, as well as with other causes with a potentially wide appeal, such as the striving for political and social emancipation and economic development. This is actually what the Flemish Movement was able to achieve.

I will now briefly describe the main factors which have contributed to the success of the Flemish Movement. Like so many other national movements, the Flemish Movement started as a small group of writers, philologists and other language lovers. As literature had to express the Volksgeist, it was quite natural for the *Maetschappij van Vlaemsche Letteroefening* [Society of Flemish Literature] (1836) in Ghent to choose as its motto *De Taal is Gantsch het Volk* [The Language is the Whole Nation].

The struggle for the national language became increasingly entangled with other factors of power and with other social and political developments. A first major factor was the Catholic faith. The church was not pleased with the secularist ideology of the French Revolution which was dominant in Liberal circles. As was pointed out above, Liberals and Catholics were the founders of the Belgian state. Governments which included members of both groups ruled Belgium in the first decades after independence. However, as the 19th century took its course, their coalition broke down and they became bitter enemies. The Flemish Movement became closely linked to the Catholic religion. Flemish priests ardently defended the traditional Christian values, which they found expressed in the language of the people. Flemish/Nederduits came to be seen as a bulwark against anti-religious French, the language of Enlightenment. Later on, in industrialized Wallonia, the Socialist Movement developed and became much stronger than in rural Flanders. French, as a result, also became the language of anti-clerical Socialism.

A second factor was the growing importance of language in social and economic life. As the modernization of the Belgian state proceeded, Flemings were more and more confronted with the second-rate position of their language. In this way, the social dimension of the Flemish struggle became quite distinct. With the modernization of the state, the democratization and the expansion of formal education, the development of the media and communication technology, language became an extremely important social and economic factor. Especially since World War Two, the number of people earning their living through language has grown exponentially. To speak of empowerment through (one's own) language is now simply, as it were, to state the obvious. This process started in the 19th century.

Of all possible nation-building factors, war is by far the most important. Both Belgian and Flemish national feelings were strengthened during World War One. At the Yser front, in that small unoccupied western corner of the country, the majority of the Belgian soldiers were Flemings. On the remains of a destroyed building was painted the slogan *Hier ons bloed! Wanneer ons recht?* [Here is our blood! When do we receive our rights?]. After the war, the first Flemish nationalist party was founded. It blamed the Belgian state for ignoring the soul, the character and the language of the majority of the population, which had defended Belgium so bravely during the war.

It was the Christian Workers' Movement which provided the Flemish Movement with a mass foundation. This movement was much stronger in Flanders than in Wallonia – and perhaps than in any other European country as well. According to Wils (1994: 248), this had everything to do with its historical linkage to the Flemish Movement. Both recruited their leaders mainly from the Flemish Student Movement. From the 1880s onwards, the latter was strongly represented in the Catholic University of Leuven. Clergymen, primary school teachers and university graduates put themselves into the service of the people through the Christian Workers' Movement. This Movement developed in constant competition with the Socialist Movement. Gerard (1998) observes that rejecting Socialism implied emphasising one's own Flemish and Christian values. The Flemings in the Christian Workers' Movement looked upon the social struggle and the Flemish national question as two sides of one coin.

An extremely important factor contributing to the success of the Flemish Movement was the numerical majority of the Flemings in Belgium. Had Flanders remained part of the French Republic, the Flemish nation would probably never have come about. Indeed, the Flemish Movement would then have had to face France, a much mightier opponent than francophile Belgium. In 1830, the Flemings already constituted the majority of the population, but this had no political consequences, as only 2% of the Belgians obtained the right to vote at this time; this thin upper layer either spoke French or identified themselves with French. It was not until 1919, when – thanks to the Walloon Socialists – universal suffrage (for men) was introduced, that the Flemish demographic majority also became the political majority in the country.

Also of great political relevance was the linguistic homogeneity of Flanders. The number of Francophones in Flanders never amounted to more than 5%; only in Brussels – the capital in which the Belgian state nestled itself – did «frenchification» occur to any significant degree. Thanks to the linguistic homogeneity of Flanders (and Wallonia), the principle of territoriality could be asserted by the Flemish leaders as early as 1932. Flanders had remained a linguistically homogeneous area because it was poor and backward. It hardly participated in the first industrial revolution. In the 19th century, and even in the first decades of this century, Flemings migrated to Wallonia (amongst other areas) to escape from the poverty at home. In Wallonia, their children became Walloons and learnt French at school – no Flemish worker or farmer dared question the superiority of French. On the other hand, very few Walloons settled in Flanders and, as a result, Flanders remained Flemish-speaking in spite of the cultural, social and political superiority of French. Had heavy industry been located not in Wallonia but in Flanders, a massive exodus from Wallonia to Flanders would have ensued; and those Walloon immigrants would not have learnt Flemish/Dutch – they would not have seen any reason to do so. The old industrial zones of Flanders – as we would have called them – would now be French-speaking. (This sort of process can be compared with the examples of Spanish-speaking Bilbao in the Basque country, and with English-speaking Cardiff in Wales.)

Belgian history took a new turn in the fifties and sixties. In the fifties, Walloon heavy industry began to encounter serious difficulties. Flanders, on the other hand, experienced an economic boom. The national bourgeoisie lost its grip on the economic development of the country and was replaced by multinational corporations. Flanders' share of foreign investment was soon larger than that of Wallonia. What made Flanders very attractive was its geographical situation, especially its ports (Antwerp, Ghent, Zeebruges). These dynamics led to the toppling of the old economic axis of the country. The economic centre of gravity shifted from Wallonia to Flanders. As a result, a territorial solution was sought for the political and economic problems engendered by this intricate unequal development. The Flemings wanted political power to match their new economic power; the Walloons wanted political power to counter their economic decline (Saey et al. 1998).

3   From a unitary to a federal state

According to Kesteloot (1998), almost all of the factors generally assumed to be at the origin of national movements in Western Europe, were quite problematic in the case of Wallonia. The Walloon provinces had had no common history before their annexation by the French Republic – as was mentioned earlier, the most important principality, the Prince Bishopric of Liège, had not been part of the Habsburg Netherlands. The French language constituted the only criterion by which all Walloon provinces could be united; still, French was not typical of Wallonia alone, but also of the Belgian bourgeoisie and of an ever increasing number of inhabitants of Brussels. Moreover, given Wallonia's prosperity, Walloon militants were only marginally concerned with economic matters.

The Walloon Movement emerged towards the end of the 19th century, above all as a political movement in defence of the interests of the Francophones in Flanders and in Brussels against the Flemish demands. However, it soon shifted its activities from Brussels to Wallonia. During the Congress of 1905, the first seeds of a Walloon cultural identity were sown. When universal suffrage was introduced in 1919, Wallonia was bound to end up in a numerically inferior position in the Belgian parliament. Anticipating the political consequences of this fundamental change the Socialist leader, J.Destrée, wrote his famous *Lettre au Roi* (1912) in which he demanded autonomy for both the Walloon and Flemish peoples; Destrée is generally considered to be the father of the Walloon movement.

During the Great War, most Flemish militants remained loyal to Belgium; a large majority of them fought in the trenches of Flanders' Fields. Yet, a small number responded favourably to the Germans' *Flamenpolitik* – a policy of giving preferential treatment to the Flemings and their language so as to incite them to collaboration (Vos 1998: 88). After the war, two opposite Flemish Movements emerged, one loyal, the other anti-Belgian. The former, the so-called minimalists, chose to strive for a monolingual status for Flanders within a Belgian framework (through language legislation). The latter, the so-called maximalists, wanted to create a Flemish state.

The minimum programme was realized in the 1930s through a series of language acts. Both Flanders and Wallonia obtained a monolingual status, whereas Brussels, the capital, became officially bilingual. Belgium thus opted for dual monolingualism instead of overall bilingualism. The Walloon politicians especially, insisted that the country be organized on the basis of the principle of territoriality; for them, the need to safeguard a monolingual Wallonia assumed far greater importance than fighting for a lost cause such as the privileges of the small Francophone minority in Flanders (less than 5% of the population). Hence, the linguistic legislation of the 1930s met with little or no objection from the Walloon Movement.

In contradistinction to the minimalists, the maximalists went off in an anti-democratic direction. They rejected the Belgian parliamentary system, in which in any event they could never have played a significant role. Not surprisingly, during the war, they opted for full collaboration with Nazi Germany.

The post-war period revealed an ever-widening divide between Flemings and Walloons/Francophones. The blowing up of the Yser Tower – a monument commemorating the Flemish sacrifices at the Yser front during the Great War – as well as the trials of the Flemish collaborators and the harsh sentences that were passed against them, shocked many Flemings. The Walloons, for their part, had again been frustrated by the German policy with regard to the two nationalities in Belgium: whereas the Flemish prisoners of war had been allowed to return home after a few months, the Walloons had been held in Germany for the entire duration of the war.

A very special prisoner of war was King Leopold III. «The Royal Question» brought Belgium to the brink of civil war. During the war, the King had remained in Belgium, whereas the Government had fled to London. Left-wing political parties considered him a traitor and claimed that he should be prevented from resuming his functions. A referendum in 1950 showed that 58% of the population was in favour of the King's return. Yet, it was mainly the Flemish votes that accounted for this majority; in Wallonia, the greater part of the population voted against his return. The King did come back, but street violence soon broke out in Wallonia, and the (Catholic) government was forced to resign. The King abdicated. Catholic public opinion in Flanders felt humiliated.

In 1945, Flemish nationalism was dead, as a result of what had happened during the war. However, the harshness of the repression and the outcome of «the Royal Question» led to the revival of a moderate Flemish nationalism. In the mid-1950s, a new Flemish nationalist party appeared on the political scene, viz. the *Volksunie* (VU); in the sixties and seventies, this party became the champion of Federalism.

During the Great Strike of 1960–61 against the so-called *Eenheidswet* [Unity Law], the Walloon trade union leader A. Renard received only limited support from the Flemish Socialists. When the strike failed, he founded the *Mouvement Populaire Wallon* (MPW). Out of the MPW there grew a genuine Walloon-nationalist party, the *Rassemblement Wallon* (RW). Given the prosperity of Wallonia and the superiority of French, the Walloon Movement had long been of interest only to an agitating minority. This changed in the sixties. As a result of the failure of the Great Strike, part of the workers' movement in Wallonia started to demand federalism as well as structural economic reforms. In 1968, the so-called *Leuven Vlaams* Question resulted in the splitting up of the old university into a Flemish and a Francophone university; the Francophone faculties had to leave Leuven and a new university was built a few kilometers south of the linguistic frontier. The impact of the Leuven crisis on the Walloon

Catholics was of the same magnitude as the impact of the Great Strike on the Walloon Socialists (Kesteloot 1998).

Due to the Leuven crisis, in 1968 the Christian-Democrats split into two autonomous political parties. The Liberals and the Socialists were to follow suit in 1972 and 1978 respectively. As a result, there are no longer any truly «Belgian» political parties in the country. The absence of any national parties is probably the weakest point in the new construction of Belgium.

Another conflict that has contributed considerably to the strengthening of the Walloon Movement was the Voeren/Fourons case. In 1963, the linguistic frontier was officially delineated. Voerens/Fourons was assigned to Flanders, against the will of the majority (some 60%) of its population. The stiff resistance against this transfer which was led by J. Happart, who became the mayor of the village, made him by far the most popular politician in Wallonia (Deprez and Wynants 1989; Ubac 1993).

In 1961–62, the Flemish Movement had organized two marches on Brussels. Its main demands were that the linguistic border be definitively established and that the bilingual Brussels agglomeration be limited to 19 municipalities, so as to stop the Brussels Francophone expansion into Flemish territory. As a reaction to the Flemish marches, French-speaking radicals founded the *Front Démocratique des Francophones* (FDF) to safeguard the interests of the French-speaking majority in Brussels.

The three linguistic parties, the VU, the RW, and the FDF, enjoyed spectacular successes in the sixties and early seventies. They reached their electoral peak at the general elections of 1974, gaining 22% of the votes (Luykx and Platel 1985: 654–659). In addition to the VU, the RW, and the FDF, the newly-formed monolingual Christian-Democrat, Liberal, and Socialist parties from now on also defended the interests of their own linguistic communities. As a result, whereas in 1945, Flemish nationalism had been dead, some 30 or 35 years later, the Flemish nationalist programme had even attracted the support of the Flemish Liberals and Socialists, and one could again speak of a mass movement – which was now even stronger than at the beginning of the century, as it was now backed by those of every ideological persuasion.

Because of the ever growing antagonism between the Flemish and Walloon/Francophone elites, the only possible solution seemed to consist in adjusting the structure of the state to reflect the new political realities. This amounted to a devolution of power to representative institutions for each nationality. Four constitutional reforms followed: in 1970, 1980, 1988, and 1993. The outcome of this vast operation is a curious mix, with confederal and federal elements, but also with a few still heavily centralized ministries and administrations which the reforms have left unchanged (Falter 1998; see also Mabille 1997: Part 5).

The Flemings constitute about 60% of the Belgian population. In the sixties, after an adjustment of the number of votes per seat, the Flemings became the absolute majority in the Belgian parliament. In 1970, the Francophone fear of becoming a minority – which was not new but which had then become acute – was partially laid to rest by three Flemish concessions: (1) parity in the national government; (2) special majorities for issues that concern the relations between the nationalities; (3) the alarm clock procedure.

Neither in the 1970 nor in the 1980 reforms did the Flemish parties accept that Brussels should become the third Belgian region, for fear of a coalition of Wallonia and Brussels against Flanders. In 1988, a compromise was reached: the Flemish minority in Brussels (about 15% of the Belgian population of the capital) was given the same guarantees as the Francophone minority had been given at the national level. In 1989, Brussels for the first time elected its own parliament and formed its own government.

Because of Brussels, a distinction had to be made between Regions and Communities. These two concepts had been introduced in 1970, but were only made operational in the 1980s. Communities are institutions which are competent for cultural matters, education, health care, family policy, welfare policy, etc. Belgium counts three Communities: the Flemish, the French, and the German-speaking. Regions, on the other hand, are geographical entities with socio-political competences. Belgium also counts three Regions: Flanders, Wallonia, and Brussels. Brussels is not a Community because people belonging to two different national communities – Flemings and Francophones – are living on its territory. The Communities were largely the result of the Flemish demand for cultural autonomy, whereas the Regions had to honour Walloon aspirations for greater regional economic power.

The Flemish Region and the Flemish Community immediately decided to merge, together becoming competent for about 6 million citizens, the sole exception being the 150 000 or so Flemings in Brussels for whom only the Community exercises power. A similar merger did not take place on the Francophone side because of its differing proportions – 3.25 million Walloons, and 600 000 Francophones in Brussels – and because of political antagonism – Republican, Socialist Wallonia distrusting the Belgium-minded Liberal capital (Fontaine 1998).

4   Can Belgium survive as a post-national state?

The history of Belgium offers a clear illustration of the fact that national identity and nationalism are not natural phenomena which have existed since time
immemorial, but that they are things which are created. This is not to say that
they are mere ideological constructions. On the contrary, they are realities that
emerge, flourish, and eventually disappear again.

Speaking of smaller nations in the 19th century, Hroch (1985: 185) stated that
the national interest was «the transformed and sublimated image of the material interests of definite concrete classes and groups, whose members took an
active part in the national movement (or had to be won over to participation
in it)».

Belgium, like Flanders and Wallonia, is a clear illustration of this point of view.
Due to divergent interests, Flemings and Walloons have divided and built up
their own networks of communication. If K.W. Deutsch – who defines a nation
by the relative efficiency of communication among its members – is right, then
there is not much left of the Belgian nation. Over the last thirty years, many of
the Belgian links have been broken off, in the first place in the fields of language, culture, and education, the nation building forces par excellence.

Belgians no longer have a common language. Dewachter (1996: 137), a Flemish
political scientist, puts it like this: «Belgium has lost its ‹most obvious› vehicu-
lar language. Both the ruling and the middle classes in the unitary Belgium have
always been able to communicate perfectly in French. Still, the knowledge of
French of the current generation of Flemish students is quite poor. Their com-
mand of English is far better; it is the language they prefer. On the other side
of the language frontier, the knowledge of Dutch is what it has always been –
it remains quasi non-existent.»

Education and media have been completely divided up so as to serve each of
the language groups separately; even in Brussels, two exclusively monolingual
networks – schools (at all levels!), cultural centres, theatres, etc. – have been
established, in spite of the city's bilingual administrative status. The result is
that Flemings and Francophones no longer know each other. They do not read
each other's newspapers, they do not watch each other's television, they no longer know each other's writers, they do not visit each other's theatres, and so on.

La Belgique sera latine ou ne sera pas was one of the typical slogans of 19th
century French-speaking Belgium. Those might have been prophetic words.
Belgium was Latin as long as the political, economic and cultural power re-

mained in the hands of the French-speaking bourgeoisie. However, those days are gone. Flanders is now far more prosperous than either Wallonia or Brussels. Still, many Francophones remain convinced of the superiority of French, and therefore do not think it necessary to learn Dutch properly. This means that the ethno-linguistic group which now dominates economic and political life is not considered to be culturally valuable by the other group. It remains to be seen whether a country with such a lack of balance can continue to exist. For how much longer will Flanders still agree to pay for Wallonia and Francophone Brussels, if these refuse to behave as true Belgians? A bilingual country cannot survive if it does not have a sufficient number of bilingual citizens in both communities.

Nevertheless, even if there were hardly a Belgian nation left, the Belgian state can probably be saved: Belgium may eventually survive as a post-national state. The latter concept emerged primarily in debates about European unification and European identity. The question is whether we can unite people from different cultural backgrounds – speaking different languages, being the products of different histories, having different traditions, cherishing different values – around a common political project so that they abide by the same European laws and become European citizens. We could think about Belgium in the same terms: can Belgium survive or make a new start on the basis of a «constitutional patriotism»? Flemings and Walloons/Francophones would then cherish their proper cultural values and identify with their own communities, but both groups would deliberately opt for a Belgian citizenship.

The Francophone jurist H. Dumont (1997) has serious reservations as to a post-national Belgian construct. In his opinion, no state, be it mononational or plurinational, can function democratically if its citizens do not have a feeling of belonging to the same historical community which surpasses the internal differences. A minimum of *identité narrative partagée* is an essential condition, together with a common political culture. According to Dumont, a post-national state requires a strong will to continue to live together under the same federal roof and, therefore, some kind of love of the Belgian state. He concludes that this transformation of the Belgian national state into a post-national state is far from having been accomplished.

I share Dumont's doubts as to whether a Belgian feeling of national cohesion can be restored. Yet, I wonder whether we actually need this sense of togetherness in order to save the Belgian state. Flemings and Walloons/Francophones might decide to stay together for pragmatic reasons. In fact, each Community/Region might have serious reasons for deciding not to separate. The Walloons undoubtedly have a financial interest in the survival of Belgium, given their economic problems. For Flanders, Brussels is Belgium's major surplus value. Some observers consider the Flemings in Brussels to be the best protected minority in the world, a status which they owe to Flanders' economic strength. If Belgium falls apart, the Flemings will cease to have any political impact in Brussels, because their numbers there have become too small. Given its attachment to French, Brussels will never side with Flanders.

From a moderate point of view, Brussels is the major surplus value for Flanders. From a radical Flemish nationalist point of view, however, Brussels is the most vulnerable link in the federal Belgian state. As a result, the extreme right-wing, separatist Flemish party *Vlaams Blok* is concentrating its efforts on blocking the Brussels model so as to blow up the Belgian federal system. Indeed, as I explained earlier, the Brussels Region cannot be governed without or against the Flemish minority in Brussels, even if the latter occupies only 10 out of the 75 seats. The *Vlaams Blok* already holds 2 seats, and hopes for a major breakthrough in the next elections in June, 1999. In order to attain this goal, it organizes bilingual campaigns – to recuperate gallicized Flemings, so to speak. If the *Vlaams Blok* obtains a majority of the Flemish seats in the Brussels parliament, the Brussels model will cease to function. The Francophone parties will refuse to co-operate with the *Vlaams Blok* and so will the other Flemish parties. In short, the Brussels model is under serious threat.

Brussels has to cope with more than just the antagonism between Flemings and Francophones. The inner city, especially, is faced with serious financial and social problems. The share of Brussels in the total national income has decreased. Within the Brussels Region itself, disparities have increased: some of the Brussels municipalities are among the richest in the country, while others are among the poorest. It is in the latter that we find the highest percentages of immigrants. The number of non-Belgians in Brussels now amounts to some 30% of the total population. The citizens of the member-states of the EU will have the right to vote at the municipal level in the year 2000, and in 2006 non-Europeans will follow suit. What role they will play on the Belgian political scene in general and on the Brussels scene in particular, it is of course still impossible to say. What is very clear, however, is that it will not take long before the «new» Belgians constitute the majority in Brussels.

It is important to understand that most immigrants are scarcely interested in the Belgian language problems. To integrate them into Belgian society should be a political priority (Club van Leuven 1990: 252). Yet this seems all the more difficult since – as is explained by Martiniello (1997) and Morelli (1998), both of Italian descent – many immigrants are insensitive to the Belgian language problems. Both Martiniello and Morelli point out that the immigrant populations have never been consulted by the Belgian authorities. Moreover, one might wonder how foreigners can possibly have the feeling of being welcome in a country where the indigenous communities fight an eternal struggle for linguistic homogeneity.

Let me conclude this contribution by observing that Flanders is not as homogeneous as it would like to be. Some Flemish municipalities around Brussels, are, like Voeren/Flourons, much disputed areas. In the former, the number of Francophones runs into tens of thousands. Voeren/Fourons is just a picturesque cluster of villages counting little more than 4 000 inhabitants, but it has a highly symbolic value for both Flemings and Walloons. As long as Belgium exists, there is considerable room for manoeuvring and for the famous Belgian compromise. It seems to me that this is the main reason why we should opt for Belgium. Belgium as a land of peace, democracy and prosperity, and as an exercise for a united, multilingual Europe.

References

Berg, C. (1998). «The Symbolic Deficit. French Literature in Belgium and 19th Century National Sentiment», pp. 61–71 in K. Deprez and L. Vos (eds.). *Nationalism in Belgium. Shifting Identities 1780–1995.* London: Macmillan.

Club van Leuven (1990). *Vlaanderen op een kruispunt. Sociologische, economische en staatsrechtelijke perspectieven.* Tielt: Lannoo.

Couttenier, P., (1998). «National Imagery in 19th Century Flemish Literature», pp. 51–60 in K. Deprez and L. Vos (eds.). *Nationalism in Belgium. Shifting Identities 1780–1995.* London: Macmillan.

Deprez, K. and L. Vos (eds.) (1998). *Nationalism in Belgium. Shifting Identities 1780–1995.* London: Macmillan.

Deprez, K. und A. Wynants (1989). «Voeren/Fourons», pp. 95–108 in P.H. Nelde (Hrsg.). *Historische Sprachkonflikte.* Bonn: Dümmler.

Dewachter, W. (1996). «La Belgique d'aujourd'hui comme société politique», pp. 105–142 in A. Dieckhoff (dir.). *Belgique. La force de la désunion.* Bruxelles: Ed. Complexe.

Dumont, H. (1997) «La Belgique, un Etat post-national?», pp. 195–206 in C. Derenne et C. De Troy (coord.). *Belgique, disparition d'une nation européenne?* Bruxelles: Luc Pire.

Falter, R. (1998). «Belgium's Peculiar Way to Federalism», pp. 177–1997 in K. Deprez and L. Vos (eds.). *Nationalism in Belgium. Shifting Identities 1780–1995.* London: Macmillan.

Fontaine, J. (1998). «Le discours anti-wallon en Belgique francophone», *Toudi* 13–14: 3–58.

Gerard, E. (1998). «The Christian Workers' Movement as a Mass Foundation of the Flemish Movement», pp. 127–138 in K. Deprez and L. Vos (eds.). *Nationalism in Belgium. Shifting Identities 1780–1995.* London: Macmillan.

Hroch, M. (1985). *Social Preconditions of National Revival in Europe.* Cambridge: Cambridge University Press.

Kesteloot, C. (1998). «The Growth of the Walloon Movement» pp. 139–152 in K. Deprez and L. Vos (eds.). *Nationalism in Belgium. Shifting Identities 1780–1995.* London: Macmillan.

Luykx, Th. en M. Platel (1985). *Politieke geschiedenis van Belgie.* Antwerp: Kluwer (2 volumes).

Mabille, X (1997). *Histoire politique de la Belgique. Facteurs et acteurs de changement.* Bruxelles: Crisp.

Martiniello, M. (1997). «L'indispensable renouveau du pluralisme à la belge», pp. 207–214 in C. Derenne et C. De Troy (coord.). *Belgique, disparition d'une nation européenne?* Bruxelles: Luc Pire.

Morelli, A. and J.P. Schreiber (1998). «Are the Immigrants the Last Belgians?», pp. 249–257 in K. Deprez and L. Vos (eds.). *Nationalism in Belgium. Shifting Identities 1780–1995.* London: Macmillan.

Pil, L. (1998). «Painting at the Service of the New Nation State», pp. 42–50 in K. Deprez and L. Vos (eds.). *Nationalism in Belgium. Shifting Identities 1780–1995.* London: Macmillan.

Saey, P., C. Kesteloot and C. Vandermotten (1998). «Unequal Economic Development at the Origin of the Federalization Process», pp. 165–176 in: Deprez and Vos (eds.). *Nationalism in Belgium. Shifting Identities 1780–1995.* London: Macmillan.

Ubac, P. (1993). *Génération Fourons.* Wesmael: De Boeck.

Vos, L. (1998). «The Flemish National Question», pp. 83–95 in: K. Deprez and L. Vos (eds.). *Nationalism in Belgium. Shifting Identities 1780–1995.* London: Macmillan.

Wils, L. (1994). *Vlaanderen, Belgie, Groot-Nederland.* Leuven: Davidsfonds.

Wils, L. (1998). «The Two Belgian Revolutions», pp. 33–41 in K. Deprez and L. Vos (eds.). *Nationalism in Belgium. Shifting Identities 1780–1995.* London: Macmillan.

Last in, First out? – Austria's Place in the Transformation of National Identity

Josef Langer

Because there seems to be a lot of confusion about what a nation is, I would like to touch on this question for a moment, although theory is not my main concern here. The everyday use of the word «nation» remains blurred and rather superficial,[1] though in some cases this can be justified from a pragmatic point of view. For example, the title «United Nations» covers every state organization, but completely neglects its inner structure: from the «grand nation» of the French, via the «socialist nation» of former East Germany, to the tribal states of Africa, every more or less sovereign political organization is considered to be a nation. To avoid confusion, I would like to outline briefly the basic theoretical assumptions which will guide my arguments. One assumption is the distinction between *national ideology* and *national identity*.[2] By national ideology, I mean the signifiers (flag, shield, name, programs, special values, narratives such as legends, etc.) by which a group asserts its existence as a nation. These signifiers provide a collectively shared store of information which makes it possible for the members of a group to imagine, feel and express their belonging to a nation. The national flag on the tail of an airplane or the name of the nation included in the name of a company could likewise be signifiers. This store of information can be transformed into national identity when it reaches the everyday existence of the people. However, one can speak of national identity only if a significant part of a population identifies with elements of a national ideology. Yet once this transformation occurs, national identity can be observed as a characteristic of an individual, whereas national ideology can exist independently as artifacts without being directly associated with a social reality.

The difference between the two is along the lines of «cultural» and «social». National ideology is the cultural and national identity the social dimension within the concept of nation. The one circumscribes the semantic options available for the expression of nationhood, the other how these options are accepted and lived out by the people. National ideology can be documented and

---

1 When I first saw that the organizers of this conference had put Belgium, Austria and Switzerland together in one cluster, I wondered why. The first rationale one might think of is size: each is a small country. But surprisingly, this was not the answer which I got when I asked a colleague about it. He argued that the choice might have been made because of Swiss Air. Why Swiss Air? SWISS AIR, the national carrier of Switzerland, more or less dominates the major airlines of the other two countries, SABENA and AUSTRIAN AIRLINES, in their joint operations. He obviously associated nations with airlines.

2 In this distinction, I follow Csepeli (1997).

passed on to anybody who is interested in it, whereas national identity is the real life of a society which has opted to become a nation. Outsiders and succeeding generations can analyze and study it, but they cannot have it for themselves (Susag 1999). Like any life, it is transient. Besides this distinction, I want to point out that if we are to speak of a nation, then a third dimension must also be considered: the presence of a special kind of political *institution*. These institutions must provide the people with the opportunity to participate in the political decision making of the whole. By definition, only those who have the status which entitles them to participate are members of the nation. Historically, the term «democracy» has been used to describe this legitimization of power.

Within the framework of this definition, a society can only be considered as a nation if all three dimensions or factors (ideology, identity and democratic institutions) are fully developed. Therefore, not every politically organized people is a nation.[3] In reality, different configurations of the factors mentioned will appear. None of them alone or in combination with only one of the other two suffices. Yet ultimately, it depends on the analyst whether a society can be considered as a nation or not. Moreover, it is assumed that the concept of «nation» is a *historical reality* which has had a beginning and will most likely have an end.[4] Though from a normative point of view one can consider the nation as the most appropriate political representation of a society, analytically the force of history cannot be neglected. All of these considerations have implications for the study of national identity. Firstly, the term national identity should be reserved for that subset of collective identity which is more or less explicitly related to the ideology of nation. Secondly, national identity is a phenomenon in a state of continuous development. No final picture of it can be drawn. Thirdly, national identity needs the support of institutions. The most appropriate structure for this is the sovereign (nation) state with its educational system. Any transfer of sovereignty to other political institutions must inevitably lead to an erosion of national identity.

---

3   It is not accidental that the Nazi regime, which is considered by many to have been a monstrous exaggeration of nationhood, usually preferred to speak of «Volk» instead of nation, though the party carried the term in its designation.

4   One of the first writers to emphasize the historical bounds of the nation was the Austrian poet and politician Guido Zernatto, who wrote an excellent text about the emergence and future of the concept (Zernatto 1966; see also Zernatto 1944, quoted in Greenfeld 1992: 4).

1   Examples of Austrian national ideology

In the stock of knowledge defined as national ideology, the *name* of a land or a people takes a prominent place. Already here it is difficult to frame the term «Austria» or «Austrians» with a national ideology. Although in 1996 the official Austria celebrated the millennium of the first appearance of «Ostarrichi» – an old form for «Österreich», which is the German name for «Austria» – in an official document, this does not necessarily reduce the difficulties. Whereas most, if not all, other European nations trace their designations back to the name of a tribe or a group of tribes (e.g. Germans), in the case of Austria it is a term most probably given by Bavarian administrators to a small stretch of land east of a small river (Enns) more than 1 000 years ago. It should be mentioned that it was not until after World War II that this event came to be considered as a significant aspect of the national ideology of Austria. For centuries, «Austria» has first of all been associated with the Habsburg family, which was also called the House of Austria. I do not have to mention here that this family originated in what is today Switzerland[5], before it began to adopt the term Austria in the 13th century. What I want to emphasize is simply that the word «Austria(n)» is not derived from the designation of a tribe like the name of most nations, but historically it has stood most prominently for the political organization of the House of Habsburg. This explains why, between the ancient Ostarrichi and the present-day Austria, the term has assumed such arbitrary or different meanings, depending upon the changing fortunes of the House of Habsburg.

Until 1918, all kinds of people with different ethnic and language backgrounds could claim to be Austrian (see Csaky 1996). When, after World War I the French politician Clemenceau coined the famous phrase «L'Autriche c'est ce qui reste!», it was the will of the constitutional assembly of this «rest» that its name should be «Deutsch-Österreich». We know that the adoption of this name was prohibited by the victors of World War I. But what is less often reflected upon is the fact that the intention to adopt this name indicates that the name «Austria» was compatible with different ethnic and linguistic groups: the choice of the term «Deutsch-Österreich» implies that one was aware of a Non-German Austria as well. One can still occasionally meet old people in the US, Canada or elsewhere, who say that they are of Austrian descent although their ancestors spoke Czech, Polish or other languages. And even now in post-89 Europe (Münch 1993), one can be confronted with similar statements. For example, only recently the president of the Republic of Slovenia said in a discussion about whether or not to recognize an ethnic group of «Altösterreicher» in

---

5   About the relationship between Switzerland and Austria today, see Altermatt/Brix (1996).

present-day Slovenia that «at one time we were all Austrians». Perhaps it was because of this multi-ethnic semantic which irritated nationalists that German was constitutionally declared the official language of Austria; and sociologically speaking, the connotation of «Austria» is closer to *Gesellschaft* than to *Gemeinschaft*, if we may use this distinction by Ferdinand Tönnies. With classical nations, it is usually the opposite.

Besides the name, *legends* are usually also a prominent part of national ideology. One such Austrian legend is about the origin of the Austrian red, white, and red flag. The legend tells of the bravery of Duke Leopold V of Babenberg: after the battle of Akkon in the year 1190, only that part of his shirt remained white which was covered by his belt, the rest was red with blood. Another more significant story is told in the play «König Ottokars Glück und Ende» by Franz Grillparzer (1791–1872). This is about the dramatic events which occurred during the transfer of Ostarrichi from the Babenberger to the Habsburg dynasty. The main protagonists of the play are Rudolf von Habsburg and King Ottokar of Bohemia. The Bohemian king was defeated in a battle by Rudolf in 1278. This is considered to be the beginning of a correspondence between the Habsburg dynasty and the term Austria. In contrast to national sagas of other countries, this play does not paint an archaic picture of the beginning of the nation (e.g. the Finnish Kalevala), nor does it praise a hero who brings his people to civilization (e.g. the Hungarian Arpad saga), but it shows the dramatic events in the process of the taking of power within a given system. It also praises the people and the landscape of Austria (along the Danube).[6] In this play (a tragedy!), Grillparzer tried with the tools of a writer to express and support an anti-nationalistic national ideology in an age when all around Austria, nationalism was flourishing. The spirit of the play can be found condensed in one sentence by Grillparzer: «Von der Humanität über die Nationalität zur Bestialität.»

To round up briefly what I wish to say about national ideology, we might mention a few other aspects. The Austrian *state eagle:* It bears on its head a golden crown similar to the tower of a city wall, in its claws a sickle and a hammer and between the claws a torn chain. This heraldic animal replaced the famous double headed eagle of the monarchy after World War I. It is said that the tower crown is intended to symbolize the bourgeoisie, the sickle the farmers, the hammer the working class, and the broken chain the liberation from Nazism in 1945. The presence of the hammer and sickle have been criticized because of their semantic proximity to the symbols of communism. After 1989, Jörg

---

6   «Schaut ringsumher, wohin der Blick sich wendet, lachts wie dem Bräutigam die Braut entgegen» or «Es ist ein gutes Land, wohl wert, dass sich ein Fürst sein unterwinde».

Haider, leader of the Freedom Party, suggested removing them. Interestingly enough, however, this proposal found no significant support either in the political elite nor in the general population.

Another element of national ideology is the saying that contemporary Austria was forged in the Nazi concentration camps. Those who had been enemies between the wars – Socialists, Christian Democrats and Communists – finally found each other between the barracks of the camps and laid the foundation for the new Austria, which should forever more exist separated from Germany. A derivation from this covenant is the Austrian version of *social partnership*.

National holiday: The Austrian national holiday is the 26th of October. This commemorates the day in 1955 when the national assembly declared «everlasting neutrality». It is also said that on this day the last soldier of the occupation (!) forces left Austria. Until the sixties, this day was called the «Day of the Flag» (Tag der Fahne), and only since 1965 has it been a national holiday (Nationalfeiertag). It is worth mentioning how the nation is celebrated on this day: there is very little martial ceremony, in contrast to how other countries so often celebrate themselves – rather, Austrians choose to relax, go hiking and play sports on their national holiday.

National anthem: Since World War II, Austria has probably had the most peaceful national anthem in Europe. It praises the location, the landscape, the culture and the genius of the people. The music is heavy, similar to a religious hymn; in fact, it is said to have been used as a hymn by the Freemasons in the 18th century. The music of the previous Austrian anthem was by Joseph Haydn, and is now used for the German national anthem.[7]

I will not continue the discussion of national ideology here, but there are certainly other elements which would deserve attention: neutrality, the Habsburg heritage, Mitteleuropa, the sense of cultural superiority, the myth of victimization, etc. Most of these last-mentioned elements are often contested today, but they are also intellectual artifacts. And this is another peculiarity of Austrian nationhood: it was only in the 1970s and 1980s that an Austrian-minded intellectual elite began to dominate the public discourse. Until then, but particularly during the 19th century and up to World War II, the dominating national ideology was German – and the Austrians were merely the «better» Germans. It sounds paradoxical, but when Austrian national ideology became more or less uncontested for the first time in the late eighties, historical events began to

---

7   The best account of the national ideology of Austria can probably be found in Heer (1981).

put the very nation as such in question. The collapse of communism in 1989 brought a great push forward towards a supranational Europe, and neutral Austria applied for membership in the European Union.

2   National institutions

Austria is usually considered as a «late nation», but unlike other late nations it had national institutions long before it accepted its own nationhood. The Austrian national assembly *(Nationalrat)* was established in 1918/1919, immediately after World War I. Paradoxically, one of the first decisions it took was to declare Austria a part of Germany. Usually, national assemblies do the opposite: they declare a country as independent from another country. The *Nationalrat* had a predecessor under the late empire: the *Reichsrat*. Although this assembly did not represent all strata of the population, it did exercise some control over the government. The *Nationalrat* inherited the representative neoclassical building on the Ringstrasse in Vienna from the Reichstag. Quite often, the names of former Imperial institutions were changed to «National...»: Nationalbank, Nationalbibliothek, etc. Two other institutions which are equally important for a modern nation also date from the 19th century. One of these is the Austrian civil code, and the other is the core of the constitution, and these are still in use today. The Austrian civil code (Allgemeines Bürgerliches Gesetzbuch) was one of the first in Europe, dating from 1811. The core of the constitution (Staatsgrundgesetz), which mainly regulates the political rights of the individual, was formulated in 1867.

In addition to these, many other institutional elements necessary for the establishment of a nation-state, even if not characteristic only of the nation-state, have continued to exist from the time of the empire. Most important among them are the structures, values and customs of the state bureaucracy. The military, for example, still cultivates the idea of continuity. At least in Central Europe, this is quite unusual for nation building (e.g. Germany, Italy), where national identity typically develops together with national mobilization before institutions are established. Perhaps it was a little different with the classical nations of Western Europe. But while in England and France, the nation inherited a more or less strong state, its institutions had to be completely remodeled; in these countries, national ideology also preceded the establishment of the modern institutions to a significant extent, or at least developed simultaneously with them (Greenfeld 1992). In the case of Austria, however, modern political institutions emerged not only long before national ideology and national identity had taken shape, but what is even more important – they showed strong loyalty to the German nation. This explains to some extent the smooth way in which some institutions were taken over by Nazi Germany in 1938, and then later and once again rather smoothly formed the administrative basis for the Second Republic. Moreover, whereas the nation building process is usually a question of integrating and expanding, Austria was pushed and broken out of a whole. First, it was pushed out of Germany by Prussia in 1866, and then it was broken off from the Danubian Monarchy and not permitted to return to Germany in 1918/19. During all of these changes, the institutions have shown a surprising durability and continuity.

Many of these peculiarities in the emergence of the national institutions are closely related to the Austrian national identity, which I will turn to in the next section. It can be observed beforehand that until 1918, Austria was a transnational designation encompassing at least eleven ethnic groups, each with more or less strong nationalistic aspirations. Austria was a state of many would-be nations, but there was no Austrian nation as such. Irrespective of this situation, an «Austrian mindedness» did exist, which meant an identification with the state institutions and with a certain way of life. This orientation could be found in all the ethnic groups. It is difficult to say whether the national identity or the Austrian mindedness was the stronger of the two, because the Austria of that time did not fall apart from within but came to an end with a lost war. The Austria which then became the First Republic had national institutions and a clear national identity, but these two things did not correspond to each other. Whereas the institutions were definitely Austrian, the national identity was German. To speak of a «second German state» as the elite did is inadequate, though, because nations must insist on unity of institutions, identity and ideology. Can anybody imagine French children singing the *Marseillaise* with the text of the *Deutschlandlied* as their national anthem in their schools? In socialist Vienna things like this happened in the thirties: because the school administration did not like the Austrian anthem, the children were ordered to sing the *Deutschlandlied* to the music of the old Austrian *Kaiserlied*.

3   National identity

A population which no longer shows or which does not yet show awareness of its national ideology or national institutions, by our definition lacks national identity. This does not mean that such a population has no collective identity at all, but only that its identity cannot be considered to be a national identity within the framework of our theoretical approach. From this point of view, the evidence of every variable concerning a politically organized people cannot be interpreted without qualification as an indicator for national identity. In each case, the association of such responses with ideology and institutions also has to be considered. To avoid confusion with terms like cultural identity, one could speak instead of nation-consciousness or nation-oriented conduct. For example, numerous studies have found that the Austrian population is very proud of its country (see Bruckmüller 1996; Haller/Gruber 1996). International comparison even shows that in this respect Austria has been among the top ranking countries for many years. This is usually interpreted as «a high degree of national pride». From what has already been said, however, it should be obvious that such hasty conclusions are not necessarily justified: not only must the wording of the question be taken into account, but also the relation of the respondent to the concept of nation as such. It is self-evident that one can appreciate a country and its people without considering it as a nation.

The question whether Austrians are a nation or not is actually another aspect for which longitudinal data are available. As already mentioned, in the fifties a substantial part of the Austrian population still considered itself as German.[8] This percentage has decreased until in 1995, it stood at about 10% of the population, whereas those who consider themselves to be Austrians has increased to almost 90% (Haller/Gruber 1996: 65).[9] The statement «Austrians are a nation» has received continuously increasing approval, from 47% in 1964 to 85% in 1995. Although the validity and reliability of such questions could be questioned, there is no doubt that the term «Austria(n)» meets with wide approval in the population today. But whether this can be interpreted as evidence of a strong sense of national identity is another matter. One could argue that at a time when every state is called a nation, the answers to such questions do not convey much information. The meaning behind «nation» itself must become a subject of study. How do the respondents understand it, and what do they associate with it?

3.1 National identity among 17–19 year-olds Austrians

We have argued that pride in citizenship or country is not necessarily an aspect of national identity, nor is it a sufficient indicator for nation-consciousness. In a study of the age group of 17–19 year-olds in Austria (Langer 1996), we have therefore applied additional empirical approaches, including content analysis of teaching materials, intensive individual and group interviews with representative members of the sample, as well as expert interviews, in order to obtain a better understanding of this question. In these enquiries, it was most important to direct attention not only to the collective consciousness, but to

---

8   Concerning the question of «Austria as a German state» in the 1980s, see Pelinka (1990).
9   In fact, whether or not Austrians consider themselves as Germans depends significantly on how the question is phrased (Ley/Gehmacher 1996: 98).

the actual concept of nation in particular. It hardly needs to be added that the attitudes of the younger generation have long been considered to be a good basis for anticipating the future. To ask this group about its perception of nation should therefore also provide some insight into the future of this type of collective identity.

It is well known that, historically, nationalism and nation-consciousness have had their most influential protagonists among the contemporaneous younger generations. Now, though, the relevant genre of studies does not emphasize this dimension very much. In the forefront of modern studies, there are usually general life-style characteristics and the specific events which produce communality among age cohorts and mold them into a generation in the sociological sense. Thus, we hear in Austria (and Germany) of the «wartime generation» *(Kriegsgeneration),* the *Flackhelfer-Generation* (those whose youth coincided with the later months of the war and was characterized by the common experience of massive air raids on cities), the «skeptical generation» (Schelsky 1957) of the fifties and, as a kind of antidote to the wartime generations, the '68ers. But it is worth mentioning that the closer one gets to the present, the less the writings about «generations» refer to the question of «nation», even though sometimes hostile attitudes and behavior towards foreigners are occasionally classified as «nationalism». The term is, for example, frequently ascribed to groups of juveniles (e.g. skinheads) acting violently against foreigners.

The primary data considered here are drawn from a study of upper secondary and vocational school students (N=262) carried out in 1995 in eastern (Vienna), western (Innsbruck) and southern (Klagenfurt) Austria. Information was gathered by questionnaires and group discussions directly with the students, as well as by content analysis of history textbooks and intensive interviews with teachers. Perhaps the most significant question in the context of national identity was that of belonging to a nation. The question was explicit and direct. It did not focus on «Austria» but on the «nation». It did not ask whether others (the Austrians) were a nation but whether the respondent himself felt that he «belonged to a nation»: «Do you have the feeling of belonging to a nation?» From those 17–19 year-olds – the «next generation» – who responded to this question (85%), almost one third (29%) indicated that they did not feel that they belonged to any nation *(Figure 1).* Only 62% felt that they belonged to one nation (predominantly Austrian), and 9% felt that they belonged to several nations. In the following discussion, we will focus on the «non-nation» oriented youth, because they are the most interesting group for testing the proposition that Austrians have a low nation-consciousness while at the same time their pride in the country is high.

First of all, the non-nation oriented group does not differ with respect to its gender distribution from the sample as a whole. Male and female students share this characteristic to the same extent. With respect to social stratification, this orientation is predominant among children of salaried employees/management (39%) and skilled workers (41%). Among those who come from a civil servant, professional or entrepreneurial family background, lack of a nation-orientation is much less frequent. Only 17% of the children whose fathers are civil servants are non-nation oriented. One could infer from this evidence that the idea of nation is in trouble, particularly with the employed social classes not protected from market competition; in the milieu of state employees and small business owners, it still seems to be a valid concept. Does the concept of nation today serve the interests of these groups?

Figure 1:   «Do you have the feeling of belonging to a nation?
I feel I belong to ...» (N = 262)

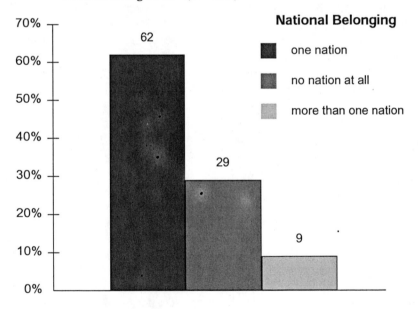

In contrast to family socio-economic background, neither the type of education nor the region differentiate the results. Whether the students are from Vienna, Innsbruck, or Klagenfurt, the distribution of the responses is similar. This also holds true for vocational schools and high schools. What does differ is the fact that students from vocational schools refuse to answer this question significantly more often than do students from high schools. We don't know whether this is because of a lack of imagination, or because of negative feelings. However, we do know that the nation-oriented students more often have (77%) a distinct cognitive concept of nation than do the non-nation oriented students (56%). The latter obviously had to answer the question more often from a mere emotional point of view. We will see later that the school seems to play an important role in providing a cognitive map for the development of nation-consciousness, though a cognitive map should not necessarily be equated with a feeling of belonging to a nation. In our study, many vocational school students do not feel that they belong to a nation because they have no clear idea of a nation, whereas high school students answer the same question from a critical evaluation of the concept.

This connection can also be seen in the responses to another question: «Are you proud of your country?» The answers correlate with nation-consciousness *(Table 1)*. Yet, although students who are nation oriented tend more often to be «very proud» of Austria (52%) than do non-nation oriented students (27%), there is not a consistent correlation between the two sets of findings. The answers clearly indicate that being proud of a country is not the same as being nation-oriented, even though it is a collective feeling and there is some correlation. One can refuse to know or simply not know the concept of nation, and still be proud of a particular society. Considerable pride in a country is compatible with a low sense of nation-consciousness, as is the inverse. We have already seen that in an international survey, a high proportion of Austrians showed great pride in their country, the older generation more, the younger less so. But from this evidence alone, we cannot automatically conclude that there exists a high degree of nation-orientation.

Table 1:   «Nation-consciousness» and «pride of being Austrian»

Pride	Feeling of belonging to ...			
	one Nation [%]	no Nation [%]	several Nations [%]	Total [%]
very proud	52	27	36	45
somewhat proud	33	36	42	33
not very proud	9	20	10	13
not proud at all	5	15	10	9
[N]	134	65	19	218
	100%	100%	100%	100%

Every collective identity includes feelings directed towards group symbols. But beyond the nation, there are few collective entities in history that have mana-

ged to attract strong feelings to symbols like the flag, shield, and anthem. Only
if that could be accomplished would such symbols begin to mobilize whole societies to move in the same direction. Do young Austrians still have considerable edifying feelings towards these symbols? If so, then the proposition that
there is a declining influence of the concept of nation on collective identity
would have to be reconsidered. From *Table 2,* we can see that of the one third
of non-nation oriented students in particular, only small proportions admit to
having edifying feelings associated with national symbols. If the Austrian flag
is raised, no more than 18% of this group show such emotions, and when they
see the army march past, the figure is even lower (14 %). More than anything
else, it is international sporting events in which Austrian teams are competing
that seem to be able to mobilize such feelings (with 68% of nation-oriented
and 51% of non-nation oriented youth). We can also see that even among those
who feel that they belong to a nation, the correlation between identification
with constituent symbols (flag, anthem, and army) and nation-consciousness is
not very frequent. We consider this as support for the proposition that there is
either no, or at least only a low level of, nation-consciousness.

Table 2:   The acceptance of nation and national symbols:
«Do you have edifying feelings at the following occasions ...?»

National Symbols	Feeling of belonging to ...			Total [%]
	one Nation [%]	no Nation [%]	several Nations [%]	
when the Austrian flag is raised	37	18	47	32
when the president hold a speech	7	2	11	6
when Austrian athlets win	68	51	58	62
when the army marches out	16	14	21	16
when the national anthem is played	46	27	11	42
I have never such feelings	13	22	11	16
[N]	138	65	20	223
	100%	100%	100%	100%

3.2 Teaching national identity

Molded within a complex historical process, it is not easy for national identity to be influenced by rational action. Nevertheless, political organizations such as governments and parties have always tried to exercise such an influence. In many countries, the state is especially tempted to do so through the educational system and through propaganda. The former German Democratic Republic, for example, tried to transform its citizens into a «socialist nation». Authors like Znaniecki (1973: 105) and Gellner (1991: 95) agree that schools and education are important instruments of the nation-state. Similarly, Francis (1965: 343) additionally emphasized the role of schools in «standardizing» the population. Today, one could oppose to this view the impact of the global media, which compete with the views of the nation-states transmitted by state schools.

For our purpose, it is important to find out how the Austrian school system imparts the concept of nation. To this end, we have analyzed history text books and carried out extended interviews with teachers. The students themselves were asked to name heroic times and important personalities in Austria's history. The results of these approaches should indicate the semantic field within which the development of nation-consciousness is embedded in Austria.

The history curriculum for the age group of 17–19 years-old covers the 19th and the 20th century. These centuries also happen to represent the high points of nationalism, of ideas of nation and the nation-state in Europe. One is all the more surprised, then, to find how little attention is paid to this phenomenon in the Austrian textbooks and in teaching. To begin with, in the vocational schools for apprentices, history is not taught at all. Instead, a course on social and institutional matters is taught in which the topic of nation is completely replaced by information about governmental institutions and the dynamic of social groups in general. In contrast, the teaching materials for history in secondary schools *(Gymnasium, Höhere Schule),* which give access to the tertiary educational system, are abundant. Teachers were almost critical of the fact that it is difficult to choose between them, because there is such a variety of documents and other materials. Yet even here, the nation is a minor theme. In the major history textbooks, only 4 to 5 percent of the content is dedicated to the nation (Langer 1996: 362). The treatment of this theme concentrates on «nationalism» and the «conflict between nationalities», which is held to have led to the end of the Habsburg monarchy. When the emergence of the nation state in Italy, Germany and Poland is discussed, the implicit evaluation is rather negative. In the case of Poland, for example, uprisings and the deportation of rebels to Siberia are emphasized. For Italy, the increase of social inequality as an outcome of nation building is stressed, and for Germany the exclusion of

Austria. Another implicit message given to the student is that «nation» is a difficult and complicated concept. All in all, what the students learn about nation is not likely to raise any enthusiasm or sympathy. From the perspective of the official textbooks, Austria does not appear to be a nation, but rather a timeless mirror in which the events of history are reflected. This is how it must appear to high school students. For the apprentices, Austria is simply a state organization.

The teachers confirm that they have problems with teaching the concept of «nation». They usually avoid speaking about «our nation», and prefer to use the term «Austria», signifying a long term historical actor. The idea of individuals and organizations is more dominant than that of a collectivity like a tribe. In the Austrian historical consciousness, the imagined scenario of a tribe (the «Austrians») taking possession of a piece of land which will then become its legitimate territory, is missing. Instead, it is the first mention of the present name of the country in a document about the passing on of a fiefdom from a feudal lord to a vassal[10] that is commemorated.

The answers of the students seem to directly reflect the teaching as described by the teachers and the content of the text books. When asked about which periods of Austria's history one could be proud of, the Second Republic after 1945 was mentioned most frequently, and in second place came the Baroque period, and the wars against the Turks and against Napoleon. Out of about sixty topics drawn from a period spanning 2 000 years, the students were proud of only two (the Viennese Congress and the Austro-Hungarian Monarchy) which fall in the 19th century. That century – the high point of nationalism in Europe – otherwise hardly seems to exist in the students' collective memory. This result is complemented by answers naming the most important personalities in Austria's history. First and second place go undisputed to Wolfgang A. Mozart and the Empress Maria Theresia, two personalities from the Baroque period. After these two, among the ten most significant figures were placed mostly personalities from this century and especially from the time after 1945, among them the former chancellor Bruno Kreisky and the movie star Arnold Schwarzenegger; from the 19th century, only the Emperor Franz Joseph was mentioned. Obviously the 19th century, which is so important with respect to nation-building for neighbors like Germany, Italy or Hungary, attracts little attention

---

10   In 1994, two-thirds of Austrians voted for membership of the country in the European Community. In no other country was a similar level of approval reached. Many reasons have been given to explain this behavior. It is most commonly accounted for by the dishonest advertising campaign of the government, or by a kind of longing for unification with Germany. We would argue rather that, unlike the Swiss, Austrians have always been affiliated with large (imperial) political organizations and prefer this to small units. In their subconscious thinking, then, the EU is simply another form of what they have been accustomed to for most of their past.

from the Austrian youth of today. Collective identity is instead gained from a combination of the Baroque period of more than 200 years ago, and the present.

3.3 Alternatives to the nation?

In his writings, Karl W. Deutsch (1972) has indicated two possible ways of transcending the nation: 1) to move one level beyond (globalism), or 2) one level below (localism). Today, the latter approach is reflected in debates about the new nationalism in post-communist countries, «small is beautiful», regionalism (Ohmae 1996) in the West, and fundamentalism in the religious sphere; the former approach is reflected in the proclamation of a «new world order», and more importantly, we can observe the formation of transnational entities at a macro-regional level. This is accompanied by the emergence of a kind of global culture made possible by a media revolution (i.e. satellite TV, Internet). We assume that these processes irritate and will finally erode the traditional nation-consciousness, especially in societies like Austria, where it was only recently consolidating and even then, only at a low level.

In our study, we looked at alternatives to the nation according to three indicators: 1) the degree of belonging to different levels of society, 2) the importance of various social circles, and 3) identification with life-style groups.

Whereas other studies (Haller/Gruber 1996: 394) have shown that the average Austrian has a kind of multiple identity with respect to territorial entities which operates at various levels, the 17–19 year-olds seem to behave somewhat differently. In other studies, «multiple identity» means that persons will identify with their local communities to the same extent as they identify with Austria or even with Europe. But in our study of 17–19 year-olds, this pattern was not observed. Here, the sense of identification with level 2 (city/community) and with level 5 (Europe) especially, is low in comparison with that with level 1 (neighborhood) and with level 4 (Austria). From this general pattern, the non-nation oriented group deviates significantly in respect of level 4, where only 9% – versus 23% of the nation oriented – feel strongly attached to Austria. Conclusion: the sense of attachment of the young is lower than that of the average Austrian throughout all territorial levels, including that of Europe.

When we come to the importance of belonging to certain social circles, the differences become more pronounced. An overwhelming majority of the students ascribes highest importance (very important) to «friends» and «family» (almost 80%). A second cluster is composed of «leisure groups» and «school classes» (35% and 17%). The lowest percentage of respondents consider «religious groups» (4%), the «population of the province» (3%), and «all Austrians» (8%) as «very important» for them. It is worth noticing that whereas the territory, with noticeable exceptions (city/Europe), attracts similar degrees of attachment on all levels in the view of the young, the importance of social circles dramatically declines as the size of the group in question increases, and generally this is strongly related to a shift from primary to secondary types of relationships. Whereas within the frame of territory, «Austria» attracts almost the same degree of attachment as «neighborhood», only a very small group of students consider the «Austrian people» to be an important social circle for them. Here, the difference between the nation oriented and the non-nation oriented is less pronounced than in other dimensions of the study. At the same time, even in this case, the social attachment of the non-nation oriented is more cautious, particularly when it comes to their peers at school: only 9% consider school to be a «very important» social circle (compared with 20% of nation-oriented students).

Besides these differences in attachment to territory and the ascription of importance to social circles, we were able to observe a variety of identifications with contemporary life-style groups as well as with more conventional associations. The fact that only 30% declared a permanent group affiliation indicates that the majority of 17–19 year-olds never or only occasionally join groups. Of those who responded to the question, three quarters mentioned membership of conventional groups (soccer clubs, fraternities, etc.), and one quarter mentioned membership of modern life-style groups (skater, techno, etc.). With respect to nation-consciousness, it was striking that the students unanimously declared that they would rather not wear national costumes to school, though in other social milieus they would do it. This also supports the view that Austrian schools today have, to put it mildly, a low profile in producing and sustaining nation-consciousness.

In group discussions and intensive interviews, many of the students expressed interest in and sympathy with a great variety of life-style categories and affiliations. Names like skater, heavy metal, hip hop, raver, techno, snowborder, skin heads, crunch, new waves, handy types, junkies, biker, and so on, were mentioned. None of these groups has anything to do with national integration: they are rather identities offered by international business and the global media. It also appears that the non-nation oriented young people are especially prone to these kinds of images. The low profile of nation among young Austrians is also indicated in other survey results which show, for example, that out of 50 popular terms, none carries a national orientation. Most of them are not even German but are rooted rather in the Anglo-Saxon culture.

4   Conclusions

The Austria of today is not a typical nation, but a society with a strong *Staats-bewusstsein* and considerable confidence in its history. The backbone of both are the state institutions. But from this I would not conclude that it is a *Staats-nation* in the theoretical sense. Austria is historically too far removed from the respective western European models to be considered as such. But that does not make Austria an Ethnonation, either. The empirical indicators produce confusing results in both directions, especially where national identity is concerned (Haller/Gruber 1996). Still, it would be rather bold to consider the Austrian nation as a «contingent event», a term recently suggested by Rogers Brubaker (1996: 18) when discussing the post-communist situation. There has been too much development and continuity in the Austrian case to justify the use of this appellation. Upon closer consideration, however, our findings do not fit neatly into any of the theoretical models of nation, «nationness», nationalism, etc. It seems to me that as a historical phenomenon, the concept of nation has just not fully taken possession of Austria.

Theoretically speaking, it was only at the end of the eighties that Austria came closest to what we usually call a nation. I have argued that this particular status in the process of nation building should make Austria prone to denationalization in the post-89 era, though empirical studies do not yet reveal any clear pattern. In part, the blurred picture is due to confusing theoretical concepts and the methodology applied. What we can say is that the young generation seems to comprise significant numbers of individuals who do not feel that they belong to a nation at all, or who even have no concept of nation whatsoever. Instead, they not only disclose high expectations with regard to European integration, but are also increasingly drawn into the segmented, individualized life-style of global culture (consumerism, media, etc.). Though the latter tendency might be even more widespread in other European societies with more extended metropolitan areas, it is the configuration of low nation-consciousness, the ambivalent and opaque character of the term «Austria», together with the steamroller of global youth culture which makes accelerated denationalization in this country one likely scenario.

To sum up, we would like to sketch a number of scenarios for the future. Each of them will have specific effects on Austrian national identity.

a) The regrouping of the *Bundesstaat* (federation)
   aa) Mild version: A new distribution of responsibilities and competences is negotiated. Strengthening of provincial authorities is intended. Such

negotiations have been going on for years now. Regional identity would benefit.

ab) Strong version: *Bundesländer* (states of the federation) are expected to merge (e.g. Styria and Carinthia) especially to reduce administrative costs. This would probably have a negative effect on regional identity. Examples exist from the Nazi era. The effect at the state level is uncertain. It is most likely that it would lose influence.

b) Transborder regions

It has even been suggested that the institutions of the central states could be completely replaced by regional transborder structures.

The *Bundesländer* would unite with provinces of the neighboring states and form a new type of political actor within the framework of the European Union. Occasionally, such ideas are mentioned in the media, but they have never been more than an intellectual exercise.

Those who consider a) and b) assume that the Austrian cultural identity will remain, even if the national (or state) identity should disappear. Those who advocate b) even expect a strengthening of this identity *(Mitteleuropa)*. Given the strong role of the state in Austria in forming collective identity in general and national identity in particular, this assumption is very questionable.

c) The German card

Since Austria has joined the EU, the already strong influence of German capital and German media in the country has further increased. Given the historical peculiarities of Austria, it is not completely impossible that in the case of a significantly weakened state structure (all power to Brussels), the country could silently be incorporated into Germany – especially if the rest of Europe, as happened in 1938, loses interest in a separate Austria. One should not forget that a sovereign Austrian republic was originally established against its own will by those powers which won World War I. This earlier interest of Western Europe could turn in the opposite direction. Though in this scenario, Germany would also have lost sovereignty to the EU, it could well be that this new powerful administration gives up Austria in order to simplify its decision making structures.

d) The EU as *Einheitsstaat*

It is not completely impossible that under certain conditions the EU might turn into a totalitarian system. This could be provoked by increasing complexity in the course of continuing enlargements. In this case, the central authorities of the EU might decide in favour of structuring the «Empire» according to technical requirements for the maintenance of power. This could lead to an artificial structure of districts as existed, for example, in the former German Democratic Republic. The ideology of the nation-state could be replaced by a European national ideology or an imperial ideology. To understand the latter, one would have to examine the ideology of earlier multi-ethnic empires.

e) Failure of European integration (or globalization)
The scenarios mentioned so far have assumed a weakening of the nation-state structures in favor of transnational government. But it is imaginable that EU integration and globalization, will fail. In this case, the nation-state could experience a revival. In a fashion similar to the new nations in eastern Europe after the disintegration of the Soviet bloc, this would lead to new opportunities for the nation-state. For Austria, it would not necessarily be the worst case, because it could give a new boost to the completion of the national project.

More so than in the old established nations in Europe, the survival of an Austrian national identity depends on the continuation of central state institutions. Otherwise, it is conceivable that the term «Austria» will only remain as the name of a Euroregion on the Danube between Passau and Vienna, and in the case of scenario d), it would not even be that. But even if the state structures remain in one way or another, the population could quite easily slip into the newly emerging identity realities of Europe, simply because of the peculiarities of its nationhood. One of the last of the old European political cultures to (almost) reach the stage of nationhood, Austria could be one of the first to adapt to the new transnational structures, which finally bear some resemblance to those of the country's past.

References

Altermatt, Urs und Emil Brix (eds.) (1996). *Schweiz und Österreich – Eine Nachbarschaft in Mitteleuropa.* Wien: Böhlau.

Brubaker, Rogers (1996). *Nationalism reframed – Nationhood and the national question in the New Europe.* Cambridge: University Press.

Bruckmüller, Ernst (1996). *Nation Österreich.* Wien: Böhlau.

Csaky, Moritz (1996). «Die Vielfalt der Habsburgermonarchie und die nationale Frage», pp. 44–64 in U. Altermatt (ed.). *Nation, Ethnizität und Staat in Mitteleuropa.* Wien: (Böhlau).

Csepeli, György (1997). *National Identity in Contemporary Hungary.* Boulder (Col.): Atlantic Research Publications.

Deutsch, Karl W. (1972). *Der Nationalismus und seine Alternativen.* München: Piper.

Francis, Emerich (1965). *Ethnos and Demos.* Berlin: Duncker&Humblot.

Gellner, Ernest (1991). *Nationalismus und Moderne.* Berlin (Rotbuch Verlag).

Greenfeld, Liah (1992). *Nationalism – Five Roads to Modernity.* Cambridge (MA): Harvard University Press.

Haller, Max (1996). «Nationale Identität in modernen Gesellschaften – eine vernachlässigte Problematik im Spannungsfeld zwischen Wirtschaft und Gesellschaft, Kultur und Politik», pp. 9–60 in M. Haller (ed.). *Identität und Nationalstolz der Österreicher (Identity and National Pride of the Austrians).* Wien: Böhlau.

Haller, Max und Stefan Gruber (1996). «Der Nationalstolz der Österreicher im internationalen Vergleich», pp. 432–499 in M. Haller (ed.). *Identität und Nationalstolz der Österreicher (Identity and National Pride of the Austrians).* Wien: Böhlau.

Heer, Friedrich (1981). *Der Kampf um die österreichische Identität.* Wien: Böhlau.

Langer, Josef (1996). «Nation – Schwindende Basis für soziale Identität», pp. 327–382 in M. Haller (ed.). *Identität und Nationalstolz der Österreicher (Identity and National Pride of the Austrians).* Wien: Böhlau.

Ley, Michael und Ernst Gehmacher (eds.) (1996). *Das Ende des Nationalismus.* Wien: WUV.

Münch, Richard (1993). *Das Projekt Europe.* Frankfurt A. M.: Suhrkamp.

Ohmae, Kenichi (1996). *The End of the Nation State.* New York: Free Press.

Pelinka, Anton (1990). *Zur österreichischen Identität.* Wien: Ueberreuter.

Schelsky, Helmut (1957). *Die skeptische Generation.* Düsseldorf: Diederichs.

Susag, Chris (1999). «Finnish American Ethnicity as Measured by Collective Self Esteem», *University of Joensuu Publications in Social Sciences,* 37.

Zernatto, Guido (1944). «Nation: The History of a Word», *Review of Politics* 6: 351–366.

Zernatto, Guido (1966). *Vom Wesen der Nation – Fragen und Antworten zum Nationalitätenproblem*. Wien: Holzhausen.
Znaniecki, Florian (1973). *Modern Nationalities*. Westport: Greenwood Press.

Collective Identification in Western and Eastern Germany

Bettina Westle

1 German identity in scholarly discussion

International observers have always regarded German identity as a fragile thing, as a permanent imbalance between an underdeveloped and an excessive national consciousness (see Greiffenhagen und Greiffenhagen 1993). As a late-comer in the process of European nation building, the roots of German natio-nal identity have been primarily of an ethnic and cultural character – similar to those in some east European countries, and different from those in coun-tries in which the nation was constructed within an already existing political unit and thus formed primarily in direct linkage with the process of democra-tic emancipation, France being the most obvious European example of this type of a political nation. Whereas some observers see the German ethnic and cultural roots as the principal reason for the development of an excessive na-tionalism, others point to the damage to German national self-esteem fol-lowing the First World War and the Treaty of Versailles, which led to the ag-gressive nationalism and disaster of Nazi Germany.

In the early years after the end of Second World War, national identity was not a topic of public or academic discussion. The German *Wirtschaftswunder,* the Cold War, and comparison with the GDR, all helped to promote acceptance of the democratic system. The politics of integration into the Western world was not seen as contradictary, but as the only way of achieving national unity in some unspecified future. In addition, the prospect of a European Union for-med an attractive alternative to national identification.

With the building of the wall in 1961, the argument that German unity could be achieved by way of integration into the West lost its credibility. Institutional problems encountered along the way to the European Union also cast doubt on the idea of Europe. With democracy and prosperity becoming common-place, people became aware of the problems and dangers of economic pro-gress. Against this background, a value shift – especially among the younger generations – began to occur. Then, with a decline in prosperity and the great coalition in 1966–69, the support of democracy by the West Germans seemed to be endangered. A radicalization on the poles of the political spectrum – gains in votes by the right wing NPD on the one hand, but also by the student movement together with its demands for a public discussion of Nazi history on the other – put the subjects of collective identity, nation and democracy on the political agenda. In the sixties, a controversy was initiated first by the president of parliament and vice-chairman of the CDU, Gerstenmeier (1965), who pleaded for a revitalization of a traditional national identity embracing the whole German nation as an indispensable basis for the continuing determination of the West Germans to achieve German unity. Left and liberal participants in the debate argued that, because of the political separation between East and West, such an identity policy at the time would not provide concrete answers to the problem of a divided Germany, but rather that it would simply reactivate dangerous nationalistic trends (Sontheimer, Stammler und Heigert 1966).

Against a background of fears about a West German crisis of legitimacy, a second controversy, with a reversal of the front-lines, soon followed. The philosopher Jaspers opined that a reunion of the two parts of Germany was an unrealistic goal: West Germany should accept itself as a complete nation-state and should develop a sense of patriotism focused only on the Federal Republic (1966). Conservatives agreed with these arguments (Freudenfeld 1966, 1977), whereas the left, represented by the chairman of its parliamentary group, promoted the idea of two parallel identities – a West German consciousness with respect to the state, and a German national consciousness which included the East German population (Schmidt 1967, 1968). This construction was widely accepted, because it seemed to allow loyalty both to the FRG and to the Germans in the GDR. However, it effectively located West German identity in nothing more than support for democracy, and it said little about the political consequences of a German national identity (Lepsius 1967, 1968).

The agreement established by the social-liberal government with the GDR in 1970–72 implied a de facto acceptance of the GDR, and was widely supported by the West Germans. However, the German high court denied to all political institutions the right to abandon the goal of German unification. Over the following years, the construction of two parallel identities – a West German state counsciousness and a German national consciousness – became widely accepted.

In the GDR, the SED also followed a two-fold course in identity policy. On the one hand, the aim of German unity was articulated, on the other hand the building of a class nation and a GDR-patriotism were promoted. The impression of a widespread German national identity in the GDR, and attempts of the SED to demarcate itself from the FRG, led to the formulation of the «Binationalization thesis of the Germans in a socialist and a bourgeois nation», formalized in modifications to the second constitution of the GDR in 1974 (Heydemann 1987).

In West Germany, a similar thesis was formulated. German reunion disappeared from the list of political priorities, and national pride came to be grounded less and less in ethnic and cultural objects while being directed increasingly towards democracy and the social welfare system. East Germans likewise seemed increasingly to support their system. This led some observers to assume that in both German states, German identity would be replaced by two new, qualitatively different forms of national identity. Therefore, the two Germanys were not only two different states, but would also form two different nations (Schweigler 1972). Others rejected this thesis, because the SED-regime was not democratically legitimated; however, they could not reasonably claim a priority of German national identity over West German identity (Ludz 1974).

One proposed solution to the problem of the political under-definition of the nation concept in the West German debate was to adopt a multiple identity: an orientation towards the political, West German state-nation together with an orientation to the transpolitical, German cultural-nation (Lepsius 1977). This proposal failed, too. Some interlocutors interpreted the construct of a transpolitical cultural nation as a dismissal of the goal of German unity (Winkler 1981), while others interpreted it as expansionism towards Austria and Switzerland (Mommsen 1981).

With the beginning of the eighties, there was wide-spread agreement on a binationalization of cultural and social consciousness between the two German states. GDR-identity was characterized as private, Prussian, and authoritarian, while social and cultural consciousness in the FRG was said to be modern and cosmopolitan, with nation and state being only two pragmatic objects of identity among many other possibilities (Pross 1982; Rudolph 1983). Given that earlier controversies had been characterized by an underlying concept of nation as a historical community of fate (defined by objective characteristics or at least considerably shaped by such characteristics), the recognition of two separate nations and the abandoning of the goal of German unification might have been the logical consequence. This step was not taken, however, because of the lack of democratic legitimation of the GDR and the assumption that the East Germans did not support their state.

Quite to the contrary, a proposal to avoid the term «nation» in inter-German communication (initiated by Gaus, the then representative of the FRG in the GDR) gave rise to a debate which linked the definition of «nation» even more closely to the questions of collective identity and of German unity (Grewe 1983; Bucerius 1984). Intermediate positions which rejected a sustained quest for unity while wanting to ensure that the German question remained open, led to a moralization of German national identity – the guardianship of identity as a duty of the more fortunate West Germans (Hättich 1983). Further attempts to moderate the debate included reference to the possibility of multiple identities (von Krockow 1983), and to European union as a means of achieving German union (Weidenfeld 1985) – no real solutions either, because of the political incompatibility of co-existing German and FRG-GDR-identities and/or because of the West-East tension, which could not have been resolved by West German or West European politics.

In spite of massive criticism, the CDU/CSU-FDP-coalition, which came into government after the collapse of the social-liberal coalition in 1982, did not change the new policy towards the GDR. Some excitement was caused by a new concept of «national neutralism», promoted not only by the extreme right, but also by the left. It aimed at finding a Third Path between socialism and democracy in a united, neutral Germany (Venohr 1982). However, these positions did not gain the support of the West German population.

In academic and in political circles, the diagnosis of a new German identity crisis, caused in turn by a crisis of orientation, found considerable agreement. The teaching of German history in the education system was looked at in an attempt to resolve this latest identity crisis. For the left, this meant FRG-history, while for the right it meant the whole of German history. Conflicts similar to those which had gone before erupted once again. The ensuing controversy culminated in the «debate of historians» («Historikerstreit» 1987). This debate was triggered by an article by Nolte (1986) in the *Frankfurter Allgemeine Zeitung,* in which he encouraged the Germans to forget about their – in his view – overwhelming sense of guilt over their Nazi past, which had caused so much self-hatred that it had resulted in a «negative nationalism» which threatened the legitimacy of the FRG. Habermas (1986) denounced inaccurate descriptions of history in this article, and criticized the attempt to relativize the crimes of the Nazis in order to reactivate a traditional national identity which is not moderated by self-criticism. Together with Habermas, other participants in the debate interpreted this approach as an attack against Western political culture, according to which collective identity should not be anchored in a particular nationalism but in universal values. In their view, the reflection about Nazi guilt and the disassociation from Nazi ideology were core elements of a development towards a new, democratic postconventional identity, for which the term *Verfassungspatriotismus* (constitutional or democratic patriotism) was coined. For some time, this concept of a democratic patriotism was highly controversial. Most participants on the right accepted it only as a makeshift substitute for a traditional national identity, which ideally should embrace Germans in both West and East. *Verfassungspatriotismus* was felt to exclude the East Germans, to dismiss the aim of national unity, and to be an effectively weak construct of intellectuals which was scarcely suited to the stabilization of democracy (Isensee 1986; Noelle-Neumann 1987; Lübbe 1989). By contrast, those on the left pleaded for *Verfassungspatriotismus* or – going even further – for a postnational identity, which they envisaged as being supportive of democracy and peace between natives and immigrants as well as between countries. A parallel duty to keep the German question open was considered unproblematic, but any idea of aiming specifically at its resolution was rejected (Bracher 1986; Glotz 1990).

With the unexpected collapse of the SED-regime and the democratization of the GDR, the question of German unity was catapulted onto the political agenda once more. The resulting controversies revealed different underlying concepts of the nation-state. Most protagonists on the left-liberal and the alternative side in the FRG, as well as the people's movements in the GDR, viewed unification with some scepticism. They feared a return to authoritarianism, economic and ethnic nationalism, and expansive ambitions. Therefore, in the beginning, they proposed two separate states or a transitional confederation, in which the East Germans should have time to realize their own political ideas without being dominated by the FRG. Later in this process, they preferred a unification according to Art. 146 GG (Grundgesetz) with a new constitution ratified by the population in both German states, rather than the accession of the GDR to the FRG according to Art. 23 GG (Habermas 1989; Offe 1990). The arguments of the wide spectrum of proponents of a rapid unification via Art. 23 GG ranged from recourse to a notion of an objective nation, anthropologically grounded in traditional ethnic identity and a natural inclination to unity and cohesion (Nipperdey 1990; Schwarz 1990), through moral appeals based on a historical responsibility and the constitutional obligation of unification (Bohrer 1990; Isensee 1990), to the pragmatic position, recognising the limited economic and political resources of the GDR, the ongoing emigration into the FRG, and the result of the *Volkskammer*-election, which was interpreted as a vote in favour of a rapid unification (Berger et al. 1990). All participants showed a strong mistrust of the general population, which was inconsistent with their former arguments – the left was afraid of a return to an ethnic nationalism, in spite of its earlier diagnosis of a strong democratic identity, and the right was afraid that the West Germans might reject the East German longing for unity in a plebiscite, in spite of its simultaneous insistence on the existence of a German national identity and its desire for unity. The elite discussion and the policy of German unification was dominated by the concept of nation as an ethnic-historical community of chance, in contrast to the democratic concept of nation as a community which is free to express and exercise its collective will.

With the realization of German unity, the question about the appropriate form of collective identity has arisen yet again, in a new light. In order to preclude further problems of domestic unity, some now propose the promotion of an ethnically and historically founded national identity (Reese-Schäfer 1991; Schäuble 1994). Others warn against such an instrumentalization of traditional national feelings and view it as an attempt to distract attention from political deficits and as a dangerous path which could lead to chauvinistic nationalism; they plead for a strong connection of traditional national feelings with universal values, or for a purely democratic patriotism (Dahrendorf 1990; Gessenharter 1997). In the normative debate of the nineties, we now find at least three orientations. The first type of argument rejects any form of a positive, constructive or democratic patriotism as an oxymoron. Patriotism is equated with particularism and an affirmative orientation towards one's own nation. Any link between universal values and striving for their realization in the particular nation is therefore seen as impossible (Burger 1994; Lauermann 1994). The second type of argument promotes a nationalistic patriotism. It tries to rehabilitate the ethnic-historical nation as the only adequate form of political organization. Ethnic-national identification is interpreted as a basic human need. Germans should dismiss their negative nationalism and their irrelevant *Verfassungspatriotismus* and develop a so-called defensive nationalism – a concept strongly reminiscent of the ethno-nationalism of the new right (Nolte 1991; Zitelmann 1993; Schwilk und Schacht 1994). The third trend is an adoption of *Verfassungspatriotismus* across the entire political spectrum. The background for this trend is that *Verfassungspatriotismus* can no longer be interpreted as being inconsistent with German unity, and that the question of support of the democratic system has gained new importance with the incorporation of the population of the former GDR, which was raised in the socialist tradition. However, the concept of *Verfassungspatriotismus* is interpreted in widely different ways, ranging from a subordination to the primary link with the nation (Kluxen-Pytha 1990), through several concepts which reject an ethnic definition of nation and try to combine a universalist orientation with a sense of civic responsibility in the particular nation (Hättich 1993; Sarcinelli 1993; Schwan 1995), to a dispensation with any national elements and a plea for a purely postnational identity, grounded in universal ideals (Oberndörfer 1991; Breit 1993).

In any case, almost everyone expected substantial changes in the form and intensity of German collective identity – some hoped for while others feared an increase of national self-consciousness. Although there are some indicators that minor changes have occurred, to date, it would seem as if these expectations were rather exaggerated. In what follows, the development and structures of some aspects of collective identity within the German population will be examined. The voting population in different representative surveys serves as a basis for this analysis[1].

2 The historical legacy of German identity

For many years, the most characteristic mark of German identity has been the low sense of national pride – low, when compared with other European countries *(Figure 1)*. German unification did not significantly affect this. At the time of unification, East Germans expressed a somewhat greater sense of national pride, but then in the aftermath in both parts of the united Germany, national pride evaporated. Only from 1994 can we observe a small tendency for it to increase once more, but the European average level has certainly still not been reached.

Figure 1:   National Pride

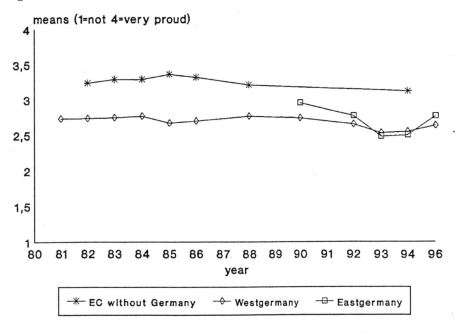

West- and Eastgermany unweighted, for EC/EU average of EC/EU-memberstates without Germany, EC/EU-weighted. 1981 and 1990 *World Value Surveys* 1 and 2, 1982 to 1988, 1994 *Eurobarometer* No. 17, 19, 21, 24, 26, 30, 42, 1992 and 1993 *Politische Kultur Studie,* 1996 Allbus.

---

1   All reported results are based on own computing.

This contradicts earlier interpretations to the effect that the low level of German national pride is caused simply by the lost war and a damaged self-esteem because of the division into two states. A more plausible explanation for the stable, low level of national pride is the scepticism of Germans with respect to intense national feelings, given their consciousness of the dangers of excessive nationalism under the Nazi regime. European comparison shows that citizens in other EU-countries usually regard national pride as something natural to everyone, or even as a duty of the good citizen, whereas in Germany large segments of the population exhibit strong reservations about national pride. The «not too proud citizens» especially, reflect an individualistic attitude and think that national pride makes no sense since nationality is caused by accident, or because people should not be judged by their nationality but by their personal qualities. Some even agree that national pride is arrogant or dangerous, because it might lead to conflicts and war. Even among the Germans who are proud, relatively few consider national pride as a duty, compared with the European average *(Table 1)*.

Table 1: Opinions on national pride

1993 + 1994 kum., EU 1994	West Germany			Est Germany			EU (without Germany)		
percentages/ column percentages	all	proud	not proud	all	proud	not proud	all	proud	not proud
duty for a good citizen	8.2	14.3	1.8	9.7	17.7	1.8	23.6	27.1	9.9
naturally for everyone	35.1	59.4	9.2	36.8	57.3	15.3	50.3	56.1	25.7
no sense/natio-nality=accident	19.6	8.1	32.0	16.5	5.6	26.7	9.0	5.2	24.4
no sense/every-one is different	11.1	3.9	18.2	7.9	5.8	10.8	6.9	4.8	15.4
arrogant towards other nations	11.4	7.5	15.9	13.8	5.3	23.4	2.6	1.3	7.9
dangerous, leads to wars	14.6	6.8	22.8	15.3	8.3	22.0	7.7	5.4	16.7

Political Cultures in Germany 1993, *Eurobarometer* No.42 (1994).

These data reveal reasons for reservation towards national pride, but they cannot answer the question of whether the scepticism with regard to national pride is generalized – which would be indicative of a reflexive or even a postnational identity – or whether it is directed exclusively towards German national pride – which would be indicative of mistrust of their own countrymen and thus, of a negative nationalism.

3 Closeness to territorial units, ethnic consciousness and ethnic identification

With respect to the territorial level of identification, most Germans feel closest to their own town or region, less so to their country, and least of all to the EC or Europe as a whole. There is still a discrepancy between Germans' feeling of closeness to their nation and the European average, but it is clearly smaller than the corresponding discrepancy in the case of national pride *(Table 2)*. Whereas the development of West Germans' feelings for the FRG before unification is quite unspectacular and correlates positively with their feelings towards united Germany, in East Germany the first years after unification show a decrease in feelings towards the former GDR, but an increase in 1992 and 1993. For most East Germans who feel close to the former GDR and/or to the new regions as a whole, this precludes a feeling of closeness to united Germany. This hints at disappointed high expectations concerning unity, problems of internal unity, and some kind of GDR-nostalgia.

Table 2:   Closeness to geo-political units

means 1 = not at all close 4 = very close	West Germany				East Germany					EC (without Germany)	
	S/ 91	S/ 92	S/ 93	A/ 95	S/ 90	S/ 91	S/ 92	S/ 93	A/ 95	A/ 91	S/ 95
town + county (index)	2.87	2.93	2.82	2.81	3.16	2.89	2.95	2.89	2.93	3.39	3.40
former FRG/GDR	2.86	2.85	2.75		3.04	2.29	2.52	2.81			
old/new counties		2.82	2.73				2.87	2.81			
Germany / nation	2.93	2.85	2.77	3.01	3.30	2.92	2.80	2.59	3.07	3.44	3.46
EC (91) / Europe (95)	2.46	2.38	2.26	2.61		2.20	2.14	1.89	2.62	2.48	2.40

S=spring, A=autumn; S/90: Lehrstuhl für Politische Wissenschaft und International Vergleichende Sozialforschung/FGW, S/91 Allbus, S/92 + S/93 *Political Cultures in Germany*, S/95 *Eurobarometer* No. 43-1b, A/95 ISSP 1995.

Very few Germans (less than 1%) do not feel close at all to the German ethnic group. Intense ethnic identifications as Germans are somewhat more frequent in East (40%) than in West Germany (33%), which might be an effect either of the less internationalized socialization in the GDR or of unification.[2] The

---

2   The conservative government (as at autumn 1998) has declared that Germany is not an immigration country. Therefore, although a great number of foreigners live in Germany, only a few obtain German citizenship and have the right to vote. Feelings of closeness to their ethnic group are somewhat less intense among these few citizens in Germany who identify themselves as belonging to ethnic groups other than that of the Germans. This might point to a low level of «ethnization» in those cases of immigrants who have obtained German citizenship.

identification with the German ethnic group is especially highly correlated with feelings of closeness to the nation and less, but not to a negative degree, to Europe. Thus, for most Germans, their ethnic identification is not associated with national isolationism (ISSP 1995). Multiple feelings of attachment to territorial units, as well as a direct question on national secession, show that separatism is not a serious issue in Germany: few West Germans (16%) and even fewer East Germans (8%) would allow parts of their country to secede, while most think it is essential that Germany remains united. Although there are remarkable reservations among the East Germans about the united Germany, and there is some nostalgia for the GDR, most do not wish to return to having a separate state. Those Germans who do not tend to identify with their ethnic group or with their country are clearly more indifferent or tolerant with respect to the question of separatism (ISSP 1995).[3]

4   Objects of national pride

In the sixties, West Germans drew their pride almost exclusively from non-political objects, which contrasted with the widespread pride in aspects of the political system in other established democracies. By the end of the seventies, however, West German pride in the political system, symbolized by the constitution and the system of social security, had increased to a level comparable with other democracies. To date, this pride has remained rather stable. In contrast, pride in the so-called German character and landmarks – objects which can be seen as representing an ethnic and traditional national identity – has decreased remarkably. From early in the post-war years until the beginning of the nineties, economic achievements constituted an important element of West German national pride, whereas other non-political objects – arts, science and sports – were and still are somewhat less significant in this respect. Finally, the parliament, possibly associated with day to day politics of incumbent authorities, is not accepted as a symbol of democracy. Reasons for these changes were the growing up of younger, democratically socialized generations, and increasing support for the democratic system, which in part at least rested upon the economic achievements. Political pride, especially that anchored in constitutional law, is typically interpreted as *Verfassungspatriotismus* (Mohler und Goetze 1992; Westle 1994). However, there was serious concern that such pride

---

3   Data surveyed in the years after unification show in both parts of Germany remarkable proportions of people who differentiate in their sympathy between West and East Germans. The rather strong feelings of closeness to Germans in 1995 do not seem not to accord with these earlier findings. However, because there were no comparable questions on ethnic identification and separation in earlier years, it must remain an open question whether or not unification has led to an increase in ethnic German identification. Further plausible reasons for a possible increase in ethnic identification might be the increase of non-German ethnic groups in Germany and the debate about a multicultural society.

might prove to be a temporary phenomenon and erode during an economic crisis (Rohe 1988). Until now, this has not been the case, as we can see in the mid-nineties when pride in the constitution remains stable while, for the first time, the economic pride of West Germans has noticeably declined because of the economic problems of a united Germany.

Table 3:   Pride in collective goods

percentages question format year	West Germany								East Germany					
	1			2					1	2				
	59	78	91a	88	91b	92	94	96	91a	90	91b	92	94	96
pol.-legal system/ constitutional law	7	31	32	51	51	48	53	53	20	23	21	17	26	24
social security system	6	18	15	39	49	45	37	49	4	31	24	15	18	23
parliament	/	/	/	10	5	5	10	6	/	11	7	3	5	3
international strength	5	9	7	/	/	/	/	/	8	/	/	/		/
German Union, Wende	/	/	6	/	/	/	/	/	14	/	/	/		/
economic achievements	33	40	33	51	64	59	46	44	60	60	60	54	36	41
scientific achievements	11	13	5	37	40	38	35	41	8	56	51	48	42	57
achievements in arts	10	16	8	22	23	22	22	31	17	47	41	44	36	53
achievements in sports	2	10	3	21	19	20	19	23	8	41	42	50	39	54
german character	36	25	16	/	/	/	/	/	19	/	/	/	/	/
geographic nature	16	14	7	/	/	/	/	/	11	/	/	/	/	/
else	4	7	4	/	/	/	/	/	5	/	/	/	/	/
nothing of these	15	21	28	20	12	12	15	13	31	6	13	13	20	10

question format 1: open ended, coding in field, question format 2: categories of answers, up to 3 mentionings, no limit of answers; /=not asked; Civic Culture 1959, Politics in the FRG 1978, 1991a Veen/Zelle 1995, Allbus 1988, 1991b, 1992, 1996, ISSP-Plus East 1990, Post-Election Study 1994 (format: rankorder of three objects).

East Germans are still predominantly proud of non-political objects. Even in the first years following unification, the democratic change in the GDR and unification were not significant sources of pride, but rather, (West German) economic achievements. In the following years, the East Germans' national pride continued to be directed primarily towards the economy and, increasingly, towards other non-political objects, to the detriment of their already low feeling of pride in democracy. The present economic crisis in Germany has adversely affected the economic pride of the East as well as of the West, and this is compensated for by a stronger concentration on other non-political objects. There are various reasons for the non-political motivation of East Germans' national pride. One is the relatively brief period thus far of their affiliation to Western democracy. Yet this does not tell the whole story, as we can see in their quickly developed economic pride. Other explanations must therefore be sought – in disappointed expectations, albeit partly unrealistic, of German democracy, and in preferences for another type of political system. Thus, those East Germans especially who feel close to the former GDR, express pride in

objects of the GDR and/or vote for the PDS, and tend to mention the constitution, the system of social security and the economy less often and the non-
political objects more frequently than do those who feel closer to the united
Germany and the EC (Westle 1999). The non-political motivation of East
Germans' national pride can only be interpreted in part as being grounded in
a traditional national identity: it must also be seen to some extent in terms of
scepticism about united Germany *(Table 3)*.

Another measure of collective goods, which includes some additional objects
and uses ratings (from 0=not at at all proud, to 3=very proud), shows a similar
distribution for the year 1995 (ISSP): West Germans are more proud of political objects (mean averages for the way democracy works West 1.77, East 1.28,
and for the social security system West 1.87, East 1.29), whereas East Germans
concentrate their pride more on non-political objects such as scientific achievements (West 2.00, East 2.10), achievements in the arts (West 1.78, East 2.02),
and in sports (West 1.72, East 2.06). The economy is for both East and West
still a source of pride (West 2.06, East 2.02). Pride in the armed forces (West
1.04, East 1.00) and in their history (both 1.13) are somewhat higher than
might have been expected, but still lower than in other European countries.
This corresponds to our earlier findings about a cautious approach to elements
of traditional national identity among many Germans (see also the similar findings of Blank/Schmidt 1993, on the basis of a slightly different index).

Relating pride in collective goods to the general sense of national pride reveals that in the West, about 80% and in the East about 90% of those citizens
who deny a general national pride, reveal pride in certain collective goods. In
both parts of Germany, general national pride and attachment to the united
Germany go together with a disproportionately high sense of pride in the economy. A general sense of national pride also corresponds to a greater degree
of pride in sports and less pride in arts and science. Citizens who admit to feeling a general national pride or closeness to Germany also mention the constitution (4% in the West, 12% in the East) and the system of social security
(around 5%) as important objects of national pride slightly more than average
(source: Allbus 1991, 1996). These results show that, today, the lack of a general sense of national pride does not necessarily imply reservations about the
democratic system, as some have previously suspected (Noelle-Neumann und
Köcher 1987), nor can the existence of general national pride be equated with
excessive nationalism, as others have suggested (Blank und Schmidt 1993).
Conclusions drawn about the underlying community ideology which are based
on evidence of a general national pride and pride in collective goods require
more qualification and sophistication.[4]

5   Criteria of being/becoming German

Exclusion is often said to be the other side of the coin of national identity. Therefore, asking questions about criteria of belonging to the German nation – whether by being «truly German» or by obtaining German citizenship – might provide further information about the national community ideology. It should be borne in mind, though, that answers to such questions might also be influenced by ongoing public debates about immigration. In the German case, respondents tend to rate all criteria in a similar way.[5] With respect to distribution, we find a high degree of support for items addressing a material dimension, and also quite high support for items intended to catch the cultural dimension, with the exception of the Christian religion. This exception may reflect the fact that until now, there has been no intensive public debate about Muslims in Germany. In the East, it might also reflect the low proportion of the population with a religious affiliation. Those items reflecting the ethnic dimension find somewhat lower levels of support. Discrepancies between West and East Germans are in the expected direction – with somewhat more support for the ethnic and the material dimensions in the East, and somewhat more for the cultural dimension in the West – but they are not very significant *(Tables 4a,b).*

---

4   The difficulty in drawing conclusions about the underlying community ideology from pride in collective goods (Easton 1965) arises from the asymmetric structure of pride and its sensitivity to contextual influences. Thus, if we observe pride in a specific object, we can take it for granted that the respondant supports this object as a positive element of the national idea and evaluates the realization of this object positively. But if we do not observe pride in a collective good, very different reasons may be responsible. First, the respondant might oppose this object as an element of national identity in principle; second, a specific object might simply have no meaning or importance for the respondant; and third, low pride in an object might correspond with situationally low achievements. Therefore, only when we observe pride in objects which are not very sensitive to situational effects – for example, constitutional law – can we draw a reasonable conclusion concerning the underlying community ideology. In all other cases, we need additional information (e.g. comparisons over time or across countries, external validation).

5   The question about criteria of being truly German proves to be one-factorial, whereas the question about criteria for obtaining German citizenship at first results in an implausible two-factorial solution, and only after further defining the number of factors does it reach an expected structure of items with one «material» (no criminal record, able to earn one's own living), one «ethnic» (born in Germany, of German origin), and one «cultural» (speaks the German language, adapts to the German life-style, and has lived in Germany for a long time) factor. This unsatisfactory outcome with respect to the question of community ideology is due to a number of methodological reasons.

Tables 4a/b: Important criteria to be truely German
and to gain German citizenship

Table 4a: Important criteria to be truely German (1995)			Table 4b: Criteria to gain German citizenship (1996)		
means: *0 = not at all important* *3 = very important*	**West** **G.**	**East** **G.**	*means:* *1 = not at all important* *7 = very important*	**West** **G.**	**East** **G.**
be born in Germany	1.6	1.8	be born in Germany	4.7	5.0
have German citizenship	2.2	2.3	be of German birth origin	4.5	4.7
speak German language	2.4	2.4	speak German language	5.4	4.5
most time of life in G.	1.8	2.0	have lived long in G.	5.5	5.2
be of christian religion	1.1	0.8	be of christian religion	2.2	1.8
respect G. institutions+law	2.5	2.3	adapt to G. life style	5.0	4.8
feel as German	2.1	2.1	have no criminal record	6.1	6.3
			able to earn own living	5.7	5.8
			meanindex ethnic criteria	*4.6*	*4.8*
			meanindex cultural criteria	*5.3*	*4.8*
			meanindex material criteria	*5.9*	*6.0*
meanindex all	*2.0*	*1.9*	*meanindex all*	*5.6*	*5.4*

ISSP 1995, Allbus 1996.

Relationships between the criteria of being/becoming German and other indicators of national identity are quite close. Citizens who identify themselves as ethnic Germans, who feel close to the Germans and to Germany, who would not allow national separation, and who express definite national pride or pride in collective goods, tend to formulate higher thresholds of requirements or expectations for belonging to the German nation. These relationships are strongest when national pride is based on objects representing a traditional nationalist attitude (history, army, and sometimes, political influence in the world), but they also exist with respect to nearly all other sources of national pride. By contrast, democratic pride (and sometimes, pride in the arts) tends to go together with lower thresholds for German nationality in general.

6   Extreme nationalism

Whereas *Verfassungspatriotismus* may be defined as a critical loyalty towards one's own nation in its democratic form, extreme nationalism can be defined as an affirmative loyalty towards one's own nation (irrespective of its political system) with a potential for aggressiveness towards other nations and their citizens. Earlier surveys among West Germans showed – depending on the index used – a nationalistic potential of between 4% and 15%. After German unification, only a slightly stronger attraction to extreme nationalism was discernible in the East than in the West. This holds true for 1995, when rather more

East Germans than West Germans strongly or at least partly agreed with nationalistic statements. These elements of the population clearly find their antinationalistic counterparts. Anti-nationalistic attitudes are stronger in the West than in the East, but almost half of the population in both parts of the country do not show very consistent and/or strong positions *(Table 5).*[6]

Table 5:   Extreme nationalism

	West Germany	East Germany
strong antinationalist	11.8	7.5
Antinationalist	19.0	16.5
Middle	45.0	46.4
Nationalist	14.3	15.7
strong nationalist	9.9	13.9

meanindex constructed from 6 items; ISSP 1995.

Extreme nationalism clearly corresponds to the other aspects of national identification. Attachment to the German ethnic group and to the nation, as well as the idea that Germany must remain a unified country, tend to be aspects of a more nationalist, though still not an extreme nationalist, position, while the opposite is true of a more anti-nationalist position. Increasing thresholds against obtaining German nationality and increasing national pride correspond to closer identification with an extreme nationalist position. This relationship is strongest with respect to ethnic criteria and pride in objects which were earlier qualified as representing a traditional national identity, but it still shows with respect to all other criteria for citizenship and objects of national pride.

7   Attitudes towards foreigners, immigration policies and integration policies

Since the early nineties, attitudes towards foreigners in Germany have become more critical, and there are increasing demands for stronger restrictions on immigration (Kühnel und Terwey 1994; Westle 1998, 1999). East Germans in general show less friendly attitudes towards foreigners than West Germans, espe-

---

6   In cross-national comparison, Germans do not show striking deviations with respect to extreme nationalism. This might come as a surprise when one considers the success of the right-wing DVU in the Saxon-Anhalt elections, or the spectacular acts of violence against foreigners especially by young Germans. Yet there are some explanations for this seeming irregularity. Individual extreme nationalism is only one determinant among others of the vote for a right wing party, for hostile attitudes or even violence directed at foreigners. Other factors include feelings of deprivation, protest motives, and a «climate» which allows for such behaviour.

cially when competition for jobs and rising criminality are at issue, more rarely with respect to the question of cultural conflicts. These observations hold true for attitudes towards foreigners in general, as well as towards specific groups of foreigners (Italians, Turks, Jews, and those of German origin coming from Russia), even though the proportion of foreigners is clearly higher in West than in East Germany, and even though West Germans more often perceive a marked difference in lifestyle between themselves and others. East Germans tend to plead more frequently for a strict immigration policy – with two consistent exceptions. First, East Germans are more open to accepting political refugees or asylum seekers, and second, they have less classical prejudices against Jews living outside of Germany (ISSP 1995; Allbus 1996). The greater degree of reserve among East Germans towards foreigners in their own country is probably linked to the more precarious economic and job situation in East Germany, and to the relative lack of familiarity of East Germans with foreigners, whereas their greater openness towards political asylum seekers could conceivably be due to their own experience of political oppression, and the lower prejudice against Jews outside Germany could be an effect of their anti-fascist socialization.

There is a continuing political debate about how to treat foreigners in Germany, especially those who have lived in the country for many years and whose children have been born in Germany. This debate concentrates primarily on two aspects: the question of legal rights and the question of a multicultural society. Whereas the SPD and the Greens argue for a law of citizenship based on country of birth, the possibility of a double citizenship, and an equalization of other rights, the CDU-FDP insist on citizenship based on ethnic criteria, reject double citizenship, and generally point to the principles of human rights embedded in the constitution as being sufficient for the status of a «guest».[7] In some respects, foreigners already have the same rights and duties as Germans (for example, in the sphere of social security), and the new EU law allows persons of EU-member-states to freely choose their working place and to vote in communal elections. The German population is almost evenly divided over these questions, tending slightly more to a rejection of equal rights for foreigners. As would be expected, opinions in favour of or against equal rights clearly correspond to respective attitudes towards foreigners and immigration policies.

---

7   The term «guest» is used by the CDU/CSU as a circumlocution to maintain their view that Germany does not have immigrants. At the time of writing this text, in January 1999, the new government (SPD and Greens) had raised the plan to legalize a double citizenship. The CDU/CSU and FDP are opposing this plan strongly and have initiated a public petition against it. This has generated considerable heat in the public debate, because the left and alternative spectrum view the right opposition as enforcing and institutionalising xenophobic fears, whereas the CDU/CSU take the line that a double citizenship would hinder integration.

The political debate is similarly structured with respect to the second aspect of integration policies, with the left showing more sympathy for concepts of a multicultural society, the right inclined to argue against, and the liberals being divided over the issue. On average, the population in both parts of Germany tends somewhat to be more in favour of assimilation, although opinions on this question are not really consistent. Correlations between different questions which are intended to catch opinions on assimilation versus multicultural society are positive, but rather moderate. Nevertheless, they are clearly linked with the attitudes towards foreigners: friendly attitudes and demands for an open immigration policy correspond to a tendency towards the multicultural society, while hostile attitudes and demands for more restricted immigration correspond with a tendency towards the assimilation of foreigners *(Table 6).[8]*

Table 6: Attitudes towards integration and integration policies: multicultural society or assimilation

Means	West G.	East G.
1995 *1 = multicultural 3 = assimilation*		
to become fully member, it is necessary to share traditions of the guest-country: *1 = reject 2= neither nor 3 = agree*	2.04	2.13
it is better for society if groups maintain their distinct customs versus if they adapt and blend into the larger society: *1 = agree 2 = don't know 3 = reject*	1.97	1.82
the state should help minorities, to preserve their own traditions: *1 = agree 2 = neither nor 3 = reject*	1.96	1.46
1996: *1 = multicultural 7 = assimilation*		
more adaption of lifestyle: *1 = reject 7 = agree*	4.88	5.00
good for culture: *1 = agree 7 = reject*	4.11	4.30

ISSP 1995, Allbus 1996.

Attitudes towards foreigners, immigration and integration policies are shaped not only by factors of circumstance such as the economic situation and the public debate, but they are also clearly linked to the intensity and nature of the individual national identity. A sense of attachment to the Germans and to Germany, of a general national pride, the opinion that it is essential to remain one nation, and most obviously, extreme nationalism, are all consistent with

8   Here we observe the inconsistent fact that citizens with a non-ethnic national identity tend to reinforce an ethnic identity of immigrants as a result of their friendly attitudes towards foreigners within a confused public discussion about multi-ethnicity and multiculturalism.

more hostile attitudes towards foreigners, and preferences for a stricter immigration policy and for assimilation rather than a multicultural society. The desire for high thresholds for belonging to the German nation is linked with reservations about foreigners in all aspects. Pride in objects of a traditional national identity regularly corresponds with reserved attitudes towards foreigners, whereas pride in democracy does not. Pride in the constitution, but also pride in the arts, go together with friendly and open attitudes towards foreigners.

8   National orientations and internal unity

Since unification, both segments of the German population have evaluated their fellow countrymen in their own part of the country more positively than they have those living in the other part, while voicing more demands towards the other part of the country. Few commentators wish to ignore the possible implications of these prejudices (Veen 1997), and it is usually perceived as an indicator of problems of national unity (Feist und Liepelt 1994; Kaase und Bauer-Kaase 1998). The hope that a stronger national orientation would reduce such prejudices between West and East Germans and thereby lead to a closer internal unity might at first sight seem quite plausible – but it has not happened. On the whole, national identification does not make much difference to domestic German prejudices. Indeed, we even find prejudices towards the other part of the country increasing slightly with stronger national identifications in nearly all aspects (Westle 1999). Encouraging national orientations therefore cannot be seen as a path to internal unity.[9]

9   Perspectives of German national identity

Half a decade after realising political unity, we do not observe disturbing changes in German national identity. Extreme nationalism and negative nationalism exist in marginal groups, but they are not wide-spread. The deeply entrenched consciousness of the crimes which resulted from the aggressive nationalism of the Nazi regime continues to shape the discreet way in which most

---

9   Consideration of demographic background variables leads to the expectation of an ongoing modernizing of German national identity, in so far as the younger generations will be educated in a democratic system. Thus, we observe that with higher education and in younger age cohorts, national identification is less intense in most aspects and attitudes towards foreigners are more friendly. Younger cohorts and the better educated especially, specify ethnic criteria for German nationality and traditional objects of national identity less frequently. Whereas in West Germany, the constituton is an object of national identity irrespective of age or education, in East Germany, derivation of a sense of national identity from the constitution nowadays correlates with higher education, but still does not reach the West German level.

Germans deal with national feelings. Yet, for the great majority of the population, the nation is an important object of identification, and more relevant than supranational communities.

However, moderation in nationalistic emotions does not automatically result in a democratic national identity or in *Verfassungspatriotismus*. This kind of constructive patriotism is more demanding. It implies an identification with the values of human rights and of democracy, and a critical loyalty to one's own nation, ideally finding expression in the implementation of these values in one's own country; a postnational identity is also linked to universal principles, but does not primarily refer to one's own country. Although the available survey results do not sufficiently capture the quality of the community ideology, they do allow some tentative conclusions to be drawn. Thus, the German population in both parts of the country shows a mix of traditional (ethnic and cultural), democratic, and postnational elements of collective identity, West Germans tending more to democratic and postnational, East Germans more to traditional elements.

Ethnic, but not cultural, elements of national identity clearly correspond to a closed concept of nation and state and hostile attitudes towards foreigners, whereas democratic elements are linked to a greater degree of openness in the concept of nation and state, and friendly attitudes towards foreigners. Certain objects of national identification, such as the economy and the system of social security, are also quite important for many Germans. At the same time, they have an ambivalent status, showing potential links with both a traditional and a democratic identity. Moreover, welfare, social security, and fair socio-economic conditions form an important basis of friendly attitudes towards others, irrespective of whether they are Germans from the other part of Germany, Germans from Russia, or people from other countries.

Internal German discrepancies and tensions, including those resulting from increasing immigration and politics *vis à vis* the European Union, should not be passed over in silence. The forms and substance of the political elites' debates in the public arena have not contributed to logical clarity in the community's ideology. Thus, for example, it is not very reasonable to appeal to domestic German solidarity, while at the same time reducing the welfare state. The same applies to the insistence on an ethnic right of citizenship, while at the same time aiming at open borders within Europe and a European identity. The concepts of assimilation, integration, and a multicultural society are still very vague and imprecise in the public mind, and citizens associate widely different things with these concepts. An open debate in Germany about the potentials and dangers of collective identity is therefore absolutely necessary. A constructive national identity must not be equated with aggressive nationalism. Instead, collective self-consciousness can be anchored in democratic values, striving for their optimal realization, and peaceful relationships within and between countries.

References

Berger, M., W. G. Gibowski und D. Roth (1990). «Ein Votum für die Einheit», *Die Zeit* 13: 5.

Blank, Th. und P. Schmidt (1993). «Verletzte oder verletzende Nation?», *Journal für Sozialforschung* 33(4): 391–415.

Bohrer, K.H. (1990). «Warum wir keine Nation sind», *Frankfurter Allgemeine Zeitung* 11 (Sondereinlage).

Bracher, K.D. (1986). «Das Modewort Identität und die deutsche Frage», *Frankfurter Allgemeine Zeitung* 182 (Sondereinlage).

Breit, G. (1993). «Verfassungspatriotismus – Eine ausreichende Zielsetzung des Politikunterrichts», pp. 181–207 in G. C. Behrmann und S. Schiele (Eds.). *Verfassungspatriotismus als Ziel politischer Bildung?* Schwalbach (Ts.): Wochenschau.

Bucerius, G. (1984). «Die deutsche Einheit ist unaufhaltsam», *Die Zeit* 35: 4.

Burger, R. (1994). «Patriotismus und Nation», *Leviathan* 22(2): 161-170.

Dahrendorf, R. (1990). «Die Sache mit der Nation», *Merkur* 44 (10/11): 823–834.

Easton, D. (1965). *A Systems Analysis of Political Life.* Chicago: The University of Chicago Press.

Feist, U. und K. Liepelt (1994). «Auseinander oder miteinander?», pp. 575–611 in H. D. Klingemann und M. Kaase (Eds.). *Wahlen und Wähler – Analysen aus Anlass der Bundestagswahl 1990.* Opladen: Westdeutscher Verlag.

Freudenfeld, B. (1966, 1967). «Das perfekte Provisorium», *Hochland* 59(5): 421–433.

Gerstenmeier, E. (1965). *Neuer Nationalismus? Von der Wandlung der Deutschen.* Stuttgart: Deutsche Verlagsanstalt.

Gessenharter, Wolfgang (1997). «Herausforderungen zur Jahrtausendwende: Kann ‹Nation› die Antwort sein?», in C. Butterwegge (Ed.). *NS-Vergangenheit, Antisemitismus und Nationalismus in Deutschland.* Baden-Baden: Nomos.

Glotz, P. (1990). *Der Irrweg des Nationalstaates.* Stuttgart: Deutsche Verlags-Anstalt.

Greiffenhagen, M. und S. Greiffenhagen (1993). *Ein schwieriges Vaterland.* München: List.

Grewe, W. (1983). «Wenn der Wille zur Einheit erlahmt», *Frankfurter Allgemeine Zeitung,* 247: 11.

Habermas, J. (1986). «Eine Art Schadenabwicklung», *Historikerstreit* 1987: 62–76 (zuerst *Die Zeit* 11.6.86).

Habermas, J. (1989). «Die Stunde der nationalen Empfindung», pp. 157–166 in J. Habermas (ed.). *Die nachholende Revolution.* Frankfurt: Suhrkamp.

Hättich, M. (1983). «Nationalbewusstsein im geteilten Deutschland», pp. 274–293 in W. Weidenfeld (Ed.). *Die Identität der Deutschen.* Bonn: Bundeszentrale für politische Bildung.

Hättich, M. (1993). «Kann Verfassungspatriotismus Gemeinschaft stiften?», pp. 25–35 in G. Behrmann und S. Schiele (Ed.). *Verfassungspatriotismus als Ziel politischer Bildung?* Schwalbach (Ts.): Wochenschau.

Heydemann, G. (1987). «Geschichtswissenschaft und Geschichtsverständnis in der DDR seit 1945», *Aus Politik und Zeitgeschichte* B13: 15–26.

Historikerstreit (1987). *Die Dokumentation der Kontroverse um die Einzigartigkeit der nationalsozialistischen Judenvernichtung.* München: Piper.

Isensee, J. (1986). «Die Verfassung als Vaterland», pp. 11–36 in A. Mohler (Ed.). *Wirklichkeit als Tabu.* München: Oldenbourg.

Isensee, J. (1990). «Verfassungsrechtliche Wege zur deutschen Einheit», *Zeitschrift für Parlamentsfragen* 21 (H.2): 309–332.

Jaspers, K. (1966). *Wohin treibt die Bundesrepublik?* München: Piper.

Kaase, M. und P. Bauer-Kaase, (1998).«Deutsche Vereinigung und innere Einheit 1990–1997», pp. 251–267 in H. Meulemann (Ed.). *Werte und nationale Identität im vereinten Deutschland, Erklärungsansätze der Umfrageforschung.* Opladen: Leske +Budrich.

Kluxen-Pyta, D. (1990). «Verfassungspatriotismus und nationale Identität», *Zeitschrift für Politik* 37 (H.2): 117–133.

Krockow, C. Graf von (1983). «Die fehlende Selbstverständlichkeit», pp. 154–169 in W. Weidenfeld (Ed.). 1983: *Die Identität der Deutschen.* Bonn: Bundeszentrale für politische Bildung.

Kühnel, S. und M Terwey (1994). «Gestörtes Verhältnis? Die Einstellungen der Deutschen zu Ausländern in der Bundesrepublik», pp. 71–105 in M. Braun und P. Ph. Mohler (Ed.). *Blickpunkt Gesellschaft 3 – Einstellungen und Verhalten der Bundesbürger.* Opladen: Westdeutscher Verlag.

Lauermann, M. (1994). «Der Nationalstaat – Ein Oxymoron», pp. 33–51 in J. Gebhardt und R. Schmalz-Bruns (Ed.). *Demokratie, Verfassung und Nation.* Baden-Baden: Nomos.

Lepsius, M.R. (1967, 1968). Die unbestimmte Identität der Bundesrepublik, *Hochland* 60 (H.2): 562-569.

Lepsius, M.R. (1977). (Ohne Titel), in Deutschlandpolitik, Öffentliche Anhörung des Ausschusses für innerdeutsche Beziehungen. Zur *Sache* 8 (H.4): S.233–239, 260–264.

Ludz, C.P. (1974). *Deutschlands doppelte Zukunft.* München: Carl Hanser.

Lübbe, H. (1989). «Patriotismus, Verfassung und verdrängte Geschichte», *Die neue Gesellschaft/Frankfurter Hefte* 36 (H.5): 408–415.

Mohler, P.Ph. und H. Götze (1992). «Worauf sind die Deutschen stolz?», pp. 45–63 in P. Ph. Mohler und W. Bandilla (Ed.). *Blickpunkt Gesellschaft 2 –*

Einstellungen und Verhalten der Bundesbürger in Ost und West. Opladen: Westdeutscher Verlag.

Mommsen, H. (1981). «Aus Eins mach Zwei», *Die Zeit* 7: 4.

Nipperdey, Th. (1990). «Die Deutschen wollen und dürfen eine Nation sein», *Frankfurter Allgemeine Zeitung* 160: 10.

Noelle-Neumann, E., R. Köcher (Eds.) (1987). *Die verletzte Nation.* Stuttgart: Deutsche Verlagsanstalt.

Noelle-Neumann, E. (1987). «Nationalgefühl und Glück», pp. 17–71 in E. Noelle-Neumann und R. Köcher. *Die verletzte Nation.* Stuttgart: Deutsche Verlagsanstalt.

Nolte, E. (1986). «Vergangenheit, die nicht vergehen will», *Historikerstreit* 1987: 39–47 (zuerst *Faz* 6.6.86).

Nolte, E. (1991). «Die unvollständige Revolution», pp. 90–100 in M. Jeismann und H. Ritter (Eds.). *Grenzfälle – über neuen und alten Nationalismus.* Leipzig: Reclam (zuerst *Faz* 24.1.1991).

Oberndörfer, D. (1991). *Die offene Republik.* Freiburg: Herder.

Offe, C. (1990). «Vom taktischen Gebrauch nationaler Gefühle», *Die Zeit* 51: 42.

Pross, H. (1982). *Was ist heute deutsch? Wertorientierungen in der Bundesrepublik.* Reinbek bei Hamburg: Rowohlt.

Reese-Schäfer, W. (1991). «Universalismus, negativer Nationalismus und die neue deutsche Einheit», pp. 39–54 in P. Braitling und W. Reese-Schäfer (Eds.). *Universalismus, Nationalismus und die neue Einheit der Deutschen.* Frankfurt: Fischer.

Rohe, K. (1988). «Die deutsche Einheit als Problem der politischen Kultur in der Bundesrepublik Deutschland», pp. 104–199 in K.-E. Jeismann (Ed.). 1988: *Einheit – Freiheit – Selbstbestimmung.* Frankfurt am Main: Campus.

Rudolph, H. (1983). «Wie sieht das Selbstverständnis der DDR-Gesellschaft aus?», pp. 193–209 in W. Weidenfeld (Ed.). *Die Identität der Deutschen.* Bonn: Bundeszentrale für politische Bildung.

Sarcinelli, U. (1993). «Verfassungspatriotismus» und «Bürgergesellschaft», *Aus Politik und Zeitgeschichte* B34: 25–37.

Schäuble, Wolfgang (1994). *Und der Zukunft zugewandt.* Berlin: Siedler.

Schmidt, H. (1967, 1968). «Bundesdeutsches Nationalbewusstsein?», *Hochland* 60 (H.6): 558-562.

Schwan, G. (1995). «Was sind die Fragen, auf die die Nation die Antwort wäre?», *Forum Locum* 2: 13.

Schwarz, H.-P. (1990). «Das Ende der Identitätsneurose», *Rheinischer Merkur/ Christ und Welt* 36: 3–4.

Schweigler, G. (1972). *Nationalbewusstsein in der BRD und der DDR.* Düsseldorf: Bertelsmann Universitätsverlag.

Schwilk, H. und U. Schacht (Eds.) (1994). *Die selbstbewusste Nation*. Frankfurt: Ullstein.

Sontheimer, K., E. Stammler und H. Heigert (1966). *Sehnsucht nach der Nation? Drei Plädoyers.* München: Juventa.

Veen, H.-J. (1997). «Innere Einheit – aber wo liegt sie?», *Aus Politik und Zeitgeschichte* B40/41: 19-28.

Veen, H.-J. und C. Zelle (1995). «Zusammenwachsen oder Auseinanderdriften?», in Konrad-Adenauer-Stiftung (Ed.). *Interne Studien* (2. überarb. Aufl.).

Venohr, W. (Ed.) (1982). *Die deutsche Einheit kommt bestimmt.* Bergisch Gladbach: Gustav Lübbe.

Weidenfeld, W. (1985). «Land im Brennpunkt Europas», pp. 69–79 in ders. (Ed.). *Nachdenken über Deutschland.* Köln: Wissenschaft und Politik.

Westle, B. (1994). «Traditionalismus, Verfassungspatriotismus und Postnationalismus im vereinigten Deutschland», pp. 43–76 in O. Niedermayer und K. von Beyme (Eds.). *Politische Kultur in Ost- und Westdeutschland.* Berlin: Akademie.

Westle, B. (1998). «Aspekte kollektiver Identifikation der Deutschen – Wandel oder Stabilität?», pp. 93–115 in R. Voigt (Ed.). *Der neue Nationalstaat – Deutschland zwischen Globalisierung und Nationalisierung.* Baden-Baden: Nomos.

Westle, B. (1999). *Kollektive Identität im vereinten Deutschland Nation und Demokratie in der Wahrnehmung der Deutschen.* Opladen: Leske+Budrich.

Winkler, A. (1981). «Nation – ja, National-Staat – nein», *Die Zeit* 8: 5–6.

Zitelmann, R. (1993). «Wiedervereinigung und deutscher Selbsthass», pp. 235–248 in W. Weidenfeld (Ed.). *Deutschland: Eine Nation, doppelte Geschichte.* Köln: Wissenschaft und Politik.

«Real» and Other Compatriots: Politics of Identity in Croatia

Vjeran Katunaric

In this paper, various aspects of national and other collective identities in Croatia are presented. In the first part, the historical and contemporary aspects are described. In the second part, the present-day situation of Croatian nationalism is explained as the incoherent result of a dynamic interplay between official and popular nationalism in the context of a country in transition.

1 The main aspects of Croatian national identity

1.1 The institutional and structural setting

Croatia is a new nation-state born out of the dissolution of and the ensuing war in ex-Yugoslavia. Its legal system is based on the constitution which was adopted in December, 1990 and amended in 1992. Croatia is constitutionally defined as a democratic republic. The supreme legislative body is a bicameral parliament. The political system is semi-presidential. The president is to be elected every five years, and he appoints a government that is confirmed by the parliament. The last elections for the Chambers of Represen-tatives were held in 1995. The Croatian Democratic Union, a center-right party, won a majority.

Divisions between political parties and among voters arise from a number of political cleavages. At first (1990), these divisions were historically determined: they opposed those in favor to those who were against Croatian independence. Later, other, more familiar polarizations developed: liberal-conservative, democratic-authoritarian, cosmopolitan-ethnocentric, religious-secular, together with regional divisions (Zakosek 1994; Rimac and Milas 1994).

The multi-ethnic composition of Croatian society has changed considerably. According to the 1991 census, the population consisted of 78.1% Croats, 12.2% Serbs, 0.9% Muslims, 0.5% Magyars, 0.4% Italians, 0.3% Albanians, etc. (24 national minorities in all). The number and position of the Serbs changed radically during the war in Croatia (1991–1995). The Serbian population lived mostly in the areas of Croatia that were occupied by the Serbian Army, formerly the Yugoslavian Army. These areas were liberated during a Croatian military operation in 1995. Today, the Serbian population in Croatia is estimated at only 3–5%.

According to Croatian constitutional law, the minorities have the right of cultural autonomy. This includes identity, culture, religion, public and private use
of language and script, education, access to the media, and protection of cultural property and heritage (Svob-Dokic 1997). The problem of establishing a
working relationship between the Croatian majority and the minorities principally concerns the Serbs and Muslims – or more recently, Bosniacs. The former
are facing the problem of returning to their home areas, which have been de-
vastated by the war. They complain that the Croatian government unofficially
puts obstacles in the way of those Serbs who want to return to Croatia. The
latter have not been officially recognized as a minority by the Croatian government, although their representatives consider Bosniacs «the second largest minority» in Croatia.

Social stratification in Croatia in the nineties is similar to that in other post-
communist countries in transition. A new class is forming at the top of the social pyramid, made up of the new political elite and the newly rich. The middle
class that emerged under the previous regime, and was largely comprised of
office employees, is today growing poorer. Middle class entrepreneurs and
owners are in a nascent stage. The lower classes – workers, peasants, pensioners, and the unemployed – carry the heaviest burden of the economic transition to a free market economy and privatization. The costs of living are almost
double the average household income. The ethnic stratification in Croatian society had almost disappeared during the communist era. Due to the Communist Party cadre policy, no major ethno-national group, whether Croat or Serb,
had enjoyed obvious privileges – with the exception of an over-representation
of Serbs in the higher echelons of the military and the police, and of Croats in
the business managerial elite. Relatively underprivileged groups included
Gypsies, Albanians, and Muslims (Katunaric 1990). Today's ethnic stratification is marked by an overwhelming predominance of elites which are purely
Croatian by national origin. The official representatives of the minorities in
the Croatian parliament are chosen according to the numerical key of the
election law. A similar representational key is implemented for local government in nationally mixed areas. Nevertheless, unlike under the previous regime, power is now completely in the hands of Croats.

1.2 Inventors and builders of Croatian identity

The «inventors» of Croatian nationality were romantic writers of the early 19th
century. The first to designate Croatia as a unique area – an area that resembles the shape of todayís Croatia – was Pavao Ritter Vitezovic (1652–1713), a
poet, historian, philologist and local politician. In his book Croatia Rediviva

(Resurrected Croatia), published in 1699, he celebrated the extent, contrasts, natural beauties, customs and vernaculars of the country (Vitezovic 1997). The political «spiritus movens» and first scholar of Croatian grammar was Ljudevit Gaj (1809–1872), a writer and savant who also co-founded the first national literary magazine, Danica. He and his followers assumed that all Southern slavs were brothers originating from a pre-Slavic ethnic substratum, the Illiri, who had lived in the Balkan area of the ancient Roman province of Illiricum (Banac 1984).

Gaj's linguistic program was opposed to the parallel Serbian linguistic program of Vuk Karadzic. The latter was sponsored by the Serbian government, which sought to unify all speakers of the Stokavian vernacular as «Serbs»; these included Croats.

These developments, which we might call the first wave of Croatian nationalism, culminated with the revolution in Hungary in 1848, when the Croatian Duke Josip Jelachic (1801–1859) intervened in favor of the Austrian monarchy, trying to obtain concessions for Croatian political autonomy within the empire, at the expense of squeezing the Hungarian hegemony over Croatia. But Jelachic's adherence to the conservative faction in Vienna did not prevent the restoration of Hungarian hegemony over Croatia, nor did it prevent the backlash of Austrian centralism.

As a result of such experiences, the new national leaders in Croatia abandoned questions of language and concentrated on political and legal issues. Croatian national identity was increasingly associated with the idea of an independent nation-state. This tendency was first formulated by Ante Starachic (1823–1896), the founder of the Party of State Right. This party came to the fore after the Croatian-Hungarian Compromise in 1868, according to which Croatia retained independence only in jurisprudence, schooling, local administration, and church affairs, while all other areas of government were controlled by the Ministry in Budapest. A few years later, the Party had lost much of its influence in the Croatian Parliament, and was overwhelmed by the Popular Party led by the Roman Catholic Bishop Josip Juraj Strossmayer (1815–1905). Strossmayer was also opposed to Hungarian rule, but he was more open-minded and pro-Yugoslav. However, by 1879, even he had realized that Serbian politicians were narrow-minded and that their idea of South Slav unity was completely different from Croatian ideas.

The next phases of the development of Croatian nationalism revolved around more or less successful attempts at transforming it into a mass movement. Mass mobilization around the national question emerged three times in the

20th century. The first episode, between the two world wars, saw a peasant-po-
pulist movement led by Stjepan Radic, who was killed by Serbian nationalists
in Belgrade in 1928. His party, however, remained the main opposition party in
the first state of Yugoslavia (1918–1941). At the beginning of the Second
World War, the party split into factions: one wing joined the government of the
pro-Nazi Independent State of Croatia (1941–1945), another group joined the
anti-fascist People's Liberation Movement led by the Communist Party, while
the rest of the party emigrated to the West.

The second mass movement, the so called «Croatian Spring,» mobilized in
1971 under the leadership of the Croatian Communist nationalists. It was suppressed in the same year by the Yugoslavian president, Tito. Finally, in 1990, a
mass movement mobilized successfully under the leadership of the Croatian
Democratic Union (CDU) and the current president of Croatia, Franjo Tudjman. But the problem of this movement's political identity was complicated by
the war and by the arrival of right-wing extremists from the Croatian diaspora.
The bulk of these extremists were political émigrés who had cherished the legacy of the Independent State of Croatia (Skrbis 1997). The resulting shift of
balance within the movement led to a bifurcation within the historical pedigree of the present Croatian state, as much as within the sense of identity of a
majority of Croats, who had learned to regard the pro-Nazi (Ustashi) government as a cause of deep national shame.

In the present Croatian constitution, the People's Liberation Struggle and the
first independent government institutions which were established during the
Second World War on the free territory in Croatia, are portrayed as a historical fact that shaped the creation and establishment of the present Croatian
state. However, this is an official truth which is scarcely accepted or reflected
in current politics. The hypocrisy of the pro-fascist elements and the confused
historicism of the CDU's politics of identity are still easily recognized.

The official national history is at present a patchwork which includes different
and often disparate founding figures and leaders. Ustashi and Communists,
Starchevic and Strossmayer, and others who are really ideologically different
from one another, are now invited, as if in a spiritualist seance, to gather together on the newly invented common ground. The fascist episode of 1941–45
is also given more favorable treatment in the current history textbooks for
schools than the history of Communist Croatia is given.

A similar revisionist approach has affected other symbolic dimensions as well:
for example, new street names dedicated to pre-Communist figures have replaced former names; there are projects for common graveyards and monu-

ments for «all the Croatian victims of the Second World War», public ceremonies commemorating the «Croatian tragedies» in the Second World War, an annual Mass for Ante Pavelic, the head of the Independent State of Croatia, and the destruction of more than a thousand monuments dedicated to the People's Liberation Struggle during the Second World War.

Admittedly, this whole tendency has recently been restrained, mainly for two reasons. First, considerable pressure has been placed on the Croatian government by Israel and by international Jewish organizations to ban the demonstration of such pro-fascist and anti-semitic sympathies. The second reason is the death of the Croatian Minister of Defense Gojko Susak, who was the leader of the extreme right-wing faction within the ruling CDU, and also a former political émigré. He was the main person in charge during the war in the nineties, who presided over financial and other transactions for the newly created Croatian army, as well as being responsible for many other provisions for the new government. His services were repaid with large political concessions to the right-wing faction, and this has contributed to the deepening ambivalence in the political position of the present Croatian president, Franjo Tudjman.

The President embodies the contradictions of the new politics of identity. He was formerly a supporter of Tito and a general in the Yugoslavian army; he was relieved of his position in the sixties, and imprisoned in the seventies under the charge of being a Croatian nationalist, and at the end of the eighties, he approached the extreme right-wing political émigrés. He therefore exemplifies the excruciating eclecticism of the new national political identity.

1.3 National identity in relation to political and social change

The political change in Croatia has brought about some major shifts with respect to the sense of national identity. According to a survey conducted on the eve of the first multi-party elections in 1990, most Croats saw the achievement of national independence as the most important political objective, and union with Europe as the second most important. The Serbs, at the same time, saw maintaining the union with Yugoslavia as the most important political objective. All other political values, including democracy and pluralism, were seen as less important by both sides (Grdesic et al. 1991). The establishment of the Republic of Croatia as independent from Yugoslavia was therefore supported by an overwhelming majority of Croats, but opposed by the Serbs. However, using the majority principle instead of the consensus or consociational principle, the CDU succeeded in proclaiming the new state. In the new Republic of Croatia, the Serbs lost the constitutional position which they had enjoyed under the previous regime as the «constitutional nationality» that had co-founded the Socialist Republic of Croatia, and were automatically given the status of a minority. The local Serbian political leadership did not want their people to lose their former privileged status and, supported by the Serbian leadership in Belgrade and the Yugoslavian army, decided to embark upon the war against Croatia.

This war in Croatia has created a new layer of symbols, heroes, and historical references that have replaced the legacy of the Second World War and the Communist past. As a consequence, for example, the higher pensions and other benefits which former Communist war veterans received, were abrogated by the new government and passed on to newly selected war veterans.

Immediately before the war, the public scene had already been invaded by a newly invented historical symbolism that blended the present with the myths and heroic figures of the medieval past. Kings, horses, parades, and other monarchical appurtenances, accompanied by symbols of the Roman Catholic tradition, were mixed up in a cocktail that lacked any folk traditional or national historical authencity (Braica 1990). This kitsch, sometimes combined with material drawn from contemporary popular culture – newly composed folk-songs and naive paintings, rather than rock and pop music and modern or postmodern visual arts – has pro-vided the scenery for every major national celebration and festivity: from victory in the war to the success of the national team in the World Cup Soccer tournament in 1998.

However, social changes resulting from the new policies of privatization and the establishment of a market economy, have produced a mood of national excitement of another sort, with a consequent impact on the sense of national identity and self-awareness (as discussed in the second part of this paper).

1.4 The nation-state as the frame of reference

The contemporary nation-state is the major frame of reference for a majority of Croats. There are a number of different ways in which the nation-state is perceived or portrayed.

The mythical-historical reference: The main reference here is to the antiquity of the Croatian nation. The official historicism has succeeded in spreading the belief that the Croats are «one of the oldest nations in Europe», and that they had a state, i.e. their own mighty kings and kingdoms, at a time when many other European peoples did not. This belief appeals to «a thousand years of the continuity of the State.» Although this belief has been seriously contested by critical national historians (Klaic 1975; Budak 1997), it has survived the criticism for an obvious reason: its mythical substance meets the need of people for extraordinary, missionary, and other secular and religious models, a need which is deep-seated in the traditional ethnic consciousness (Smith 1986).

The metaphysical reference: Today's most repeated slogan, especially in the public speeches of the Croatian president, is «Long live the Eternal Croatia!». This use of a religious notion has a double origin. One source dates from the time of the Habsburg empire, when Croatia was subjected to a foreign, absolutist monarchy. Ante Starachevic, unlike his predecessor, Ljudevit Gaj, did not believe anymore in the goodness of the «Father in Vienna», but he continued to believe in the real Father, the Lord (Starachevic 1897/1995). Hence his slogan «God and Croats,» which became the most reiterated cry in subsequent waves of right-wing Croatian nationalism. Today's slogan of «eternal Croatia» is a paraphrase that blends Starachevic's slogan with the earlier «Croatia rediviva» of Vitezovic.

The other source of the slogan is more political but no less illusory. It is derived from a nebulous idea spawned by the leaders of the ruling party, who imagine that Croatia should be organized into social estates or orders similar to those of the 18th century under the Austrian empire of Maria Theresa. Some critics now see this idea as an echo of Mussolini's corporatist state, others as a more regressive, traditional monarchic vision of society as a «King's body» (Vijenac 1998).

The modern constitutional and the traditional possessive references: Closely related to the metaphysical reference is that to the nation-state as the property of the titular nation, i.e. Croats. This reference is directly opposed to the modern idea of citizenship, according to which the state, as far as groups residing within it are concerned, is neither legally nor in practical terms anybody's property, but simply a guarantor of the basic equality of citizens. According to its constitution, Croatia is defined as «the state of Croats and of other citizens living within it …». The names of only some of the 24 minorities are then listed, but the national or ethnic groups are declared to be equal in all respects. Nevertheless, to some extent, such a definition of the state is traditional and ambiguous, and it includes no statement of principles or constitutional consequences regarding human rights, for example. The simple classification of citizenship would appear to have been all that was considered important.

Yet people's constitutional rights will, in the end, be observed according to this more traditional understanding of citizenship, and this could lead to some social discrimination. For example, being a Croat by origin might give one an informal advantage over those belonging to other nationalities in employment, the distribution of appointments, and on other occasions. Admittedly, though, such potential advantages are at present of little value to most Croats because of the dire shortage of employment opportunities.

The discriminatory political reference: Associated with the possessive assumption of statehood is the drawing of concentric circles of national political identity. These are the circles of favoritism and exclusion among Croats. The first and largest circle is made up of «real Croats» («Pravi Hrvati»), who are characterized by their «Croatness» («Hrvatstvo»). This designation embraces those Croats whose attitude toward the Croatian state is affirmative and who are conveniently Roman Catholic, yet it is not particularly exclusive, for it includes people who are not necessarily politically active but merely sympathizers and supporters of the Croatian cause. The next, and more exclusive, circle consists of the «state-generating Croats» («Drzavot-vorni Hrvati») or «Great Croats» («Veliki Hrvati»). This category is restricted in a double sense. It designates the right-wing group within the Croatian political elite, and those who are loyal to the ruling party or who are more of a «vanguard» in some aspects of current politics – that is, those who are more expansionist and aggressive, albeit not always in a clearly defined way; who subscribe, for instance, to the idea of «Greater Croatia» (i.e. the annexation of the Croatian part of Bosnia and Herzegovina).

Who makes up the rest of this identity game? The Croatian president is accustomed to saying that there are «about 20% of Croatian citizens who do not accept the Croatian state.» By itself, this figure is not particularly important, in so far as the way in which it has been arrived at remains a mystery. The meaning of this statement, however, is very important, because it reveals a certain logic of exclusive identity and political discrimination. It implies that, in addition to the remaining Serbian minority, there still are Croats who have not completely accepted the new Croatian state. Either they still prefer the idea of a multi-ethnic Yugoslavia, or they are attracted to a more cosmopolitan, European vision. To some extent, this suspicion presumably refers to the small number of remaining Communists and old war veterans, and to the quite small number of liberal intellectuals in Croatia. But this suspicion is also politically manipulative, for it is a way of derogating and stigmatizing a considerable number of people – ordinary people, intellectuals, and politicians, both Croats and non-Croats – who are critical of various policies of the Croatian Government, of its «Bosnian adventures» and its headlong rush into primitive capitalism.

The social-psychological reference: The new Croatian state has enlarged the sphere of national identity at the expense of other social identities. A sense of national identity is most salient among less educated people of rural origin, among the religious, and among those who have been directly affected by the war (refugees and veterans). It is less meaningful among the more educated, those of urban origin, the non-religious, and among residents of regions far from the war zones (e.g. Istria). There are, though, statistical variations in both categories (Katunaric 1998). Moreover, the degree of significance which is attached to a sense of national identity is not necessarily correlated to whether or not one supports the new government in Croatia; this discrepancy is especially clear among the lower social strata (Sekulic and Sporer 1997).

Nevertheless, with the passing of time, the sense of national identity may become more balanced with other identities (political, professional, generational, gender, regional, etc.), and naturally less homogeneous in itself. One brief example may illustrate the decline of the possessive meaning of the nation-state. In 1990, when the new constitution of the Republic of Croatia was adopted by parliament, a number of the leading politicians from the Croatian Democratic Union came to the main square in Zagreb to share their expression of joy with the crowd. They shouted: «Do we have it, finally?» (meaning the constitution), and the crowd responded unanimously: «Yes, we have it!». The same scene, this time more spectacularly organized, occurred the following year upon the proclamation of the independence of Croatia. The leadership shouted: «Finally, we have Croatia!», and the crowd responded in the same way. The last episode of mass enthusiasm occurred immediately after the final operation of Croatian troops in the summer of 1995, which ended with the liberation of the territory which had been occupied by rebellious Serbs.

Over the last couple of years, however, a rising number of mass protests of workers, teachers, pensioners, and other dissatisfied Croats have replaced the gatherings which celebrated national unity and independence. Now, the most frequently heard slogan echoes the earlier cry: «This is your Croatia and not ours!». Such a contesting of the meaning of the nation-state reminds us of the historical divergence between offical nationalism, and popular nationalism's tendency towards egalitarianism and harmony (Anderson 1991). Or is it, in this case, really a reflection of an old and deep-seated resentment of the masses against the others? It seems that both tendencies, i.e. utopian and nationalistic, co-exist and cannot be separated, at least not under the present conditions of social development in the context of persistent major antagonisms against neighboring nations. In any case, this is evidence of the fact that the process of developing a national identity does not terminate with the establishment of a nation-state.

1.5 Social distance and images

According to a number of surveys conducted in the nineties (Katunaric 1995a,
1997a; Domovic et al. 1997; Stulhofer and Karajic 1997), a majority of Croats
prefer close contacts with Americans, Germans, Italians, Austrians, and
Hungarians, while they least like contacts with Serbs, Montenegrins, Gypsies,
Russians, Albanians, and Muslims/Bosniacs. Such polarization is primarily the
consequence of the war and the projection of «friends» and «enemies.» At the
same time, it is also the result of the cultural transmission of stereotypes, and
of acceptance of the pervasive geo-political rhetoric which claims that Croatia
is a Western, middle-European, and not a Balkan country.

Nevertheless, there is some variation among these findings, and the rejection
of the Serbs is not a universal tendency. According to a survey carried out in
the summer of 1996, around 50% of the respondents in the national sample
did not want to see the Serbs in their country (Katunaric 1997a), but the percentage of such responses was much higher in areas of Croatia directly affected by the war than in other areas.

1.6 Exclusion and inclusion

The practice of social inclusion and exclusion might be a direct consequence
of the categorical construction of reality presented by current political rhetoric
and its media. The case of the Muslims/Bosniacs illustrates the point. At the
beginning of the war in Bosnia and Herzegovina, the Croats and Muslims/
Bosniacs were allies confronting the Serbs. This created a climate of solidarity
among the Muslims in Croatia, and many of them joined the Croatian army
which fought against the Yugoslavian army and the Serbs in Croatia. In accordance with an old political idea, stemming from Staracevic, the Muslims were
unofficially still considered as «the flowers of the Croatian people in Bosnia»,
and not as a separate nationality as they had been regarded in ex-Yugoslavia
since 1981. As far as the Croats were concerned, the meaning of such a political image was not pejorative: if someone is considered as the «best part» of
one's nation, then of course they cannot be treated as inferior, as an enemy or
a stranger, but they belong to the same group. Unfortunately, however, the
Muslim/Bosniac leadership in Bosnia and Hezegovina saw this designation of
the Muslims by the Croatian nationalists as an offense, but they suppressed
their anger while hoping that new alliances during the war would help to resolve the tension.

A turn came in 1993, when the war between the Croats and the Muslims exploded in Bosnia and Herzegovina. A strong propaganda campaign against the Muslims/Bosniacs was immediately unleashed in Croatia. It employed dirty old nicknames, like «Balije» (used by Serbs and Croats for Turks in 19th century Bosnia). The legal position of Muslim refugees in Croatia also deteriorated, due to the official interpretation according to which they, unlike Croatian refugees, belonged to another state and nationality, which justified treating them as foreigners. In this way, a reversal of the practice of inclusion occurred: former «brothers» and «allies» became hereditary enemies. Such a story is much the same, for example, as that of the oscillating relationships between Italians and Germans (Reich 1976), or Croats and Serbs in the present century (Roksandic 1991).

The strongest regional identity that challenges the exclusiveness of the national identity is certainly the Istrian. Although a majority of inhabitants were Croats, until 1945, Istria had rarely been part of the territory of Croatia. Instead, it had in turn belonged to Venice, Italy, and Austria. Italian irredentism in the 19th century in particular provoked the rise of Croatian nationalism in Istria and its collaboration with the Slovenian nationalist movement. This collaboration, however, weakened the impact of Staracevic's legalistic nationalism emanating from the Croatian mainland, and gave rise to pro-Yugoslavian factions in Istria (Banovac 1996). After 1945, the ethnic map of Istria changed: 100 000 Italians emigrated to Italy, and a number of Croats also opted to accept Italian citizenship (Zerjavic, 1993).

In the 1991 census, 16.1% of the residents of Istria declared their regional attachment, «Istrianness», as the only socio-political identity. The remainder declared themselves to be Croats (57.7%), Italians (6.7%), Slovenians (1.6%), or «other» (17.9%). According to a survey taken in 1996, only 2.4% of those who declared themselves to be Istrians were separatist, i.e. wanted to see Istria as an independent country. The vast majority supported the idea of Istrian autonomy within Croatia (Banovac 1996). This autonomy was the major objective of the regional party, the IDS (Istarski Demokratski Sabor), who took some 70% of the votes in Istria in the last national parliamentary election. More recently, the IDS has joined a coalition of the national left and centrist parties, and has since postponed resolution of the goal of autonomy until «some other and better time».

The example of Istria and the IDS is not just politically peculiar, but represents a telling chapter in the dynamics of national and subnational identities. The fact is that a majority of Istrians do not see their regional identity in exclusive terms: «Istrianness» and «Croatness» are not held to be mutually exclusive. Again, the social distance of Istrians toward other nationalities, including the Serbs, is significantly lower than in the rest of Croatia (Katunaric 1995b). This is evidence that «Istrian multi-culturalism» is not merely a rhetorical ploy of the IDS, but a living socio-cultural pattern. At the same time, the ruling and other right-wing parties remain suspicious of Istrian patriotism and loyalty, and are strongly opposed to the autonomous tendencies of Istrians.

Movements for autonomy in other historical regions of Croatia, such as Dalmatian Action in Dalmatia, were defeated in the parliamentary elections and today exist only as non-parliamentary parties with small numbers of followers. Although Dalmatia has a historical record of rather strong movements and parties in favour of autonomy in the 19th and 20th centuries, the centrist national parties prevailed there this time. This happened primarily because the war had severely hit a large part of the region, such that it became completely dependent on the central government; this was not the case in Istria. Moreover, the favorable geographic position of Istria (near Slovenia, Italy, and Austria), good tourist seasons, and industry that is relatively protected by the regional party trustees – constitute utilitarian reasons for seeking autonomy.

2   A dialectic of resentment and identity

Properly understood, national identity corresponds neither to a simple, categorical identity (Billig 1995), nor to a «prototypical identity» (Turner 1989). However, during ethnic or international conflicts, for example, childish images of «Us» and «Them» invade common sense (Spillmann and Spillmann 1991). Similarly, the use of a facile, categorical notion of national identity characterizes the rhetoric of authoritarian regimes which threaten political opponents, ethnic, sexual, and other minorities, as enemies of the nation (Calhoun 1993).

The political rhetoric of the Croatian government, particularly in the early nineties, abounds with such tendencies (Katunaric 1997b). But this is not the end of the story. «Real Croats» and similar prototypical notions were also adopted by the political opposition in Croatia – for example, the workers, trade unions, and the representatives of almost a million retired people. In their hands, nationalist notions have returned with a vengeance. These critics of the official nationalism usually claim that the «most deserving Croats» are those who suffered most during the war and those who suffer from the government's harsh economic policy. Naturally, these victims are not the newly privileged, but the many young soldiers who were disabled in the war, pensioners on very low incomes, the growing mass of unemployed, those who work for months without receiving their wages or salaries, and so on.

It is not the aspect of social revolt which makes this collision of perspectives unusual, so much as the form of its expression. The rhetorical «Croatization» of the social conflict has become the fundamental issue at stake. This development builds on two more general unresolved problems. One of these problems is ideological in a proper sense, and stems from the programmatic discourses of socialism and liberalism. On the one hand, the socialist discourse has placed the class conflict and working class interests at the programmatic core of its politics, but it has not permanently resolved the conflict, especially not in less developed countries. The discourse of liberalism, on the other hand, gives the advantage to private investors and profit-makers as the essential motors of a community's prosperity and development. But liberalism does not have all the answers, either, especially not for less developed countries.

The discourse of nationalism employs a local, domestic mixture of both of these ideologies in its language of identity. Sometimes, enrichment of the wealthy is proclaimed as the primary national interest, because it is «better for Us»; sometimes, the common good for the majority, and social welfare, are declared to be priorities. Essentially, nationalism is a modern form of magic that eclectically mixes parts of a complex and conflict-ridden society on the basis of emotional attachment and familiar language.

A second problem that contributes to the rhetorical «Croatization» of the social conflict stems from the resentment involved. Resentment is a complex social emotion. Initially – on the eve of the ethnic conflict in Croatia, and particularly during the war – resentment spread nationwide and provided a fundamental ingredient in the narrative about Serbian aggression, which was seen as the latest chapter in the century-old attempt to conquer Croatia. This was magnified on the assumption that all Serbian political elites or regimes, along with all members of the Serbian minority in Croatia, were potential or actual aggressors – a typical example of the weakness of categorical logic.

Upon resolution of the conflict with Serbia and the Serbs, the initial, concentrated feeling of resentment began to be diffused into a cluster of similar tendencies directed at more diverse targets.

The «Serbian threat» weakened but still virulent: It is unlikely that the hatred of the Old Enemy will soon disappear, at least among those who have directly experienced losses during the recent war. The return of Serbs to their home areas in Croatia, which has been improving lately, may also provoke or just keep the flame burning among Croats who live side by side with Serb returnees.

Neither will the anti-Serbian feeling disappear among those who traditionally equate «Croatness» with being anti-Serbian. Several decades ago, the Croatian writer Miroslav Krleza described this equation as a sacrosanct ingredient of the provincial nationalism of the Croatian petite-bourgeoisie (Krleza 1972).

«The threat of Herzegovinian Croats»: This focus of resentment has replaced the anti-Serbian attitude amongst a large part of the population in Croatia. It has been supported, at least until recently, by part of the political opposition, but most strongly by independent newspapers. The Herzegovinian Croats are seen both as the seedbed of neo-fascist tendencies in Croatian politics, and as the bulk of the nouveau riche who executed «the robbery of the century» in . Croatia. The latter stereotype highly exaggerates the real proportion of power of the Herzegovinian lobby within the national economy, as much as the former assumes that neo-fascist tendencies are virtually and exclusively «imported» from Herzegovina.

The anti-regime attitude: This attitude is close to the anti-Herzegovinian sentiment, but it is more encompassing and in a sense semi-official. It claims that the ruling party, the Croatian Democratic Union, is to be blamed for all that has gone wrong in Croatia in the nineties. This is, of course, the favourite ploy of the political opposition, and the main issue for the next election campaign. The idea of the «Second Republic» (alluding to France in 1848) which was launched in 1997 by a centrist coalition, implies an expectation of the triumph of an alternative Croatia – pro-Western and non-Balkan, democratic and non-authoritarian. Admittedly, on the face of it, this does not sound «resentful», but the idea of a «Second Republic» of Croatia seems to be derived more from a certain sense of national pride than from a seriously prepared political program.

National Pride: The sense of national pride could ultimately become the most sublime product of the old national resentment. It would amount to a shift from «what we have» to «what we can be». Here, there is too a question of political corruption and inversion. There is a reaction of disbelief and offence against what the president of Croatia and the cabinet of ministers present to the public as a taken-for-granted narrative of the transition. They say: «We are aware of the hardships of post-communism, but all other Eastern countries are in the same or an even worse position. Besides, we cannot avoid the market economy and privatization, which determine that some can survive and become successful, while others, presumably many, cannot». Such crude and unpopular language as this neo-Darwinism is not often used, and certainly not on the eve of elections. It is heard only sporadically. At the same time, the proponents of neo-Darwinist policies accuse the welfare-focused opposition among the political parties and economists of «selling a cheap populism».

Such an argument is common enough and quite unexceptional on Western political agendas. In Croatia, though, such messages hit the newly forming sense of national pride hard. Maintaining that «the other countries suffer as we do» or that «we cannot break market and development principles», the leading politicians offer a lesson from neo-classical economics and the social sciences to an uninformed public. But the pretension of deflating the sense of national strength and power in the midst of international storms, seems to be rather misplaced. Popular wisdom simply does not believe that such pervasive social inequalities are necessary and that a more egalitarian (re-)distribution of revenues is impossible, that the former is a «scientific truth» and the latter reflects a relic of «the communist consciousness». Nor can the popular nationalism grasp that, if a weak Croatia won the war against a much stronger enemy, nevertheless the «strong» and «independent Croatia» cannot beat the anonymous market forces, and that social injustice is unavoidable.

There are many more examples of such a blending of populist and nationalist rhetoric which might be cited. The main point that we can observe is that national identity acquires different meanings, and that it may expand in various and sometimes self-contradictory directions. Neither national identity nor subnational identities are fossilized and superseded by overarching identities: there is no such evolutionary or ontological privilege or disadvantage on either side. All of them are parts of a common dynamic, interacting within the realm of individual and collective imagination around the question of what would constitute the most comfortable possible community. «Nation» is one historic name and place around which such images are often gathered. There are other such sites: for example, «Europe». Both Croatia and Europe have changed their size and teleological shape on many occasions – from small to big, from the emotional homeland to the cradle of civilization, to the imagined, the virtual, or the purely monetaristic community – and they continue to change and reshape. This is similar to the experience of the Croats living in Yugoslavia under socialism. Contrary to the current political rhetoric in Croatia, it was not a lost time in «the age of darkness», nor is living in the new Croatia equal to living in an «age of light». Croats have learned much, both from what was wrong and, however limited, what was good in the former period. One of the positive «Croatian» experiences then was certainly the stability of the employment market: those who were employed were accustomed to keeping their jobs or to finding another job relatively easily. Now, they do not want to lose this stability in the name of national independence and transition, as part of the bewildering price to pay for democracy, capitalism, and nationalism. Croats are the same as they were before only in name: in any other sense, in the content of their social and international experience, much has changed, and much will no doubt continue to change in the foreseeable future.

References

Anderson, B. (1991). *Imagined Communities.* London: Verso.

Banovac, B (1996). Etnichki identitet i teritorijalna pripadnost: sluchaj Istre. *Migracijske teme.* Vol. 12, No. 3–4.

Billig, M. (1995). *Banal Nationalism.* London: Sage.

Braica, S. (1990). Obichaj i kriza. *Etnoloska tribina.* Vol. 20, No.13.

Budak, N. (1997). Mit i povijest. *Lettre International.* Vol. 11, No. 3–4.

Calhoun, C. (1993). Nationalism and Ethnicity. *Annual Review of Sociology.* Vol. 19.

Domovic, V. et al. (1997). High School Students' Intercultural Predispositions: an Empirical Research. In V. Katunari (ed.). *Multicultural reality and Perspectives in Croatia.* Zagreb: Interkultura.

Grdesic, I. et al. (1991). *Hrvatska u izborima '90.* Zagreb: Naprijed.

Katunaric V. (1995a). Ethnic Distance and Intercultural Preferences in Croatia. In S. Kubatova and B. Machova (eds.). *Uniqueness in Unity.* Prague: SIETAR Europe.

Katunaric, V. (1995b). Exotic Friends and Real Enemies: The Impact of the War on the Image of Others in Croatia. In B. Cvjetichanin (ed.). *Dynamics of Communication and Cultural Change: The Role of Networks.* Culturelink – Special Issue. Zagreb: Institute for International Relations.

Katunaric, V. (1997a). The Meanings of Culture in the European Core and Periphery. In Nada Svob-Dokic (ed.) *The Cultural Identity of Central Europe.* Culturelink – Special Issue. Zagreb: Institute for International Relations.

Katunaric, V. (1997b). Une folie categorielle. In C. Levy-Vroelant et I. Joseph (eds.). *La guerre aux civils. Bosnie-Herzegovine 1992–1996.* Paris: L' Harmattan.

Katunaric, V. (1998). «Mostovi» i «vrata»: socijalna distanca u Hrvatskoj 90-tih. In A. Hodzic. (ed.). *Proces tranzicije i demokracija u Hrvatskoj.* Zagreb: Centar za istrazivanje tranzicije i demokracije. Forthcoming.

Klaic, N. (1975). *Povijest Hrvata u razvijenom srednjem vijeku.* Zagreb: Liber, Naprijed.

Krleza, M. (1972). *99 varijacija.* Beograd: Duga.

Reich, W. (1976). *The Mass Psychology of Fascism.* New York: Pocket Books.

Rimac, I., Milas, G. (1994). Model hrvatskog politichkog prostora dimenzioniran glasovima biracha. *Revija za sociologiju,* Vol. 25, No 1–2.

Roksandic, D. (1991). *Srbi u Hrvatskoj.* Zagreb: Vjesnik.

Sekulic, D., Sporer, Z. (1997). Regime Support in Croatia. *Revija za sociologiju,* Vol. 28, No. 1-2.

Skrbis, Z. (1997). The Distant Observers? Towards the Politics of Diasporic Identification. *Nationality Papers.* Vol. 25, No. 3.

Smith, A.D. (1986). *The Ethnic Origins of Nations.* Oxford: Basil Blackwell.

Spillmann, K.R.. and Spillmann, K. (1991). On Enemy Images and Conflict Escalation. *International Social Science Journal,* No. 127.

Stulhofer, A., Karacic, N. (1997). *Sociokulturni aspekti tranzicije – Hrvatska 1996.* Zagreb: Ekonomski institut.

Svob-Dokic, N. (1997). Multicultural Mosaic in Croatia. In B. Cvjetichanin and V. Katunaric, (eds.). *Cultural Policy of the Republic of Croatia.* Zagreb: Institute for International Relations.

Turner, J.C. (1988). *Rediscovering the Social Group. A Self-Categorization Theory.* Oxford: Basil Blackwell.

Vijenac (1998). Vol. 6, No.109, March 12.

Zakosek, N. (1997). Struktura i dinamika hrvatskog stranachkog sustava. *Revija za sociologiju.* Vol. 25, No. 1–2.

Zerjavic, V. (1993). Doseljavanja i iseljavanja s podruchja Istre, Rijeke i Zadra u razdoblju 1910–1971. *Drustvena istrasivanja,* Vol. 2, No. 4–5.

Israel: The Pluralization of a National Identity

Alain Dieckhoff

The Jewish State celebrated its fiftieth anniversary in Israel in 1998, in a peculiar atmosphere in which jubilation over the undeniable achievements of the Jewish national project was to a large extent overshadowed by the bitter uncertainties about the future of Israeli society. The commemorative ceremonies for the Jubilee projected at once a cruel and pathetic image of these doubts and divisions. The committee in charge of organizing the year-long festivities was something of a gymnastic feat to set up, with the resignation of one director after another because of lack of funding, conflicts with the supervising authorities, and above all, disagreement over exactly what was to be celebrated and how it should be celebrated.

The «Batsheva affair» was an almost comic illustration of just how strong the internal divisions were. The famous Israeli dance troupe had planned to give a modern dance performance inspired by a traditional chant of the Passover seder. In the course of the performance, the male dancers would gradually remove their black coats, the female dancers their long dresses, until they were in their underclothes. Cries of outrage came from the ultra-orthodox, who filed a petition with the Supreme Court, then threatened to bring down the government. Finally, the president suggested a compromise that was rejected by the Batsheva, which cancelled its participation in what should have been a high point of the celebrations. For secular Jews, individual creative freedom was at stake; for the religious, it was a matter of defending a central value of the Jewish community: a sense of decency.

The conflict between the two values of freedom and respect involves different conceptions of what the State of Israel should be. For some, in its normalization process as a nation, it should above all enable Jews to fulfill themselves as free individuals; for others, it should defend, if not a collective life project, at least a solid base of values that are specific to the community as a whole. Divergences over the objectives of the State of Israel are not new, but what is new is the more cut-and-dried aspect which they have assumed within the context of a blurred sense of national identity.

1   The problematic quest for a national identity

The term «identity» is, as it were, booby-trapped. It too often implies that the subject (be it individual or collective) has a sort of timeless permanence. But identity is not primordial, static, intangible: it shifts as it relates to others. The capacity for identity to change is even more true of the nation, which, even though it draws on a stock of ancient myths to legitimate and explain itself, is fundamentally a modern political category. Still, there is no doubt that the state has an essential function of assigning and consolidating national identities, which involves marginalizing «borderline» identities (ethnic, regional, etc.) and inculcating a generic identity that encompasses all of its citizens (Coulon 1994).

The State of Israel is not exempt from this logic of shaping national identity. During the founding period, when Ben Gurion was prime minister almost without interruption from 1948 to 1963, the purpose of *mamlakhtiut* («statism») ideology was precisely to make the state the supreme organ of reference and the ideal tool for national integration. To accomplish this task of «blending the exiles» *(mizug galuyot)*, schools, and to a greater extent the army, were expected to play a decisive role in implementing the Israeli-style «melting pot» which invited new immigrants to let themselves slowly become absorbed into their new host society. This model of nation building was based on a functionalist paradigm which assumes that a principle of cohesion can regulate society in such a way that it becomes a co-ordinated and integrated whole. In the case of Israel, the political center and the locus of definition of norms and values with which newcomers were requested to comply were developed out of the pioneer *yishuv* of the second and third migratory waves (1904–1923) (Eisenstadt 1954 & 1967).

In the early years of the young state, this project of creating a strong national identity might have seemed achievable. In 1948, the Jews constituted a community of 650 000 people, over 80% of whom were of European stock (mostly Russian-Polish) and who had a clear secular bent. This group of people all came from the same Ashkenazi world and shared the same vision of Zionism as a means of modernizing the Jews – even if there were ideological divergences between those who, on the left, envisaged a profound social transformation and those on the right, who wanted to see the Jews build a Western-style bourgeois society.

This relatively compact society was confronted with a new challenge as early as 1949: the mass immigration of Jews from Islamic countries (Yemen, Iraq, and later, from Egypt and North Africa). The government offered these immigrants from a much more traditional Jewish environment a single alternative: they had to move quickly into a modernization process by adapting to the existing social and cultural model. This undertaking was partly successful, in that it gave rise to a common sense of «Israeliness». Although it is not easy to give this Israeli identity a specific content, some features can be identified: use of an oral language widely disseminated by the mass media, attachment to a specific territorial idea (fostered by Bible study, archaeology, travels through the country); common experiences (particularly compulsory military service, from which only the ultra-orthodox are exempt); and behavior (rejection of overly formal conduct, directness in speech). But the integration process, supervised from the top, did not quite achieve the aims which it had been intended to achieve: to produce, through progressive assimilation, the *homo israelicus*. This project might have been successful if the «average Israeli» had really been a synthetic product, created out of a harmonious combination of various human elements and cultural heritages. In fact, the absorption of Sephardic immigrants was governed by a desire to impose conformity with a normative – Russian-Polish – Israeli identity. The considerable resistance that this integration from the top encountered eventually led to its being officially abandoned in the mid-1960s, and gave rise to a greater acknowledgement of the socio-cultural diversity of Israeli society.

The episode of Sephardic immigration revealed an inherent tension in the building of the Israeli nation. On one hand, Zionist ideology required the constant immigration of the Diaspora Jews so that Jewish life would become normalized within a specific state framework. But on the other hand, the constant demographic influx made the stabilization of a national identity extremely problematic, because each new migratory wave to some extent challenged the general economy of the national plan. Given that the consolidation of a national identity remains a precarious undertaking, «ethnicity» – taken to mean a form of differentiation based on cultural, religious, and other «markers» – has major social effects in Israel, and this all the more since it is formally validated by the state.

2 Israel as the state of the Jewish nation

By defining the State of Israel as «a Jewish state in the land of Israel», the declaration of independence did not adopt an innocuous formula. On the contrary, with its founding act, the state set itself a specific mission: to provide, through its institutions, a means by which Jews could live together. The state undertook to defend certain values, both Jewish (Jewish culture, the Hebrew language, biblical tradition) and Zionist (uniting dispersed populations, political sovereignty). In other words, the state which would allow the *Jewish* people to assert its right to self-determination was to be necessarily a *Jewish* state (Klein 1977).

Among the numerous aspects which highlight the state's Jewish nature, two are particularly significant. Firstly, both the public sphere and family law are partly governed by legislation that is based in religion. The social presence of Judaism is ensured by a series of laws passed since 1948 which, for example, regulate observance of the Shabbat, the distribution of kosher food to soldiers, forbid El Al airlines from scheduling flights on the Shabbat and religious holidays, ban the public display of bread during Passover, and the breeding and sale of pork, and so on. As for marriage and divorce, these are solely in the competence of rabbis, who in this way were given an essential role in the establishment of the national bond among Jews, since the marriage ceremony makes membership of the Jewish nation official. This is not without consequence for an individual's legal status.

Secondly, the state's Jewishness is extremely visible in the absolute freedom to immigrate that Jews all over the world have. This literal «right to return», established by law in 1950, also automatically entitles people to citizenship.

The state's role in attributing identity to its members is therefore vital, since it entitles the Jewish ethno-national group to specific rights (such as the freedom to immigrate) which other ethno-national groups (particularly the Arabs) do not enjoy. The 850 000 Israeli Arabs (not to mention those in East Jerusalem) – approximately one-sixth of Israel's population – are actually in an extremely ambivalent position with regard to the State of Israel. As citizens in a democratic state, they have the same formal rights, at least since the late 1960s, as their Jewish counterparts – the right to vote and be elected, and the protection of public freedoms. But as Arabs in a Jewish state, they are outsiders in a state with which they cannot fully identify (if only because of its national symbolism) and which, moreover, has often treated them unequally. This was particularly true during the first twenty years of the state's existence. So, although the Arabs who remained in Israeli territory received citizenship, they were subjected, until 1966, to a military government that seriously restricted their civil liberties. What is more, their status as citizens in no way helped them to oppose the string of landownership laws passed in the 1950s that gradually led to the expropriation of most of the land which had been privately owned by Arabs, on highly contestable legal grounds. In this case, Israeli Arabs were clearly no better treated than their brothers who had gone into exile in Lebanon or Syria, since the state considered them first and foremost not as Israeli citizens whose rights were to be respected, but as Palestinian Arabs, members of an ethno-national group that had to be transformed into a dominated minority (Dieckhoff 1993).

Although in principle the situation of Israeli Arabs has improved considerably since the 1970s, both because their political mobilization became more effective and because the Zionist activism of the State of Israel has become less virulent, the structural discrimination of which they are victims remains a reality, though it is more veiled than explicit (Kretzmer 1990). In this context, the bitter remark made by novelist David Grossman is hardly surprising: «There has never been an Arab minister in the Israeli cabinet ... in 1989, out of 1 310 top civil servant positions in the government and related agencies, only 17 were occupied by Arabs ... among the national health doctors, 2% were Arab» (Grossman 1993: 110).

The Arab elite has had two sorts of responses to this situation. Some demand the «de-ethnicization» of the state, in other words, that the link between Jewishness and the state be broken and a «state of citizens» be established in which all individuals enjoy identical rights and in which the state no longer has a hold over collective identity. Their aim is thus to achieve maximum integration, which in fact would also imply the acceptance of additional obligations, such as military service. Others, convinced that the «de-Zionization» of the state is a utopian dream, want to see the Arabs fully and properly recognized as a national minority with the establishment of a cultural, even territorial autonomy. Such demands, however, have no possibility of being accepted. The first Arab response probably arouses some interest amongst the radical left, which is sympathetic to the transformation of Israel into a state of citizens, but it provokes staunch opposition from the majority of Jews, who wish to preserve the Zionist nature of the state and hence, its ethnic foundation (Smooha 1990). The second alternative is almost unanimously rejected by the Jewish people, who see any sort of autonomy as a serious threat to the country's unity and detect therein signs of irredentism (wouldn't an even partially independent Galilee try to establish ties with the Palestinian Authority?).

As any profound transformation of the State of Israel is at present highly unlikely, Israeli Arabs are pursuing their strategy of community consolidation. Both the rise of political Islam in traditional Muslim areas, and the struggle of the communists, who have a strong presence in the modern Arab milieu, for the recognition of specific cultural rights, are part of this trend.

3   Jewish ethnicities

As much as prescribed ethnicity is of decisive importance when it is a question of distinguishing Jews from non-Jews, the ethnic rationale is clearly rejected by the state when speaking solely of Jews. The central postulate of Zionism being the unity of the Jewish people throughout the world, the state can only deny ethno-cultural cleavages within the Jewish population. The emphasis is placed on unifying elements (the same religion – despite different ritual practices, and the same historic experiences – anti-Semitism, the status of minorities in the Diaspora), while conversely, differences between, for instance, a Moroccan Jew and a German Jew are viewed as transient phenomena produced by the dispersion and bound to dissolve in the Israeli «melting pot».

Although ethnicity is officially denied, it still produces effects. Firstly, it is sur-reptitiously reintroduced in statistics which distinguish Jews born in Europe or America from those born in Asia or Africa. This differentiation largely, but not entirely, reflects the standard distinction between Ashkenazi and Sephardic Jews. To some extent, it even tends to reinforce this partition, since it amalga-mates subgroups of Jews which are relatively different (Italian and Russian Jews on one hand, Moroccan and Indian Jews on the other) within two broad categories. Secondly, and more significantly, ethnicity continues to be a struc-turing element in Israeli society. For those who adhere to the functionalist school, the modernization process should gradually equalize conditions and so diminish the significance of ethnic distinctions. Both the political ascension of Sephardic Jews, who are now represented by more deputies and mayors, and the increase in mixed marriages between Jews of different origins, are two par-ticularly remarkable signs of the enduring effectiveness of the Israeli «melting pot» (Ben-Rafael 1982). Conversely, partisans of the pluralist approach feel that ethnicity remains an essential dimension in Israel's social dynamics.

According to observations made over the past twenty years, it seems impos-sible to deny the persistence of ethnicity in Israel (Smooha 1978). Convergent phenomena can probably be identified in lifestyles and family habits, but in many areas, the ethnic gap remains a reality. For instance, although in secon-dary school the Sephardic rate of attendance approximates to that of the Ash-kenazim, the former are still highly concentrated in vocational school, whereas the latter are better represented in general education. Consequently, the Sephardim are five times less likely to acquire a university degree than the Ashkenazim. The occupational structure naturally reflects this differing educa-tional profile, Jews from Islamic countries being more concentrated in «blue collar» activities, whereas Western Jews constitute most of the middle class and dominate the economic, academic, and media elites in Israeli society.

Although in absolute terms the Sephardim have made considerable progress, for example, in education and an improved standard of living, the differential with Ashkenazim, rather than diminishing, has remained stable or even increased. A comparative study conducted over a thirty year period to assess the accomplishments of the Iraqi and Romanian communities which, at the time of their respective immigrations, were at approximately the same socio-economic level, has shown that the average income gap has gone from 15% to 30% in favor of Romanian Jews. On the professional level, whereas in 1961 the Romanians and Iraqis had near equal representation in the professions (about 10%) and among «blue collar» workers (around 50%), thirty years later the former were 35% in the first category and 30% in the second, whereas the latter were respectively 16% and 50% (*Jerusalem Post*, 7.6.1991). The evidence is categorical: socio-economic discrepancies are «handed down» from one generation to the next and thus maintain a persistent ethnic cleavage between Ashkenazim and Sephardim.

This ethnic configuration can be explained for the most part by the way in which Israeli society was built. The foundations of this society having been laid by Eastern European Jews, the European imprint was naturally preponderant, and the new immigrants from the old continent found their bearings much faster than those who came from Islamic countries. Furthermore, the former could take advantage of previously established networks of elites, whereas the latter only rarely took advantage of this possibility (Goldscheider 1996: 55–57). In building ethnicity in Israel around the binomial Europe-America/Africa-Asia distinction, the prejudice against orientalism as a mental framework which shaped the Orient (characterized by backwardness and irrationality) in contrast to the West (a land of progress and rationality), came fully into play (Said 1995). In this context, the new immigrants from Islamic countries were quite naturally urged to abandon their «primitive cultures» and to be absorbed by the surrounding modern society built by Zionist leaders of Russian-Polish origin. Symptomatically, the Sephardim were considered as members of «oriental communities» *(edot ha-mizrah),* but it never occurred to anyone to refer to the Ashkenazim as «occidental communities» *(edot ha-maarav)* – despite the fact that some Ashkenazim no longer hesitate to play the card of ethnicity.

In fact, the political mobilization of ethnicity has been the most significant development over the past fifteen years. In addition to the Shas party, whose score among the Sephardic population has been growing with each election, there is now the Israel ba-Aliyah party, which garners most of the votes of Jews from the former USSR. Such phenomena would have been unthinkable in the founding years of the state, when the strength of the national integration ideology disqualified any attempt to mobilize on an ethnic basis. This is no longer the case, at a time when the strategy of absorption into a common «melting pot» has been shown to have obvious limitations. The most remarkable community-forming phenomenon is the Shas party («Sephardic guardians of the Torah») which, since its emergence in 1984, has offered an original identity to the public. Its revivalist type of message, stressing the need for Sephardim to revert to a rigorous practice of Judaism, is linked to an enhancement of «oriental ethnicity» that has supposedly been systematically devalued in an Israel dominated by an Ashkenazi elite. This restoration talk is finding a growing audience, especially in development towns and the «oriental» neighborhoods of Israeli towns plagued with economic troubles and social restructuring. The Shas owes its success particularly to its strong local presence (networks of kindergartens, youth clubs, etc.). By fulfilling an everyday social function that the state does not fulfill, the Shas is striving to strengthen its political base, thus establishing itself as the spokesman of the other, economically and culturally marginalized, Israel.

Yet mobilizing ethnicity is not a Sephardic specialty. When seven «Russian» deputies entered the Knesset in 1996 under the banner «Israel ba-Aliyah», led by the former «prisoner of Zion,» Nathan Sharansky, it showed that the wave of migration from the former Soviet Union which began in 1989 had led to the creation of a strong, highly structured community that (at least for the moment) had no intention of relinquishing its specificity. Several factors ensure that this trend is sustained: their demographic numbers (over 700 000 immigrants), the identity profile (highly de-Judaicized, together with the promotion of a Russian cultural identity), and highly effective internal organization (associations, Russian-language press and television). In addition, the fact that a large number of these new immigrants are not at all Jewish or are not considered as such by religious law (perhaps as many as 300 000 of them) contributes to the perpetuation of a specific Russian identity. This ethnic identity, in which the cultural dimension plays a central role, is accompanied by an «integration without acculturation» (Horowitz 1982). Although the new immigrants in fact have encountered various problems (such as difficulties in occupational retraining, and lower qualifications), on the whole, economically they have adapted very quickly to their new environment, and their material situation appears to be quite satisfactory: 80% of Russian immigrants now own their own apartment.

Successful economic integration, however, does not necessarily go hand in hand with significant cultural assimilation. Shaped by the rich and diversified Russian culture, the new immigrants find Israeli culture unattractive and tend to move about in a social environment composed essentially of Russian speakers. At the same time, «Russian» community building does not necessarily imply a sense of alienation from Israeli society. Studies show that five years after their arrival, over 80% of them feel at home in Israel, and almost 90% say that if they had to do it over again, they would migrate a second time (Damian & Rosenbaum-Tamari 1996: 34). This high satisfaction index indeed seems to confirm that ethnicity is not used in a dissident strategy, but is in fact an instrument «that Russian immigrants use with the aim of improving their status and increasing their power within Israeli society» (Al-Haj 1996: 148). This observation holds true *mutatis mutandis* for all Jewish ethnic groups in Israel that use their ethnicity as a resource to win recognition and concessions from the political center in a quest for social ascension. For instance, there is little doubt that Sephardic ethnicity is used as a resource by the Shas in order to have the terms of integration revised (reduction of the socio-ethnic fracture, more explicit legitimization of oriental cultures, etc.), and not simply as a rejection of the very principle of integration. In sum, integration is a process that no longer occurs through the constitution of a homogeneous Israeli nation, but through the acceptance of socio-cultural plurality within a vague, sufficiently loose «Israeliness» which includes all facets of society and transcends, in particular, an increasingly salient cleavage – that between religious and secular.

4 Religious and secular reaffirmations

In June 1947, David Ben Gurion sent a letter to the representatives of the Agudat Israel ultra-orthodox party stipulating that in the future, the Jewish State government would respect certain principles (a legal day of rest on the Shabbat, kashruth in public kitchens, the independence of religious school systems, and individual status handled by the religious community). Ben Gurion's commitment appeared to be motivated by tactical considerations: to win the support of the ultra-orthodox so as to preserve the greatest possible consensus in the Jewish camp. But this concession was more than a simple political expedient: it reflected the inherent ambivalence of the Zionist national project. For Israel's founding fathers – Russian Jews imbued with a strong awareness of their Jewishness – the independent state was not to be simply a framework for the guarantee of political sovereignty, but also the instrument with which to protect a specific culture. In other words, Zionism was certainly an aspiration to political freedom, but equally, if not more so, the preservation of a collective identity which, even reshaped by the Jewish intelligentsia, explicitly claimed a certain historical continuity.

Although as a democratic movement, Zionism made the people themselves the primary actors in Jewish history and asserted their entitlement to political rights, it was based on the reappropriation of fundamental elements of Jewish identity – for instance, the Land of Israel/Bible/Hebrew language triad – and could not conceive of the national bond as entirely detached from any religious referent. This impossibility of emancipating Zionism from Judaism explains precisely why the rabbis were granted a monopoly on pronouncing marriages between Jews: although Zionism had as its aim the re-establishment of modern Jews on a state basis, it was ultimately only able to define membership of the Jewish nation by religious criteria. In fact, the socialist bent that dominated Zionism for half a century (1933–1977) always displayed an ambiguous attitude with regard to religious tradition. Although Judaism was generally rejected as a restrictive normative system and the Jewish religion vigorously condemned as a system of subservience, socialist Zionism retained the traditional priority of the community over the individual. It may have been a question of refounding the Jewish community as a nation instead of as «God's servant», but the desire to preserve a solid collective identity nourished by a strong Jewish awareness amounted to the same thing. In this attempt at political mobilization, nationalism played an essential role, and the young State of Israel was the ideal active promoter of a project for Jewish collective living. Despite the ideological differences separating Ben Gurion from Begin and Rabbi Maimon, the leader of religious Zionism, these men found themselves allied by the same national consensus based on common values (patriotism, reclaiming the land, bringing together the exiles, etc.) in which religion had an acknowledged place in society (Dieckhoff 1997). In the late sixties, the advent of a new civil religion in which religious symbolism achieved a new degree of salience, helped to strengthen Israelis' sense of unity, the Shoah having become the major traumatic event that underlined the exceptional singularity of Jewish fate (Liebman & Don-Yehiya 1983).

There is good reason to think that this all-encompassing civil religion is losing its meaning today, and that it is no longer able to serve as effectively as in the past as a cement between the religious and secular population. A methodological remark is in order here before proceeding further. Separating the religious and the secular into two distinct camps is inevitably reductive and does not do justice to the internal complexity of these two groups[1]. Nevertheless, this distinction must be maintained because it allows us to draw a demarcation line between two subgroups of approximately equal size which are different with regard both to practices (strict or regular observance vs. none or irregular observance) and to relationships between politics and religion (public space marked by religion vs. neutral public space). These two groups have evolved in

---

1   Within the religious population, it is common to distinguish the ultra-orthodox (8%), the religious Zionists (15%), and the traditionalists (30%). Among the secular Jews, we can distinguish the moderates (30%) from the intransigents (20%).

different ways over the past fifteen years, crystallizing within them two distinct poles that have radically different visions of Israel's future.

On the one hand, the two trends within the religious constellation – ultra-orthodoxy and religious Zionism – that were for decades divided by major controversies over what theological signification should be given to the Zionist project, began to find common ground around a shared intransigence. Religious Zionism, which defended an open orthodoxy in which strict respect for the *halakhah* was combined with a positive attitude towards modernity, identified closely with ultra-orthodox positions by advocating a more strict practice of Judaism. Significantly, religious Zionism, which had always purported to be a bridge with the secular world, has today aligned itself with the institutional separatism of the men in black. Since 1948, religious Zionists have had their own schools and press, and they now tend to live in their own neighborhoods and have specific structures for performing their military service (*hesder yeshivot, mekhinot,* etc.). At the same time, the *haredim* (God-fearers), more and more financially dependent on the state and institutionally integrated into it, have become «Zionized» by adopting an uncompromising territorial nationalism that is now shared by practically all the religious Zionists. The opposition of the Hassidic Habad (Lubavitch) and Gur groups to any Israeli withdrawal from Judaea and Samaria is almost as radical as that of the Gush Emunim, the militant wing of Messianic religious Zionism. As Charles Liebman writes, the tradeoff for *haredim* nationalization has been, to some extent, the *haredization* of religious Zionists (Liebman 1993: 72). This rapprochement between two former adversaries, which also facilitates greater co-operation within government coalitions, is obviously also a defense measure against any deepening of secularization in Israeli society.

Indeed, the vitality of the religious subculture has tended to conceal the activities of a secularization movement that is nevertheless quite real and that has caused a staunchly secular current of opinion to emerge. A world divides Ben Gurion's era – when the small state of Israel, isolated in the Middle East, mobilized in its nation-building enterprise on the basis of a collectivist ethos – and that of Netanyahu in which Israel, fully integrated in the world economy, has seen a rise in the individualistic rationale not only in the economic (encouragement of free enterprise) and material realms (consumer society), but also in the legal realm (increased protection of individual rights) (Ezrahi 1997).

This modern Israel, in which hedonism is now a fully established value, in which the quest for individual satisfaction is no longer taboo, is seen by «the new seculars» as a denationalized society. Contrary to the socialist Zionists, who had wanted to rebuild Jewish collective existence on a national foundation, preserving a link of continuity with the past, the «radical seculars» think in post-national terms, both individually and globally. Their priority is not for Israel to be a primarily Jewish society, but rather a Western society, integrated in advanced modernity, firmly established in the contemporary world. Not surprisingly, they are also in favor of a separation between religion and state, and the more politically involved would like to see Israel transformed into a state of citizens[2].

These two contradictory tendencies, according to which some advocate a state according to the Torah *(medinat ha-torah)* and others advocate a post-Zionist Israel, largely dominate public debate, but they are far from summarizing the positions on the «religious content» of national identity. In fact, the majority of Israeli Jews belong to the «forgotten center» (Liebman & Susser 1997) – people who are neither religiously observant, nor in favor of wholesale secularism, but who want to see the State of Israel maintain its Jewish character in one way or another. This center is made up, in my opinion, of two distinct categories: the traditionalists and the moderate seculars[3]. The former display, in a sort of family loyalty, a respect for religious tradition. Yet their observance of religious rites is selective, and attending synagogue on Saturday morning does not prevent them from going to a soccer match in the afternoon. Many of them are from a Sephardic background. The moderate seculars are more detached from any religious observance, and feel that the presence of religious markers in the public sphere should be strictly limited. They nevertheless feel that the State of Israel should maintain its Jewish nature, expressed through the dissemination of the Hebrew language, the existence of a Jewish education (in which the history of the Jewish people is taught), the persistence of strong ties with Jews of the Diaspora (hence the need to preserve the Law of Return), and even maintaining certain ties between Judaism and the state – so long as these ties do not interfere with individual freedoms (Yehoshua 1992). This moderate secularism remains pervasive among the political elites of the two main Israeli parties, Likud and the Labor Party, and has long found a definite resonance among European Jews imbued with *yiddishkeit.*

This «silent majority» is, basically, attached to the hybrid nature of the State of Israel as a Jewish and democratic state, even if reconciling these two principles is far from being an easy task. Yet its future is uncertain. Traditionalists are

---

2   The advocates of this «republican secularity» are particularly well represented in the media and in intellectual spheres. To name a few among many: Idith Zertal, Amos Elon, and Zeev Sternhell.

3   Although in their previously quoted article, Liebman and Susser were right to draw attention to this «silent majority», they define it in such a way as to hypertrophy its religious character. Some people in this middle way maintain links with religious tradition in a highly individual way, others express an attachment to the state's Jewish nature without feeling that it has to involve even a minimal degree of religious conduct.

tending to diminish in numbers, some becoming orthodox in their religious practices, while many others have been won over to the process of secularization (this is true especially of the *sabras* from Sephardic families). Moderate seculars are confronted with the same phenomenon of attrition: though some are making spectacular returns to religion, those who succumb to the «sirens of secular life» do so more discreetly but in greater numbers, and demand to be recognized above all as individuals. They take their Israeli identity for granted (by the very fact of their birth on Israeli soil and their socialization) and are unburdened by a specific Jewish awareness. Furthermore, the future of this «forgotten center» is also compromised by the political partition of Israeli society (in particular on the decisive question of the peace process) which maintains a polarization between a «normalizing» current (regrouping secular Jews of all kinds) and an «identitarian» current (ranging from the ultra-orthodox to the traditionalists) (Dieckhoff 1998).

If we take into account the various factors which we have discussed – the existence of an Arab national minority that has begun a process of identity reaffirmation (which in particular relies on Islam), a resurgence of ethnicity among the Jewish population, and increasing divergences with regard to the role of Judaism in the state – then the dream of the founding fathers of building a new, more homogeneous Hebrew nation seems more utopian than ever. But it was probably chimerical and excessively Promethean to begin with. Lacking this ambition for a refoundation, today's Israeli state has probably become more «ordinary», but it is also more attentive to social diversity. It is doubtless through a subtle balance between «soft Israelity» and respect for true (ethnic, cultural, and religious) pluralism that Israel will find a new way to pursue the project of living together.

References

Al-Haj, Majid (1996). «Attitudes et manières de se situer des immigrants so-
viétiques: l'émergence d'un nouveau groupe ethnique en Israel», *Revue européenne des migrations internationales,* vol.12, no. 3: 139–152.

Ben-Rafael, Eliezer (1982). *The Emergence of Ethnicity: Cultural Groups and
Social Conflict in Israel.* Westport & London: Greenwood Press.

Coulon, Christian (1994). «Etat et identités», pp. 283–298 in Denis-Constant
Martin (ed.). *Cartes d'identité. Comment dit-on «nous» en politique?* Paris:
Presses de Sciences-Politique.

Damian, Natalia & Rosenbaum-Tamari, Yehudit (1996). *The Current Wave of
Former Soviet Union Immigrants: Their Absorption Process in Israel.* Jerusalem: Ministry of Immigrant Absorption.

Dieckhoff, Alain (1993). «La maturation politique d'une minorité ethnique»,
Revue du monde musulman et de la Méditerranée, no. 68–69: 99–106.

Dieckhoff, Alain (1997). «Nationalisme d'Etat et intégrisme nationaliste: le cas
d'Israel», pp. 145–162 in Pierre Birnbaum (ed.). *Sociologie des nationalismes,* Paris: PUF.

Dieckhoff, Alain (1998). «Les deux Israels», *Politique internationale,* no. 80,
summer: 218–227.

Eisenstadt, Shmuel (1954). *The Absorption of Immigrants.* London: Routledge
and Kegan Paul.

Eisenstadt, Shmuel (1967). *Israeli Society.* London: Weidenfeld & Nicolson.

Ezrahi, Yaron (1997). *Rubber Bullets. Power and Conscience in Modern Israel.*
New York: Farrar, Straus & Giroux.

Goldscheider, Calvin (1996). *Israel's Changing Society. Population, Ethnicity
and Development.* Boulder: Westview.

Grossman, David (1993). *Slipping on a Wire. Conversations with Palestinians in
Israel.* London: Jonathan Cape.

Horowitz, Tamar (1982). «Integration Without Acculturation: The Absorption
of Soviet Immigrants», *Soviet Jewish Affairs,* vol.12 (3): 19–33.

Jerusalem Post, 7 June 1991.

Klein, Claude (1977). *Le caractère juif de l'Etat d'Israel.* Paris: Cujas.

Kretzmer, David (1990). *The Legal Status of the Arabs in Israel.* Boulder:
Westview.

Liebman, Charles and Don-Yehiya, Eliezer (1983). *Civil Religion in Israel.*
Berkeley: University of California Press.

Liebman, Charles (1993). «Jewish Fundamentalism and the Israeli Polity», pp.
68–87 in Martin Marty & Scott Appleby (eds.). *Fundamentalisms and the
State.* Chicago & London: University of Chicago Press.

Liebman, Charles & Susser, Bernard (1997). «The Forgotten Center: Traditional Jewishness in Israel», *Modern Judaism,* vol.17 (3): 211–220.

Smooha, Sammy (1978). *Israel:Pluralism and Conflict.* London: Routledge & Kegan Paul.

Smooha, Sammy (1990). «Minority Status in an Ethnic Democracy: the Status of the Arab Minority in Israel», *Ethnic and Racial Studies,* vol.13 (3), July: 388–413.

Said, Edward (1995). *Orientalism. Western Conceptions of the Orient.* London: Penguin.

Yehoshua, Abraham (1992). *Pour une normalité juive.* Paris: Liana Levi.

Part III

From the Europe
of Nations
to the
European Nation

Introduction

Klaus Armingeon

1   The contributions by Robert Hettlage and Max Haller

Do we observe the emergence of a European identity, comparable to national identity? Can this be traced over time in data from international surveys such as the Eurobarometer or the International Survey Program? These were the guiding questions, posed by the steering committee of the conference. Both contributors to this section, Max Haller and Robert Hettlage give the same answer: not at all. In so doing, they are in agreement with comparative research, based on survey data (Niedermayer and Sinnott 1995). This raises the question, why no such identity has emerged after more than forty years of European integration.

The functional logic, according to which economic integration spills over to politico-institutional integration, does not apply to a third layer of integration, Robert Hettlage holds. This layer consists of strong feelings of belonging together, a common consciousness or – defined in more general terms – the socio-psychological dimension of international integration. Creating a common identity is a complex task, contingent on favourable circumstances. European politicians have failed in achieving these ends, Hettlage argues. From his perspective, two major avenues lead to the creation of European identity. The first avenue is built on the restructuring of public education; the second avenue involves constructing a complex identity, which is composed of regional, national and European elements.

For Max Haller, European integration means different things for different peoples under the same European flag. It can be the cure for problems, which cannot be solved on the national level, it is considered a necessary evil, it substitutes for a lacking national identity or it serves particular economic, cultural and political goals. In addition, European integration can be seen as the creation of a super-bureaucracy, which is not in the interest of the people. Hence a common denominator for a European identity across all member countries of the Union is lacking. Given this heterogeneity of attitudes and interests toward the European Union, Haller sees the sole solution in the renouncing of the claim that the European Union will be more than a community of nations.

While according to Hettlage, it depends on the – hitherto missing – political will and skill to bring about a European identity, in the perspective of Max

Haller the best that political will and skill can achieve is limiting the process of European integration to a community of nations. Further integration, the aim of replacing the nation-state as the dominant form of political organization and the claim of becoming something like a European state will overextend the repertoire of common beliefs and attitudes among the European public.

2   Does the European Union really need a collective identity?

These findings raise questions about whether and to what extent the present European Union is in need of a collective identity of European citizens. Stated in a positive way, for Haller, identity is a precondition for consistent and forceful behaviour. In a much more restricted sense, national identity defines the group of people among whom one could expect the feeling of mutual solidarity (Weber 1980: 528). As long as the European Union does not require extensive and far-reaching solidaristic behaviour from its citizens or require forceful and consistent behaviour from its peoples, full-fledged collective identity is hardly needed. This would change dramatically if the Union begins to levy high taxes and to redistribute major resources. However, judged by national tax loads and national welfare states, European redistributive action is still severely limited. In addition, on the national level it is a widely accepted idea that in case of war and crisis, the society can demand that its citizens give their lives for the public interest. This idea has no basis on the European level, since the European Union does not have international relations and a foreign policy, comparable to the external relations of the nation-state. Hence, since the Union is far from being something like a state, there is no urgent need for a developed collective identity.

In addition, European politicians concerned about European identity expect Europeans to have an emotional commitment to Europe which citizens seldom have with regard to their own nation. As a rule, the overwhelming majority of citizens in surveys state that in the first instance, they identify with their town or region. The nation comes second *(Table 1)*. This does not imply that national identity is unimportant. Rather, in «settled» European democracies, national identification is dormant in the everyday life of ordinary citizens. It comes to the fore only in exceptional circumstances, such as domestic conflicts with foreigners (e.g. immigrants), in major conflicts with other states or once a citizen moves across national borders. In that case, citizens easily detect their own nationality by not belonging to the nation, where that person is at the moment: You feel Swiss, once you are outside Switzerland. At home and under ordinary circumstances, you don't care that much about your nationality. And perhaps the European Union requires an even less intense permanent emotional attachment of Europeans – as long as it rarely demands solidaristic behaviour from them.

Table 1: Primary sentiment of belonging to the following geographical units (% respondents)

Country	locality or town	region	country	Europe	world
Belgium	47	14	22	7	10
Canada	31	16	40	3	10
Denmark	52	22	22	2	2
France	41	14	28	8	10
Germany	39	33	16	6	7
Great Britain	40	17	32	3	10
Iceland	41	6	48	1	5
Ireland	44	14	37	3	3
Italy	41	11	28	5	15
Netherlands	44	7	36	4	9
Northern Ireland	48	23	22	1	6
Norway	70	13	14	1	2
Portugal	40	19	27	4	10
Spain	43	19	31	1	6
Sweden	56	13	25	3	3
United States	38	12	30	4	16
Switzerland 1	50	20	16	4	8
Switzerland 2	27	20	30	8	15
Mean*	44	16	29	3	8

* excl. Switzerland

Source: European Value Study 1990; Les valeurs des Suisse (Enquête Valeurs) 1988/89 (Switzerland 1); World Value Survey 1996 (Switzerland 2)

For Switzerland 1:
«locality or town» = «commune d'origine» + «commune d'habitat»;
«region»   = «canton d'origine» + «canton d'habitat» + «region linguistique»
for Switzerland 2:
«region»   = «canton» + «region linguistique»

3   If the European Union does need a collective identity, on what could it be based?

Such a minimalist position stands in stark contrast to the visions of some European politicians who seem to dream of a European political system taking over most of the functions of the then defunct, superfluous or at least degraded nation-state. Once the European Union is pushed in that direction, it will depend on a certain amount of collective definition of its citizens, doubtless exceeding the present, limited European identity. Here the major questions relate to the foundations of such an identity. Clearly it cannot replicate the building of national identity in the typical Western nation. Contrary to most nation-states, in the EU there is no common or widely shared culture; Europe is not a community of communication, nor a community of positively valued remembrance, nor a community of positively valued experiences (Kielmansegg 1996).

Considering this missing basis of European identity, it is often argued that Europe as a peace project is an alternative seed crystal of collective identification («We are Europeans, since by institutional design we want to prevent another European war»). However, international relations research points to findings that democracies do not fight democracies (Lake 1992; Czempiel 1996). According to this perspective, the West European peace after 1945 is primarily due to the democratic character of its nation-states rather than to the existence of the European communities. This does not imply, that European integration has not had a supportive function for the maintenance of peace; but it has probably not been the primary cause. Hence, building up the European identity on Europe as a peace project risks to base the feeling of belonging together on a partial myth. This may work, as the Swiss example demonstrates, but it is not without dangers.

Finally, some authors argue that a European identity could be built on constitutional patriotism. This is a feeling of solidarity based on the attachment to legitimized democratic institutions. («Since we share the same good, democratic institutions, we belong together.») The idea has been proposed by Dolf Sternberger (1990), to address the non-feasibility of «nation» or «national history» for the building of a positive national identity. This applies to the Federal Republic of Germany, where both terms are inseparable from the horrors and outrages against humanity of the Nazi regime. It is also the case in countries, where there is hardly a common culture on which a national identity can be built; Switzerland and the USA being prime examples.

Operationalization of constitutional patriotism for international comparisons is difficult, in particular if analysis is restricted to existing data sets which can be used in secondary data analysis. As a proxy, I used the trust in those core institutions of democracy, which are somewhat detached from political conflict and societal cleavages (i.e. neither political parties, nor interest organizations, nor party government) and which can be considered to secure the public interest. The legislative body (parliament), public administration and the legal system belong to this constitutional centre of a democratic polity. Those persons having confidence in at least two of these institutions, were coded as «constitutional patriots». This trust in institutions, however, is a minimal requirement for meeting the criteria listed by Sternberger. One might add that this confidence should go together with pride of belonging to the country which has these institutions. Hence, I constructed a second indicator. Those persons who have had confidence in at least two of the core constitutional institutions of democracy and who were proud of belonging to that country were classified as constitutional patriots.

Some years after Sternberger proposed the term, Jürgen Habermas added to it another meaning: those who are attached to the democratic institutions and practice democracy, i.e. are active participants in the democratic process, are constitutional patriots (Habermas 1991:9). Thus, according to a third operationalization, a citizen is coded as a «constitutional patriot» if he or she trusts in two of the three core institutions, discusses politics sometimes or frequently with friends and does not refuse, in principle, to participate in legal demonstrations.

Table 2 is based on secondary analyses of the European Value Survey 1990 and the Swiss Value Survey 1988/89 (Armingeon 1999). It shows the percentages of the national samples meeting the criteria of the three different operationalizations of constitutional patriots. On the basis of the national outcomes, the Habermasian constitutional patriotism is unlikely to be a model for Europe. Even on the national level, attachment to democratic institutions with active involvement in the democratic process is a rare phenomenon. In all countries under consideration, only a minority of the population meets Haberma's criteria. Sternberger's vision seems more appropriate, particularly with regard to the «sober» version of an attachment to the core institutions of the particular political system. Switzerland, having no common culture, language or idea of common origins, is a case in point.

Table 2:   Constitutional patriots (% respondents)

Country	Constitutional patriots (Sternberger)	Constitutional patriots with national pride (Sternberger)	Constitutional patriots (Habermas)
Belgium	42	34	14
Canada	45	42	22
Denmark	56	48	30
France	47	39	22
Germany	50	35	26
Great Britain	45	41	27
Iceland	55	52	34
Ireland	51	50	20
Italy	26	24	10
Netherlands	54	40	31
Norway	60	50	42
Portugal	36	34	14
Spain	38	35	12
Sweden	44	36	30
Switzerland	71	59	17
United States	52	50	22
Mean	48	42	23

Source:
European Value Study 1990; Les valeurs des Suisse (Enquête Valeurs) 1988/89.

From this perspective, a European identity could be based on the attachment to the core institutions of a working European democracy. However, the crucial point is that these efficient and legitimized institutions must first be built before they can meet the European political system's need for a consolidated third layer of integration, namely a European identity. According to Max Haller, intensifying the process of social, economic and political integration of the EU will increase the need for solidaristic attitudes and behaviour among the citizens of Europe. A crucial precondition for this European identity, however, is a European democratic polity. As long as this is missing, further integration is highly risky. Considering the prospects for enlargement of the Union towards Eastern Europe and the concomitant failure to bring about substantial institutional reform and a working democratic system in the EU, one could anticipate major crises in the medium to long run.

4 Muddling through by inertia and adaptation

At the end of the 1990s, such major crises still seem to be a long way off. Although in certain areas, EU policies have an enormous impact on the life of the ordinary citizen, they do not seem to be a particularly salient issue for most people most of the time. Much European integration still occurs «behind the backs» of citizens, without Europeans being aware of it. In addition, inertia and adaptation might partially substitute for the function of a European identity. In the long run, support for EU integration is slowly increasing, as more people become accustomed to that political system and its policies (Bosch and Newton 1995). A case in point is the introduction of the Euro in 1999. There were hot debates and various attempts at political mobilization in the course of the abolition of national currencies. Once the transition had occurred, the theme had virtually disappeared from the headlines in a short period of itme. It was only a few weeks later that public discussion began on whether national coins and notes could not be replaced earlier than planned.

From a normative point of view, it may be disappointing that the major federation of democratic states is not supported by a collective identity and an emotional attachment on the part of its citizens but rather by inertia and adaptation. On the other hand, this substitute for collective identity can give the European Union another couple of years of muddling through. In that regard, Max Haller's well founded warnings might be basically true, but still premature.

References

Armingeon, Klaus (1999). «Nationalismus und Verfassungspatriotismus. Die Schweiz im internationalen Vergleich», pp. 219–238 in Rupert Moser (ed.). *Traditionen der Republik – Wege zur Demokratie.* Bern, Berlin: Peter Lang.

Bosch, Agusti and Kenneth Newton (1995). «Economic Calculus or Familiarity Breeds Content?», pp. 73–104 in Oskar Niedermayer and Richard Sinnott (eds.). *Public Opinion and Internationalized Governance. Beliefs in Government* Vol. 2. New York: Oxford University Press.

Czempiel, Ernst-Otto (1996). «Kants Theorem. Oder: Warum sind Demokratien (noch immer) nicht friedlich?», *Zeitschrift für Internationale Beziehungen* 3(1): 79–101.

Habermas, Jürgen (1991). *Staatsbürgerschaft und nationale Identität. Überlegungen zur europäischen Zukunft.* St. Gallen: Erker.

Kielmansegg, Peter Graf (1996). «Integration und Demokratie», pp. 47–71 in Beate Kohler-Koch und Markus Jachtenfuchs (eds.). *Europäische Integration.* Opladen: Leske + Budrich.

Lake, David A. (1992). «Powerful Pacifists: Democratic States and War», *American Political Science Review* 86(1): 24–37.

Niedermayer, Oskar and Richard Sinnott (1995). «Public opinion and internationalized governance. Beliefs in Government» Vol. 2, in Oskar Niedermayer and Richard Sinnott (eds.). *Beliefs in government.* Oxford: Oxford University Press.

Sternberger, Dolf (1990). «Verfassungspatriotismus. Rede bei der 25-Jahr-Feier der ‹Akademie für Politische Bildung›», pp. 17–31 in: Sternberger, Dolf (ed.). *Verfassungspatriotismus.* Frankfurt am Main: Insel.

Weber, Max (1980). *Wirtschaft und Gesellschaft. Grundriss der verstehenden Soziologie (5., rev. Auflage).* Tübingen: Mohr (Siebeck).

European Identity – Between Inclusion and Exclusion

Robert Hettlage

In 1997, the Treaties of Rome, the basis for the ambitious project of European integration, were forty years old. Taken together with the earlier organization of the coal and steel union, this makes the modern European unification process almost half a century old. The successes of these projects are unquestionable. In any case, with the establishment of the European single market between fifteen participating states in 1991, the most successful process of deregulation in economic history was achieved (see Ambrosius 1996). The introduction of the single currency will change Europe still more dramatically from the year 2002.

Admittedly, nobody has ever been unreservedly enthusiastic about this vision of Europe. Even so, it would seem that Europe is once again facing a crisis of identity. Economic unification is proceeding well, but the political objectives which were expected to follow are only beginning to be achieved, if they are at all. There is no real plan for the development of the institutions, no political federation, and with respect to its international position, this project has still not, after forty years, developed as an independent and coherent entity capable of exerting influence.

One asks why this is so. The standard answer, which is doubtless correct, is that the several national consciousnesses have been found to be much more resilient than had been supposed. The development of a common European identity will therefore not succeed in the foreseeable future. This needs further explanation, because after so many successes and such great upheavals, it is not yet perfectly clear why the European Union is still in search of a self. Nonetheless, one was from the beginning quite certain of having chosen the right course: if economic unification could be achieved, then everything else would fall into place. Yet, to date, there has still not been any definite development of a European identity. In order to see precisely what this means, we must first outline the meaning of individual and collective identity (Part One). We will then propose ten theses about how the EU stands in relation to this question of identity, which means of achieving an identity it chose, and which problems must be faced in pursuit of this strategy (Part Two).

1 Identity and the representation of identity –
a process with surprises!

Nothing seems so easy at first sight, and so difficult upon further reflection, as to say who one is. And even if one enjoyed a consistent self-image, one would still have to persuade everybody else to accept it, because as recipients and audience, they are not without some importance. The difficulty is that identity is not a once for all granted reality, but:

1) it is composed of various constituents or aspects of identity called «partial identities» (i.e. the problem of complexity);
2) it is an ongoing process throughout one's whole life (i.e. the problem of provisionality);
3) in attempting to describe it, one does not feel that one's knowledge of oneself is sufficient (i.e. the problem of transcendence).

1.1 Identity and the framing of the self

Whoever thinks about one's own existence and claims a certain form for it, must not forget the question of time. Because one cannot understand and evaluate one's self without taking into consideration who and how one was previously, it follows that identity involves the totality of one's self-images in all of its inter-connections. This is probably what was meant by Erikson (1966) when he described the self as the ability to experience one's self as the continuity and confluence of partial and provisional versions.

At the same time, it is irritating but sociologically obvious that the production of such self-images does not occur entirely autonomously. At least, the autonomy is limited by circumstance or «situated». In order to recognize myself, I need the other. The self is always directed to an audience, and through this, the view of the self-image returns. Identity is therefore simultaneously bound up with evaluation by others. There is a connection between recognising oneself (the concept of) the «I», being recognized, and being accepted («Me»). As Mead has shown, there is a permanent balance between them (which constitutes the «self»).

Within this process, certain partners are more important than others for one's self-confidence. Through them i.e. sociologically speaking by the hindering or the support of certain reference groups, as also through our grounding in space, time, culture, law, language, customs, religion, and so on, we come to know what we are, what we can be, and what we should be (secondary social «fixing»). Identity is therefore not only a particular personal style, but also a reflexive act which occurs within a context of interacting stimuli and reactions. Although, or even because, we are in a continuing process of interaction with others, identity can be described as the sum of our knowledge of our reference points (Weidenfeld 1984: 10), which includes both the private and public spheres. As is well known, Elias calls this the «We-I-balance» (1987: 209ff.).

It is part of the dynamics of this balance of identity not only that it has to be continuously negotiated according to chance encounters, but that it also employs strategies of presentation. Because the reactions of the vis-à-vis in the social environment are never entirely predictable or consistent, everybody will have an interest in portraying himself as far as possible with a distinctive profile. This is the point of Goffman's «impression management» (1969) and «frame analysis» (1977).

«Frames» refer to schemata of interpretation for the identification of events (or people with their self-images), and they therefore promote inter-subjective perception. Generally, we tend to assume a strongly regulated and predictable world and the rational behaviour of human beings, so that the elementary strategies of reality construction (primary frames) need not be discussed at any given time. Our everyday sense of security («natural attitude»: Schütz) disappears rather quickly, though, if these expectations are not satisfied, whether intentionally or by chance, i.e. if the events are ambiguous (modulations), or if deceptions become apparent (fabrications). In this case, one needs a precisely profiled self-image and a corresponding representation (performance), which will not always succeed, because one can never be sure how the intended performance will be received by the audience (Goffman 1969).

1.2 Collective identity and performance compulsion

Within a group, as in an individual, there is a double performance compulsion. On the one hand, members need to obtain a feeling of security by belonging to the group; on the other hand, the group needs to convey its collective identity to its social environment. Frequently, ethnic, religious, national or other political memberships, serve as acceptable embodiments and affirmations of established traditions, as responses to historically changing circumstances, material conditions, and changing discourses. Especially in unsettled times, it is important to construct and preserve the image (face) of a group or community.

Once more, within the group, the questions inevitably arise: Who are we? Where did we come from? Where are we going? These questions are a constant of all political life (Weidenfeld 1984: 9). Materials for the construction of collective identity are symbols, values, and norms, which define the vital community and distinguish it from all others. This kind of self-description has to be re-discovered by each new generation, i.e. the members of the group have to be made conscious of it, it has to be named and anchored. The collective self, like that of the individual, is therefore in a continuous process of construction and articulation. Historical events, geographical features, material conditions of life, cultural particularities, and political experiences and institutions are never given as «objective» circumstances, but first have to find the acceptance of the group. This is the task and the sphere of activity of collective actors («performers») that make use of a certain inward- and outward-directed dramaturgy on various levels of relationship, community, country, nation and religion.

By modelling (and stereotyping) the presumed or real characteristics in distinction from others (both within and without of the group), an emotional bonding between the individual and the actual group or community is achieved. The success of the collective formation of identity depends essentially on the success of fixing these constructions («frames») by means of specific institutions within the various reference-groups, and being able to introduce them into everyday speech so that they assume the nature of something unquestionable, unchangeable and natural (the principle of the naturalization of the artificial). By means of this social establishment, a knowledge of certain reference points, and therewith a horizon of comprehension, is mediated to the actual recipients.

1.3 Collective self-representation between inclusion and exclusion

It is one of the peculiarities and paradoxes of both individual and collective self-description that it needs not only the other as adressee, but that it must also give itself an image and profile in opposition to the other. It would seem that identity is not to be defined as something positive in itself, but only in distinction from others.

Ethnic and national aspects of identity, for example, not only produce emotional membership, but are at the same time an element of distinction from, of tension between, or even pose a threat towards those who do not share in those aspects (within as without). This is connected with the fact that the work of constructing each identity or We-(I-) assertion is necessarily a binary construction: the function of binding together or inclusion makes possible social relationships with other people on the basis of pre-defined common features, while a function of difference or exclusion perceives these relationships as what distinguishes those within the group from those who are, on this definition, outside it («non-members»).

Identity is therefore necessarily drawn into a dialectic between inclusion and exclusion, for those who are identical are only recognizable by being defined in contrast to those who are not identical. In that very moment, when the integrity of relations is constituted for the activity of the community, the basis for possible exclusions is marked out – whether according to the factors of space, or ethnicity, or race, or history, etc. – and it is irrelevant whether these self-portrayals are real or merely imagined.

Concurrently with the question of identity, another problem arises: how to fix, to maintain, or to discard boundaries. Such boundaries can be exaggerated (e.g. nationalism), or kept more open (e.g. European integration), but they are basically flexible. They can be hastened or postponed, kept slack within one sub-system while being emphasized within other sub-systems, sometimes be forgotten, and then accentuated once more. «Inclusion» and «exclusion» are therefore flexible strategies which are used to designate exaggerations of values inwards and, in a negative sense, outwards (labelling effect). Quite often, the basis for the use of these strategies is rather arbitrary, because the «inherited space» cannot always be precisely delineated. The boundaries or distinctions between ethnic group and race are often as fluid as those between ethnicity and nation, and one often encounters inappropriate categorising and mythologising or racial-cultural redefinitions of originally political communities (see Weber 1972: 234ff.).

This does not prevent the stranger who is by definition excluded from being involved in processes of integration to be positively «functional» for this very process, and, indeed, the mobilization of such ethnic or cultural labelling to this end is often quite successful. This occurs especially in times of general insecurity. Typically, crises are welcome opportunities for the formulation of strategies of inclusion and exclusion (which are justified by the location of the «actual» causes and the «really responsible» groups or persons within or without).

Crises are often precipitated precisely in order to mobilise such strategies. Yet even without this trick, it is obvious that the compulsion to consolidate the self which results from old and new socializations produces enduring strategies of identity management. Therefore, the institution building between attempts at unification and the desire to differentiate, centralization and federalization, integration, inclusion and separation, nation and regional autonomy, framing and reframing, is never really completed.

The EU is involved in a particular way in this identity dialectic. Its history is one of continuous disagreement between economic and political union, between small and larger geographical definitions of Europe, between the opening and closing of borders, between centralization and federalization, between globalization and a sense of «Europeanness», but also between re-nationalization and regionalization.

2 «European Identity» between inclusion and exclusion

The problem of the collective framing of the identity of the EU can be illustrated with ten theses:

2.1 Until now, the EU has concentrated on the economic mechanism of inclusion

As is well known, the present EU emerged out of the EEC, and this background remains a significant factor. The aim then was to break down the economic barriers between a certain number of member-states in order to create one single large internal market. But this could only be achieved if administrative obstacles of all kinds, including customs and quotas, could be eliminated. Therefore, in order not to manipulate the competition, commercial law and trade regulations had to be modified or adapted.

Behind these developments lies the idea of a functional integration which is to lead to further inter-governmental agreements and, eventually, to a political integration due to the logic of the domino effect. A system of integration was employed which began with the easiest steps, i.e. the economic arrangements, from which it was expected that a greater sense of political community would emerge. The success of this process can certainly be seen in the case of the achievement of the European single market. It is also obvious that with economic integration, pressure between member-states to make tax, budget and financial agreements has increased. The EEC and the establishment of a single currency show that the original idea of the market mechanism was not mistaken.

At the same time, it is striking that important aspects of shared politics – social, internal and external politics, to name but a few – have thus far been excluded from the process of integration and have led to only isolated agreements. One rather has the impression that the process of integration will always be more difficult, the more it involves the political sphere. It is not so surprising, then, if only a limited «spill-over effect» from the economic to the political process of integration has really been felt.

2.2 The economic process of integration only exercises limited political influence

In the course of its history, the EU has been forced to deviate from its programme of integration on more than one occasion, and this reveals the limitations of its theory of the economic mechanism of integration. The extension of the EEC to include Greece, Portugal, and Spain was an early breach of principle: for the first time, members were accepted into the community for political reasons who had not satisfied the economic requirements.

These new members were, at the time of their acceptance, by no means equal and competitive market partners, though this was then precisely the condition for EEC membership. Through this extension, in fact, the principle was stood on its head. Political considerations, such as the encouragement of democratization, now had priority, whilst the economic process of change and adaptation was relegated to long transition periods. To date, this policy has only been successful in the case of Spain, and then, only partially. Spain is also the country which profits most from EU financial assistance (European Structural Fund). Perhaps the combination of political co-operation and economic integration suffices to guarantee prosperity and security. But, as Aron had already demonstrated in 1964, this combination proves to be insufficient for more far-reaching political integration or even for the establishment of a European state.

This problem will increase as former eastern-bloc countries are accepted into the EU. In such cases, the original conditions for inclusion are completely ignored. Similarly, the economic indicators of the new applicants for membership – Poland, the Czech Republic, and Hungary – fall far short of the EU standard, so they are clearly not being integrated on economic grounds. The difficulty with this project is that, not only are the limited common funds being extensively exploited and the allocation of transferable funds is resulting from this, which should ordinarily be associated with a demonstrable improvement in performance – a condition which is rejected by the benefitting southern European member-states – but the already highly complicated and delicate voting procedures between the fifteen members are also being threatened.

The formula that expansion will inevitably place stress upon the institutions, cannot conceal the fact that now, all the weaker members, including the new applicants, will be over-powered by the more powerful member-states. The latter wish to work more closely together in order to prescribe the direction of integration to the new members (compliance with the so called «acquis communautaire», i.e. the already attained achievements of the integration process). In any case, the possibility of political integration will paradoxically be made even more difficult as a result of this political tendency of the EU.

2.3 The EU thus produces more problems of exclusion

As the economic mechanisms of integration at best have only an indirect influence, one can no longer assume that political integration will inevitably result from them. On the contrary, political integration is, in effect, almost assumed to be an accomplished reality.

But this is an unproven assumption. According to this assumption, the member-states have already reached a consensus about Europe, without having clearly decided upon the concrete establishment of institutions. And if necessary, common market interests can be subordinated to political priorities. Yet such a reversal of policy was not planned by the founders of the EEC. They knew that the inclusion of completely unequal members would lead to the establishment of new discriminations or boundaries within the community, and so to concealed or open exclusions. This can be illustrated with some examples.

If extremely unequal partners – powerful and weak – come to be associated within a union, two results are possible. In the first scenario, the powerful attempt to dominate the weaker partners by retaining control of the purse strings and by extending their domination of the market, whereupon the weaker partners feel deceived in respect of their interests and abandon their loyalty to the union.

The example of German unification shows that this can happen even if the more powerful partner offers considerable financial assistance. The attitudes underlying such patronage were so provocative that a long-lasting cultural and group-psychological tendency of self-exclusion followed.

In the second scenario, the weaker partners come to accept their position – that they will never achieve the degree of efficiency of the stronger partners – and then develop strategies of maximum exploitation of the stronger partners. In turn, the powerful partners will combine to resist these strategies, thereby further increasing the inequalities between the members of the union. Incidentally, this characterization is one of the reasons why waves of immigration of people from economically weaker to economically stronger states, lead quickly to considerable oppositions – racism, xenophobia, and the exclusion of the foreign cultures of immigrants. A strong and confident sense of political identity is essential for the reining in of these tensions, but to date we have not seen such firm handling within the EU. Kielmannsegg (1996) also pointed out that the fact of the existence of democratic majority decisions in political controversies is only accepted if «there is a consciousness of shared political identity which includes both majorities and minorities, and which prevents majority decisions from being regarded as heteronomy». This observation is also applicable to the relationship between powerful and weaker members of the EU.

2.4 Tendencies of disintegration and exclusion endanger the EU and strengthen the nationalist «revival»

The still unresolved problems of inclusion and exclusion within the EU could easily lead to a deepening crisis in the process of integration. Thus far, we have been able to see that the idea of the nation-state has been carved out of hardwood, and it has not yet disappeared as a political factor even after forty years' history of efforts toward integration and ensuing losses of national competences.

It is clearly observable that in western Europe, anxiety in face of the next stages of integration has increased and has thus resulted in the national state once more styling itself as the anchor of a common collective identity. But the EU was founded precisely in order to prevent this. It has not been successful in obliging the nation-states to relinquish their position as guarantors of collective identity (including security, the articulation of interests, the ensuring of prosperity, the symbolising of cultural unity).

In eastern Europe, things are different. There, the nationalist movement is historically more recent because it was suppressed for decades beneath the heel of the USSR. Following the disintegration of the hegemony of the USSR, it has once more become possible to follow the longed for path to nationhood. What the nation-states in the West had achieved much earlier should now likewise be possible in central and eastern Europe. The arguments in favour of the nationalist revival are the same everywhere – excepting the aims of welfare, the achievement of which is rather hoped for by joining the EU of the rich. Otherwise, it was not obvious why, in spite of this momentous opportunity for the acquisition of national identity, the eastern states should immediately steer a different course towards trans-nationality. It is therefore not yet clear how strong is the intention to integrate of the eastern states which are applying for membership.

In the event of the EU encountering another crisis due to extension without real or effective integration, the tendency of national states in both the West and the East to go their separate ways will increase – which is, as we have said, precisely what the foundation of the EU aimed at avoiding. Paradoxically, the need for national identification and sovereignty increases not only when political and economic inequalities increase, but equally when processes of levelling in Europe increase. Korte (1993: 27) wrote: «The more that diversity in Europe is eroded, the more a feeling of disquiet towards integration increases. Western Europe has long been a production- and market-community. But people are resisting the levelling of their national cultures. The more confused and controversial the common European future seems to people, the more the idea of nations recurs in discussions about Europe.» Such nationalist tendencies employ a double strategy against the EU: on the one hand, they affirm the economic integration, but on the other hand, they style themselves once again as representatives of political-cultural identity. National governments are thus able to remain the central agents of collective self-representation. In the case of the new members, nothing else is to be expected.

2.5 The reason for the deepening problems of the EU is its lack of identity management

The EU is now beginning to suffer from the history of its foundation. Initially, it seemed logical to use market interests as a motor for European unification. However, further political developments did not automatically follow, nor could they have occurred, for down to the present day, the several European states have only been able to agree to co-operate in opposition to something, but not in order to achieve something positive for themselves (Korte 1993: 27).

The history of the post-war period shows that the EEC and the EU achieved their unity and self-definition only in response to perceived threats and enemies from outside, but not from any positive attempt to define criteria of political, social, and cultural togetherness.

Particular tendencies towards exclusion without intensive efforts to achieve inclusion, do not work. This is now being recognized, because the perceived external threats have disappeared. And to date, the EU has not discovered a new sense of vocation which is independent of any perception of external opposition.

It has often been overlooked that interests and ideas, according to Weber, are closely connected with each other. Political, and even economic, interests are by no means a priori, but are rather narratives of foregoing or presupposed political-cultural self-portrayals, processes of reflections, and suggestions (Reese-Schäfer 1997: 321). Today, many people are warning that the EU does not offer anything to people, especially to younger people, and is therefore in danger of not achieving its political aims. Recently, Jack Lang (1998: 63) called upon people «to give Europe a soul» once more – a literary formula meaning that sooner or later, a European self-consciousness must be developed. Pfetsch (1998: 8) has sketched six means of constructing a European basis of values: the participation of the citizen, a philosophical anchoring (e.g. in classical and later antique philosophy, in Christianity, in the Enlightenment), the humanistic ideal of education, the balance of interests within the welfare state, and the legal and cultural community. Only through these means can Europe as a whole achieve something of the dignity which is appropriate to the modern national state and which has made it so vital.

The nation-states have also understood that politics per se and a politics of identity are intertwined. History shows that these states have worked intensively to manifest their common self-consciousness in certain fields of activity and institutions by deliberate use of symbols and socialising agents. In our terminology, this is precisely a politics of inclusion. At the same time, the EU as a single entity or group of national states, has failed to establish any equivalent shared sense of self-consciousness, and it should therefore not be surprised if it receives only diffuse support (Immerfall and Sobisch 1997: 36). It has become merely a community of profit, perhaps also a fortuitous political community, but by no means a real community of values and experiences. Because the EU as an all-embracing identifying point of reference does not exist, future decision-making will be permanently endangered, and it will fall short of the goal of limiting national profiles. If majority decisions are to be recognized and accepted by all, including the weaker states, and if a policy of balance between the powerful and the weaker states in Europe is to be successful, then it is obvious that the various short-term interests of the nation-states must be subordinated to the common goals of the EU, and even that this re-prioritization is to be considered worthy of support. Otherwise, how should a welfare politics – such a considerable transfer of national resources from the powerful to the weaker states – even be possible? From this, it is obvious that the EU member states need still more to bring themselves together in a cultural unity which transcends a preoccupation with national profit-making.

2.6 Vis à vis cultural policies, the EU relies upon the regions in order to avoid dealing with the problems of nation-states

In order to avoid the nation-state and its position as guarantor of cultural identity, the EU has invented the «Europe of Regions». For the EU recognizes the cultural vacuum and the historical weakness of the modern idea of Europe, and the consequent power of the nation-states, and it therefore seeks to circumvent the latter and to anchor an ersatz guarantor of the historical memory and collective self-consciousness. The EU expects that the cultural vacuum will be compensated for by the cultures of the smaller geographical and ethnic entities of the regions. Regions are seen as being appropriate channels for the guaranteeing of effective membership, security, and sense, as over against the imposing yet remote, impersonal machinery of the state. In people's local space, our sensual culture should be dominant. Identity becomes more tangible through folk lore, shared customs, dialects, «Volksgeschichte», local memorabilia, stories and traditions. Everything is emotional, and draws its continuing life from the unmediated knowledge of individuals, groups, festivals and temporal rituals, and the continuity of time and space. Place, buildings, the physical settlement of the local community (private and public areas, etc.), and even the climate, all belong to the regional sphere of experience. People feel more closely bound to their immediate environment than to more distant places, which are, in relative terms, devoid of significance.

Regions, with their cultural distinctiveness – their ethnic groups with their bases in shared language and a «natural» way of life, and the resilience of their cultural habits – should be more deeply appreciated as crystalization points of things held in common, common desires, and inner coherences. If opportunities to dominate, as within Europe, are newly distributed, territorial identity (or «historical territoriality») becomes a political resource. So anxieties about a competition between or a submersion of cultures, about domination and loss of homeland (as a result of globalization and Europeanization), might prove to be unfounded.

Through such an emphasis, one hopes to see, then, on the one hand, the EU relieved of the charge that it is remote from its citizens; on the other hand, the nation-states relinquishing some of their competences in favour of their constituent parts – the regions. National citizenship is obviously not to be dissolved trans-nationally: rather, through a deepening appreciation of the ability of the regions to make decisions, a new approach to sub-national, and at the same time, European inclusion, is to be attempted. If the capacities of cultural identity manufacture can be harnessed at a regional level, and at the same time, political and economic powers of decision are at least partly transferred upwards,

then, so it is hoped, the original idea of a de-nationalization of Europe might
be achieved.

2.7 Regionalization is not a solution to the problem, but only a transfer of it

The regionalized Europe has thus far failed to achieve any communal reality.
It has not even been clearly defined what a European region is. This failure results from political indolence, while many different administrative entities
smaller than the level of a state have simply been declared to be regions. Some
of these entities are, for example, German states («Länder»), historical nationalities (Spain), French Départements, and districts. These 180 or so areas, because of their considerably differing degrees of competence, cannot possibly
build the longed-for «Europe of Regions».

Furthermore, these regions inevitably disappoint the hopes which are placed
in them, because as a result of these differences, they do not all enjoy equal representation, or representation at all, within the organs of the EU. Stronger regions are well represented, the weaker ones are not. The European Commission supports regionalization, but for the moment intends nothing more than
the integration of the weaker regions into the European lobby. Naturally, the
EU need not be concerned about the stronger states. But it wishes to help the
weaker states, to compensate them for the disadvantages which they encounter due to the single market, by skillful manoeuvring in Brussels. This concern
crystallises, for example, in the question of where to locate new investments.
As markets expand, the capacity to compete becomes increasingly, for the
companies, cities, districts, and larger sub-national entities, a question of advantages of location, that is to say, the compensation of the disadvantages. This
is the function of the concept of the region: it is a means of placing one's self
well in the competition for premier locations. Apart from this role, however,
the regions, with the help of the Committee of the Regions, have only a con-
sulting function, and therefore do not relieve the EU of the demands of the
national states. Therefore, it is easy for the member-states to adapt themselves
flexibly to this situation. It seems obvious that the nation-states do not feel
themselves to be curtailed in respect of their competences by the regions.

In another sense, too, regionalization is not a solution to the problem of cultural identity in Europe, but only transfers it. If the regions are economically
strong, if they are successful in their identity management, and if they are well-
provided with political administrative rights, then they show a tendency for
mini-nationalism, as is exemplified by Scotland (see Mccrone 1996: 42ff.) and
Catalonia (see Moreno and Arriba 1996: 79ff.), and so the barriers are strength-

ened between the regions, and between such sub-nations and the actual nations. The conflict between the Spanish state and its «historical nations» – regions in the EU's sense – mirrors this tendency towards double exclusion. To
date, neither Spain nor the EU has found a way to channel this inherent dynamics. For it obviously fails to restrict the stronger regions mainly to cultural
identity management; consequently, there could emerge a new problem of nationality within the traditional nation-states. This tendency is also now endemic
to central and eastern Europe (see Schwarz 1997; Buchowski 1997).

A superficial regionalization therefore does not solve the problem, any more
than a strong regionalization will solve it. In either case, the question of inclusion and exclusion increases the problem, which to date has been a problem at
the national level. Stronger regions tend, like nations, to assume a more central role and thus a certain degree of superiority within the EU. Weaker regions are then obliged to accept a more marginal position and, lacking a sense
of belonging, tend to attempt to achieve more autonomy. Through the regionalization of Europe, the problem of integration might become even more critical and more pervasive. At least, as important as it is, regionalization can only
make use of its integrative power if it is developed within an already existing
framework of identity.

2.8 The EU therefore needs a new methodology of cultural self-definition

The construction of Europe has for too long been governed by the expectation
that its cultural definition would somehow result from the workings of the
other sub-systems, and too little attention has therefore been given to the symbolic level of reference. It was left unclear how the single market should achieve this, and how it could prevent the loss of its legitimation.

It is well-known that large spaces produce opaque abstraction and detract from
any sense of solidarity. Through the complexity of the inter-governmental
agreements, the opportunities of the regions to participate are even fewer than
is the case at a national level. Consequently, Europe, in the perception of its
citizens, reduces itself to an institution for the organization of competition and
financial transfers. Other functions of the state are outside general experience.
It then becomes increasingly difficult to extend the basis of loyalty from the
nation-state to the wider community, so that nothing other than the EU takes
this loyalty away from its original basis of legitimation, and yet it must do so.

Modern community development in the West encounters this in an unfortu-
nate way. The connection between globalization and post-modernity produces

a world picture of radical surprise and openness. One can only survive or be functionally adapted by resisting determinations of any kind. This attitude supports, on the one hand, a de-institutionalization, on the other hand, privatization to an ill-advised and cynical degree (see Bauman 1993). In the case of the EU, this can mean that the great vision of European unity disappears over the horizon of possibilities before it can be realized. Although we still see a general affirmation of the idea of Europe, we notice in the concrete case a considerable lack of acceptance of and support for this idea, especially concerning particular decisions. The Euro-barometer reveals a dangerous lack of interest not in Europe in general, but in European politics (see Hübner-Funk 1992: 222). There is no particular interest, either, in an extension and deepening of its unity. If it became necessary to make demonstrable sacrifices in order to consolidate the unity of Europe, it is all but certain that people's support for Europe would evaporate altogether. It is obvious that one has failed to anticipate that, despite all the economic successes, the process of European unification could find itself stuck half way down the road.

Although European integration is based on considerable shared cultural foundations, these foundations have almost never been formulated. The integrating bonds which could help to balance the loads and offset the disintegrating tendencies are therefore weakened. It is not, as one is so often tempted to believe, a divergence of ideas from which Europe suffers, but the lack of binding force of the concepts (Weidenfeld 1984: 9). A rethinking is only hesitantly beginning. The Maasstricht agreement of 1991 for the first time formulates conditions of acceptance for new members which embrace more than merely economic criteria.

It has long been believed that one could avoid further trouble by placing confidence in the formula «Diversity within Unity». But this formula fails to adequately explain anything beyond the fact that Europe cannot be constructed by pathetic formulas of unity and inappropriate homogenizations. Although it is necessary to formulate catalogues of values which make inclusion and exclusion, and therefore the finding of identity possible at all, in the area of culture in the wider sense, only loose frameworks envisaging a trans-national, but not a supra-national and unitary identification, are being brought into play. Anything else, given the historical starting point, would be unrealistic and unacceptable. In this sense, paradoxically enough, support for the single region also supports the unity of Europe (Lang 1998).

2.9 The identity management of Europe needs a new organization of the system of education

To date, Europe has – with the exception of the Council of Europe – developed very few forums for the identification of its cultural identity. The Council of Ministers has to date pursued a different concept. The parliament has few powers of initiative and can – more or less – ratify the decisions of the council.

The media, and therefore the public, are fascinated rather by globalization. The EU is simply not an interesting subject. From their side, then, no «Euro-socialization» (Mann 1998: 203) is occurring. The example of German unification shows that Interrail and Interfood do not make a European community. Neither a transfer of financial resources, nor the shared language and history, could really bring together both parts of the country. There also needed to be an exchange of information and understanding, from which interests, intimacies, sympathies, and feelings of having things in common develop. Integration in this sense is a learning process on different levels. And such a learning process needs to be guaranteed by sustained efforts for the improvement of the education system.

Apart from inter-school exchanges, there is very little effort at improvement, for the schools have always been closely linked with the national government. The information about Europe which is available in schools is, to say the least, poor. There is no teaching of a deeper knowledge about other countries, nor about Europe as a whole. One example of this is the history programme in schools which, until now, has been unable to liberate itself from the blinkers of the national perspective. In a list of topics of general interest presented to a sample of adults in the different European countries, Europe only ranks in the 30th place. Less than 10% of people questioned were able to name all of the member-states of the EU (see Weidenfeld and Piepenschneider 1987; Hübner-Funk 1992: 218ff.; Kommission der Europäischen Gemeinschaften 1991). This is already a declaration of the bankruptcy of the integration concept.

Equally dramatic is the problem of the language courses. To discuss tourism is not to address the real questions. To organize a Europe of interpreters might be possible in Brussels, but not across the whole of Europe. Switzerland – faced with and experienced in questions of cultural differentiation – realizes, too, that the education towards polyglot citizens has to be emphasized in order to prevent tendencies of separation of the regions.

Tolerance and solidarity are needed in Europe not simply because of its sad history. There is, potentially, always a certain tension in contacts with foreigners. At present, xenophobia in Germany is directed outwards against the culturally foreign (e.g. immigrants, asylum seekers, and immigrants of German origin who return to settle in Germany). But inward-directed xenophobia has not disappeared – it is merely dormant. Again, it is not so long ago that the other Europeans were perceived as culturally distant as it is the case now with the Turkish population.

The need for the increasing mobility of people as part of the single market cannot be achieved without respecting the regulations and without normalising and relaxing contacts with the neighbouring member-states. But appreciation, helping each other, and closeness, is more than that. In the course of the Mezzogiorno-problem, Italy experienced just how latent the danger of de-solidarization can be. An extended world has to learn to more than tolerate the inevitable proximity of the foreigner in one's living space.

2.10   A trans-national politics of identity involves working towards a multi-layered identity

All human beings and constructions must strive towards a definition of their respective selves. The EU has not yet found its definition. It has to decide how it is going to define itself, and then it must anchor this image clearly in the minds of its members. One of its difficulties is that it cannot demand any priority or exclusivism. (The latter caused the outburst of extreme nationalism everywhere in the world in the course of the 20th century.)

Every pursuit of particular goals by a collective is necessarily a limitation both inwards and outwards. One only has to ask how strict or loose this limitation is intended to be, for often identities, despite their being bound up with specific denotations, are not exclusive but compatible with other self-images.

Human beings always live in tension with various such definitions, obligations, and loyalties (family, friends, occupation, politics, leisure time, etc.). This is similarly true for the European collective. It should be possible, then, and it is certainly desirable, to find a balance between the various bonds (place, region, nation, Europe, world).

The question therefore is whether it is possible to achieve a European identity which does not inevitably end with separations – e.g. between a sense of homeland, national consciousness, and cosmopolitanism. This is a question of self-discipline (i.e. civilized identity).

To date, the nation-state has assumed that it is entitled to claim to be the only collective vessel and co-ordinate of the sub-national part-identities (Marden 1997: 60). The EU attempts to extend the insular consensus, and therefore either has to construct an alternative collective vessel or itself to become this vessel. This extension can be achieved by striving not for an exclusive but for a multi-layered identity – at least a tri-identity between region, nation, and Europe.

In order to make these identities compatible with each other, one needs political structures which tolerate and support such a complex development of identity (Reese-Schäfer 1997: 326f.). In this very sense, and not in a sense of relativized values, the European identity is basically multicultural. The bracketing together of different levels will only be accepted if part-identities and self-identities are allowed to remain overt.

Despite all the piling up of instances and self-images, this process still retains a considerable degree of ambiguity. As was shown at the outset, it is a process which is inevitably held in tension between inclusion and exclusion, rigidity and flexibility, extension and limitation of the boundaries. It might be the necessary task of every instance of identity management, at whichever level, to somehow bring these opposite poles together. The way in which this bringing together succeeds will determine the vitality and even the very ability of the European union to survive. Let me conclude with a recent statement of Michael Mann (1998: 205):

> «Euro(-land) is much more a network of upper social classes and elites than of the masses. Yet even they are not specifically committed to it alone. … Euro is a rather specialized set of power networks, formed as a response to rather specialized social interests and constituencies. Though all «societies» are composed of multiple, overlapping, intersecting networks of interaction, Euro seems especially to lack overall internal cohesion and external closure. Doubtless, it will gain both in the foreseeable future. Perhaps it will eventually attain the moderate degree of cohesion and closure attained by nation-states during the relatively transnational phases of modern development – in the period after 1815, for example, or around 1900. My own guess is that Euro will be less than this, less salient as a network of interaction than networks constituted both by the North as a whole and by the more successful nation-states of the world.»

Will this outcome prove to be enough in the next century?

References

Ambrosius, Gerold (1996). *Wirtschaftsraum Europa. Vom Ende der National-ökonomien.* Frankfurt.

Aron, Raymond (1964). «Old Nations, New Europe», *Daedalus* 93(1).

Bauman, Zygmunt (1993). *Postmodern Ethics.* Oxford.

Buchowski, Michal (1997). «Neue kollektive Identitäten in Mittel- und Ost-europa», *WeltTrends* 15: 25–37.

Elias, Norbert (1987). *Die Gesellschaft der Individuen.* Frankfurt.

Erikson, Erik H. (1966). *Identität und Lebenszyklus.* Frankfurt.

Goffman, Erving (1969). *Wir alle spielen Theater. Die Selbstdarstellung im All-tag.* München.

Goffman, Erving (1977). *Rahmen-Analyse. Ein Versuch über die Organisation von Alltagserfahrungen.* Frankfurt.

Hübner-Funk, Sybille (1992). «Quo vadis, Jugend Europas? Visionen ihrer ‹eu-ropäischen Identität›», *Berliner Journal für Soziologie* 2: 215–227.

Immerfall, Stefan und Andreas Sobisch (1997). «Europäische Integration und europäische Identität. Die Europäische Union im Bewusstsein ihrer Bür-ger», *Aus Politik und Zeitgeschichte* B10/97: 25–37.

Kielmannsegg, Peter Graf (1996). «Integration und Demokratie», pp. 47–71 in Jachtenfuchs, Markus und Beate Kohler-Koch (Hg.). *Europäische Integra-tion.* Opladen.

Kommission der Europäischen Gemeinschaften (Hg.) (1991). *The Young Europeans in 1990.* Brussels.

Korte, Karl-Rudolf (1993). «Das Dilemma des Nationalstaats in Westeuropa. Zur Identitätsproblematik der europäischen Integration», *Aus Politik und Zeitgeschichte* B14/93: 21–28.

Lang, Jack (September 24, 1998). «Eurovisionen», *Die Zeit* 40.

Mann, Michael (1998). «Is there a Society called Euro?» pp. 184–207 in Axt-mann, R. (Ed.). *Globalization and Europe.* London.

Marden, Peter (1997). «Geographies of dissent: globalization, identity and the nation», *Political Geography* 16: 37–64.

McCrone, David (1996). «Autonomy and national identity in stateless nations: Scotland, Catalonia and Quebec», *Scottish Affairs* 17: 42–48.

Moreno, Luis and Ana Arriba (1996), «Dual identity in autonomous Catalo-nia», *Scottish Affairs* 17: 78–97.

Pfetsch, Frank R. (1998). «Die Problematik der europäischen Identität», *Aus Politik und Zeitgeschichte* B25-26/98: 3–9.

Reese-Schäfer, Walter (1997). «Supranationale oder transnationale Identität – zwei Modelle kultureller Integration in Europa», *Politische Vierteljahres-schrift* 38: 318–329.

Schütz, Alfred (1972). «Das Problem der Rationalität in der sozialen Welt», Ders., *Gesammelte Aufsätze Bd. 2.* Den Haag: 22–50.

Schütz, Alfred (1974). *Der sinnhafte Aufbau der sozialen Welt. Eine Einleitung in die verstehende Soziologie.* Frankfurt.

Schwarz, Siegfried (1997). «Von nationaler zu europäischer Identität», *Welt-Trends* 15: 51–63.

Weber, Max (1972). *Wirtschaft und Gesellschaft.* Tübingen.

Weidenfeld, Werner (1984). «Was ist die Idee Europas?», *Aus Politik und Zeitgeschichte* B23-24/84: 3–11.

Weidenfeld, Werner und Martina Piepenschneider (1987). *Jugend in Europa. Die Einstellungen der jungen Generation in der Bundesrepublik Deutschland zur europäischen Einigung.* Bonn.

Voiceless Submission or Deliberate Choice?
European Integration and the Relation between
National and European Identity

Max Haller

The coming into existence of the European Union can be considered as a large scale experiment in social and political integration with historically unique features: (1) it is one of the largest in terms of the numbers of countries and people involved; (2) it is occurring peacefully, with the voluntary agreement of all participating governments; (3) it involves only states with democratic systems of government. All these characteristics indicate that the process of European integration must be considered as a secular achievement on this continent which has experienced massive and destructive wars in the last hundred years. Yet, it is also clear that this process shows characteristics which might raise doubts about its success and about the supposedly positive consequences which are expected to flow from it. Given the very different consequences of other large scale experiments in political and socio-economic integration, it is essential to pinpoint potentially problematic consequences. In this contribution, I will focus on one possible reason for outcomes which might not be expected by many of the actors involved in this process. This is the fact that the governments and the people of different European nation-states in part expect rather different outcomes from the same process of integration.

This chapter consists of two parts. In the first part, the issues of national identity and European integration are discussed from a more general point of view. For this purpose, the concepts of «nation» and «national identity» are introduced and defined, as well as their relation to «European identity». In the second part, a typology of the different outlooks of the individual nation-states and their citizens towards the European Union is developed. Empirical data from different sources, large-scale international population surveys, results of Referenda, official declarations are used in order to show the existence of these differing expectations regarding European integration. In the concluding remarks, the implications of these findings for the further development of the European Union are discussed.

1   National identity and its relation to European integration

1.1 The present-day relevance of the concepts of nation and national identity

In recent decades, fundamental transformations have been occurring in the social, economic and political situation of Europe, its nation-states and regions.
With the Maastricht *Treaty for the European Union* (1992), Western European
integration reached a new stage. The full realization of the «four freedoms» in
the market sphere – unlimited exchange and movement of goods, services, labour and capital within the European Union – and the introduction of the monetary union with the common currency, the Euro, at the end of the decade,
constitute epochal achievements which will profoundly reshape the future of
this continent. In Eastern Europe, the late Eighties and early Nineties brought
the downfall of the communist regimes and the removal of the Iron Curtain
which had constituted an unnatural barrier running through the heart of this
continent. While these historical events have been occurring in Europe, a
world-wide process of globalization has also been taking place which means
that private and business travel and tourism, economic relations and transactions, cultural and scientific communication through mass media, Internet and
other means, are beginning to embrace the whole world. As a consequence, the
autonomy and sovereignty of nation-states is being significantly undermined,
and many people begin to think about alternatives to this globalization (Galli
1991; Knieper 1991; Wehner 1992).

In spite of these developments, however, there is no indication that the problems of national autonomy and independence are disappearing from the agendas of Europe and of the present-day world as a whole. The downfall of the
communist regimes in the Czech Republic, Yugoslavia and the Soviet Union
has led to the emergence of more than a dozen new nation-states, some of
which were prepared to fight for their independence. But even in Western
Europe, movements for more local political and cultural autonomy, or even for
the independence and secession of whole regions – in Spain, Belgium, Scotland and Italy – are gaining ground. Strong subnational regions, such as Bava-
ria and Catalonia, are quite critical not only of their national capitals, but also
of all trends toward a new centralization at the EU-level in Brussels. The process of regional, ethnic and national revival is therefore not simply a remnant
of traditional patterns of localism and parochialism, but must be considered as
a concomitant of the process of modernization itself. Many aspects of this process lead towards a revival of regional, ethnic and national movements. We can
mention here, for example, the expansion of middle and higher education to
include larger segments of the general population; the revival by scientists, his-

torians and intellectuals of traditional languages, customs and cultures (which had often already passed out of use); the increasing political education and critical participation (or abstention) of citizens in political affairs; and the growing competition of nation-states, regions and cities for industrial investments from multinational corporations (see also van Deth 1995).

I would like to argue, then, that the nation-state – in spite of the tendencies which seem to undermine its potential for action – remains one of the most important actors at the level of regional, state and international political affairs. This is so not least because to date, there exists no alternative – a fact which is simply overlooked by proponents of the globalization thesis (Martin/ Schumann 1996). If multinational corporations, financiers, brokers and speculators are able to put whole nationstates and national banks under pressure, they can do so only because no adequate means of international political control of their actions have so far been developed.

Western Europe seems to have responded in an adequate way to these new problems by beginning to integrate the continent into a wholly new kind of economic and political union. In fact, it is the first time in its history that the countries of Western and Central Europe have entered into such a close a relationship that an armed conflict between them seems impossible to imagine in the foreseeable future. Nevertheless, I would like to argue that at present, the European political elites have no clear and coherent idea of the ultimate goal of European integration toward which they should move. The integration achievements in economic terms have not been aspired to for their own sake, but primarily for political reasons. Only if Europeans are able to develop a clear concept about the final form of political integration will this provide for longlasting, fruitful co-operation, a balance of interests between its nation-states, and a peaceful role for Europe in the wider world. A very useful tool for helping us to understand these problems is the concept of «identity». Let us look more closely at its significance for the process of European integration.

1.2 The significance of the issue of identity for the European Union

The problem of identity constitutes a central issue of the European Union.[1] In the Maastricht *Treaty for the European Union*, the concept of «identity» is mentioned explicitly in the Preamble and in several paragraphs:

---

1   In this section, I am following closely the arguments in a recent publication by Pfetsch (1997: 97ff.; see also Weidenfeld 1985; Delanty 1995).

Preamble: The undersigned, resolved to implement a common foreign and security policy including the eventual framing of a common defence policy,
which might in time lead to a common defence, thereby reinforcing the European identity and its independence in order to promote peace, security and
progress in Europe and in the world, (...) have decided to establish a European Union (...).

Art. B: The Union shall set itself the following objectives:
to assert its identity on the international scene, in particular through the implementation of a common foreign and security policy including the eventual
framing of a common defence policy, which might in time lead to a common
defence;

Art. F.1: The Union shall respect the national identities of its Member States,
whose systems of government are founded on the principles of democracy.

What is «national identity», and what could a «European identity» be? As
Pfetsch (1997: 97) rightly observes, all of the above-quoted statements show
that the identity concept of the European Union is primarily related to foreign
policy, but not to positive self-determination concerning its internal affairs.
The same is true for the *Document on European Identity* passed by the Foreign Ministers of the European Community in 1973. In this document, too, the
Community is defined primarily in terms of its relation to the other countries
of the world. At the centre of European identity are «its common heritage, its
own interests, the particular obligations of the community.» It is stated that the
Europe of the Nine is conscious of the world-political obligations which spring
from its unification, that this unification is not directed against anybody else,
and that the European Community will play an active role in world politics.
Concerning the evolution of a European identity, the document states (Pfetsch
1997: 98, my translation from German):

> The development of a European identity will follow the dynamics of the
> work of European unification. In their foreign relations, the Nine will
> be anxious to determine their identity in relation to the other political
> units step by step. In this way, they consciously strengthen their internal
> unity and contribute to the formulation of a truly European politics.

This seems to be a rather vague, if not empty definition. And, indeed, its vacuity
has been proven in practical experience, which has shown that the European
Community and the European Union are still far from being able to follow a
determined common foreign policy. Significant examples of this weakness are
the passive and dissenting political role which the European Union and its

member-states played in two profound crises which more or less directly affected Europe: the occupation of Kuwait by Iraq and the subsequent Gulf war in
1991, and the social and political disintegration and subsequent civil war in
Yugoslavia in the early Nineties. In the latter case, the lack of unanimity
among the major Western European states – the early recognition of the independence of Slovenia and Croatia by Germany, in contrast to France and
England and most of the other EU-states – was directly connected with the
outbreak of war in Yugoslavia and Bosnia. In the Gulf war, most European
leaders were initially opposed to the all-out military invasion of Iraq by the
United States (which, as we know today, resulted in the deaths of over 100 000
Iraqi soldiers, but did not overthrow the dictatorial government of Saddam
Hussein).

In both cases, the lack of unanimity among the leading politicians of the member-states of the EU has led to a deep disillusionment among European populations about their leaders and about the prospects of arriving at a coherent
and efficient policy of the European Union in the face of serious political crises (Arnold 1993; Newhouse 1998: 93 ff.). Thus, in regard to the action potential of the European Union in its foreign relations, we must conclude: Great
hopes have been awakened, but little has so far been achieved. Why is this the
case? I would like to suggest that this failure is closely connected to the lack of
unanimity and precision among the member-states over the anticipated ultimate shape of its internal institutional structure. This institutional structure is
in turn closely related to the concepts of national and European identity.

1.3 The concepts of «nation» and «national identity»

In order to understand the astonishing contradiction between the success of
the Union in achieving economic integration[2], and its profound difficulty in arriving at a common «foreign policy», we have to look more closely at the concepts of «nation» and «national identity». What is a nation and a nation-state,
and what might a «European nation» be? We can distinguish two main approaches to this concept (see Haller 1996). The first may be called the *ontological-
substantivist approach*. This approach posits that we can enumerate a series of

---

2   If I use the word «success» here, I intend it to denote only the progress towards the realization of economic
     and market integration, the introduction of the common currency, etc. Whether or not this economic inte-
     gration overall can be considered a success, in the sense of having contributed significantly to economic
     progress, increase of wealth, etc. can only be decided after several decades. At least in one important res-
     pect – the high and persistent rates of unemployment in the European Union – economic integration has
     not been successful. For discussions of the potential negative effects of integration from the economic and
     political-democratic point of view, see Kohr (1983); Cutler et al. (1989); several contributions to Weber
     (1991).

attributes which together constitute a nation if they are fully present. Anthony Smith (1991) gives a rather exhaustive list of the relevant components: common history and territory, an «ethnic core», a common culture, a developed and integrated economy, and a coherent constitutional and political system. The strength of this definition is that it clearly indicates all those factors which in fact characterize most nations; at the same time, we can find existing nations which lack at least one of these criteria, and this shows that none of them is indispensable to the existence of a nation.

Against this characterization, I would prefer to define *nation as a self-chosen object of political identification (a political community) whose members aspire to become politically independent or politically self-determined.* There are three essential elements in this definition: the first is the understanding of a nation as a *political community,* not just as a bureaucratic apparatus or a system based simply on power. The second is the fact that its elites and populations have the will to determine their own fate (see also Heller 1934; Weber 1964: 313, 675; Elwert 1999). A nation in this sense will tend to become an independent state (if it is not yet one), but it can also confine itself to gaining extensive political autonomy within an existing nation-state (as, for example, Catalonia has done). Central to this concept of nation is, therefore, a third element, the idea of *legitimacy:* A well-established nation-state enjoys a high degree of approval from its citizens, they are prepared to engage themselves in the political affairs of their political community, and they would even be willing to defend the nation against any attack from outside.

Such a concept of «nation» can be used both as an explanatory, independent variable and as a dependent variable (in this regard, we can speak of differing degrees of nationhood). Thus, a nation is not defined as a more or less clearly circumscribed (ontological) entity, but rather as a social and politically relevant idea (*idee directrice,* as Hauriou has called it) or as a *field of forces* (Kräftefeld). The idea behind the general concept of «identity» is that a person or a nation with a strongly developed self-image or identity will behave in a much more consistent and forceful way than one which does not have such an identity (Habermas 1976: 92 ff.). With the concept of national identity, it becomes possible to see how nations can use or even create their own great history, their common language and culture, and their self-preserving economy. It can also be easily understood how nations can establish their claims to independence or their right to continue to exist, even if they seem non-viable from an economic point of view. Again, it can be seen why nations whose pride has been wounded, are able to follow irresponsible nationalistic and chauvinistic leaders (Scheff 1994). We can observe and investigate empirically to what extent factors such as a common culture, an integrated economy and the like, can contribute to the arousal of national sentiments and, eventually, to the emergence of new nations.

The concepts of «nation» and «national identity» comprise two dimensions which have to be systematically distinguished from each other (see *Synopsis 1*). The first dimension includes three components: cognitive goals, actions or experiences related to the nation, and emotional attachment to a nation; the second dimension concerns the distinction between the micro and macro levels. At both levels, similar issues and questions arise. With respect to the central aims and the self-image of a nation, we can ask, for instance: What kind of self-image is developed and propounded by the political leaders and by the cultural elites of a nation (macro level)? How are these official aims and images reflected in the minds of their populations (micro level)? How are national symbols and ways of thinking transmitted to individual feelings and behaviours (Billig (1995) shows the forcefulness of such processes).

Synopsis 1: The two dimensions of «nation» and «national identity»

	Cognitive component	Component of action and experience	Emotional-affective component
Macro Level	«Official» ideas, self-images and aims concerning the nation; perceived economic, political and cultural interests of the nation	Official politics and other actions concerning the foundation, maintenance and strengthening of the nation	Official symbols of the nation (national holidays, arms and flags, memorial days, etc.)
Micro Level	Images and expectations of the individual members of a nation concerning their political community	Nation-related experiences of the individual members of the nation-state	Emotional attachment of the individual members toward the nation

Let us now look at the central topic of this contribution, namely, the question of how the individual European nations and the national identities of their citizens are related to the new potential nation of the European Community.

1.4 Relationships between national identity and European identity

Three hypotheses concerning the relation between local-regional identities and national identity can be distinguished (Haller et al. 1996: 384 ff.). These hypotheses, which I have developed elsewhere in the context of Austria, can also be applied to the relations between national and European identity.

First, there is the possibility of a *neutral relation* between the two. This would mean that European integration will not affect the identity of the single nation states and their citizens. This hypothesis can probably be excluded immediately, since European integration affects both the action potential and the autonomy of nation-states at the level of governments as well as the daily lives of their citizens in many ways. It is very significant here that the introduction of the common currency, the Euro, has been motivated explicitly by political considerations. It is expected (and hoped) that a common currency will function as an efficient *symbol* of European unity, and that in so doing, it will strengthen European identity among the citizens of the member-states.

The second thesis posits that there exists a *complementary relationship* between national and European identity. This thesis may be considered as the «official doctrine» of the national governments and the EU-bureaucrats and politicians. It is well known that they never tire of swearing to the Europeans that integration will not lead to an elimination of the individual nation-states. Rather, it is said, it will only complement national identity and, in the final analysis, that it will even be necessary for the preservation of their independence in a changing world. This is certainly an attractive hypothesis. As long as the constitution of the European Union considers the individual nation-states as essential components of its system, these components will not be wholly assimilated into a new super-state. From this point of view, the European Union would have to declare itself clearly as a *state of nationalities* or a *union of nation states* (Nationalitätenstaat) rather than as a new nation-state in its own right (on these concepts, see also Francis 1965; Lepsius 1988, 1992; Haller 1995, 1996). Historical research on the emergence of the European Union shows that such an interpretation approximates to the reality. According to Milward (1992: 18), European integration was not an overriding of the nation-state but a conscious «creation of the European nationstates themselves for their own purposes», an effort to preserve their action potential in a globalized world. Europe can be considered as an *emergent nation* if a nation is not understood as a «close-knit political and cultural unit» – such as Britain, France or Germany – but as «a complex and vast entity, such as India» (Friedrich 1969: 213f.).

In so far as this description is true, the feeling of being a member of the Union could well develop among the citizens of the single nation-states alongside a continuation of their nation-state consciousness (Nationalstaatsbewusstsein). That both feelings can co-exist quite well, or that they could even strengthen each other, is proved by theoretical and empirical sociological considerations. From the theoretical point of view, it has been argued that modern men and women are characterized by their capacity to develop *multiple identities* – identities which, to a considerable degree, they can choose themselves (Simmel 1923; von Krockow 1970). From the empirical point of view, it is a fact that in countries with federal political systems – like Germany, Switzerland or Austria – a strong local-regional identity is combined *positively* with a sense of national pride and identity (Bruckmüller 1996; Haller et al. 1996).

There is no guarantee, however, that national and European identity will go together in such a smooth and conflict-free fashion. A third hypothesis, positing a *competitive* or *exclusive relationship* between the two, must also be seriously considered. The main argument in favour of this hypothesis is that a strong national identity can only survive the process of European integration if it is related to continuing and positive political experiences and the provision of services by the nation-states to its citizens. If European integration significantly undermines the autonomous action potential of individual nation states, this would in the long run also undermine the attachment of individual citizens to their state. Such tendencies are obvious. They are the other side of the coin of the aforementioned success of integration: the loss of the action potential of national governments; the reduction of national parliaments to the role of mere «state notaries» rubber stamping the decrees enacted by Brussels; the loss of significant national symbols; the trends toward a linguistic-cultural homogenization of Europe, etc. The thesis of an evolutionary drive towards European integration (Campbell 1994) sees such tendencies as more or less necessary reactions to and outcomes of world-wide processes. National governments, as well as individual citizens, however, might fear such tendencies and therefore oppose European integration.[3]

The central question to be investigated in the following section is therefore: To what extent are national identity and European integration and identity complementary to or competitive with each other? My general hypothesis here is that the more the new European institutions are able to preserve significant action potentials for nation-states, or to restrict themselves to the function of

---

3   These trends can be perceived most sharply in France, whose language has experienced a secular decline in
     international usage compared with English. This led the French parliament to enact a «Law for the protec-
     tion of the French language» in 1994 (Der Fischer Weltalmanach '95: 259).

complementing but not replacing nation-states, the more it will be possible for national and European identity to develop in a complementary way.

As a corollary of this hypothesis, we need to investigate the predominant visions of the future shape of the European Union, and their relation to the images and expectations which are entertained by the single nation-states. In this respect, I would like to propose the following three more specific theses:

1) We can see no consistent or coherent image or vision of a «European nation» among the present-day political elites of Europe. Rather, there exist significant differences in their ideas, both among political leaders and elites in different European nation-states, and between different political parties, as well as between the economic, political and cultural elites.

2) In so far as such visions do exist, we must say that the actual strategies and behaviours of the political elites do not correspond to them in any coherent way.

3) There also exist considerable divergences in the visions about Europe among leaders and elites on the one side, and the populations at large on the other side (see also Bach 1993; Giesen 1993; Puntscher-Riekmann 1998). Political leaders typically attribute the relatively modest popular support for their efforts at integration to a lack of information among the population, or they imply that European integration can only be a matter of emotions among «ordinary people».

Bearing these general remarks in mind, we can now proceed to the development of a typology and the presentation of some empirical data on the different images of Europe in different nation-states and among elites and populations at large.

1.5 Interests behind and functions of European integration

European integration fulfils different purposes for different nation-states and social groups and people. The first step towards an explanation is to conceptualize these different functions in a typology. This typology has been developed by systematically combining (a) the structural positions and interests of different social groups and nation-states with (b) the ideas, values and aims associated with this process of European integration. Behind this procedure lies the idea of sociology as a science of social reality (Wirklichkeitswissenschaft), which sees its main aim as being the elaboration of systematic relationships between interests, values, and institutions. In elaborating such relationships, it does not aim at the development or testing of very general theories (as the natural sciences do). Rather, it aims at understanding and interpreting social processes in a reflexive way, that is, by taking into consideration the aims of the actors themselves, their historical and structural constraints, and universal ideas and values (see Weber 1964; Lepsius 1988; Haller 1999a).

I start from the assumption that we can identitfy at least three main interests or motives behind European integration:

1) *Economic interests,* particularly concerning economic growth, enlargement of markets, improvement of the supply of goods and services, and the like.
2) *Political interests,* which can be subdivided into three more specific interests: (a) the interest in maintaining a lasting peace in Europe; (b) the interest (mainly of the political elites) in an enlargement of the free scope of their political action at home; and (c) the interest (again mainly of the political elites) in the regaining of world power for Europe.
3) *Cultural interests* in the preservation of the Christian Occident (Abendland).

In attempting to relate these motives and interests to the specific structural conditions in different European countries and regions and to different social groups, we may begin by distinguishing the following five functions of European integration:

1) *European integration as a prop or a crutch* which should help to overcome domestic insecurities, dependencies on other nations, and enduring economic and political problems which cannot be solved by the national political elites within the context of their single nation-state alone.
2) *European integration as a necessary evil* which is assumed to be unavoidable, given a lack of viable alternatives.
3) *European integration as the creation of a new kind of bureaucratized superstate* which must be rejected.
4) *European integration as a substitute for a weak sense of national identity.*
5) *European integration as a positive vehicle for the realization of particular economic, political and/or cultural interests.*

My thesis is that strategies (1) through (4) constitute a problematic basis for the development of a stable and enduring European identity. Strategies subsumable under (5) are problematic if they are not declared and openly discussed. A corollary of the latter point is that the more such interests and strategies are in the interests only of particular groups, especially elites (economic, political and cultural elites), the less openly they tend to be discussed. I will come back to these theses at the end of this essay. In the next section, more detailed justifications of these theses are given, together with some empirical evidence concerning the relations between national and European identity.

2 Functions of European integration for different nation-states and social groups: a sociological typology

In this section, I will show that these strategies can really be detected in the present-day process of European integration. Throughout these considerations, we need to look both at the macrosocial, official level of politics, and at the microsocial level of the perceptions and attitudes of the individual members of the different European populations (on the variations see also Estel/ Mayer 1994; Therborn 1995; Deflem/Pampel 1996; Pfetsch 1997; Schauer 1997).

2.1 European integration as a prop or a crutch

Several countries look to European integration primarily in the hope that through the process of integration, domestic problems can be solved which they have been unable to solve by themselves in their post-war history. There are two main areas in which European integration might serve as a panacea for nation-states.

First, *in economic terms:* Countries lying somewhat behind the «European core» in terms of socio-economic development (GNP/capita), and characterized by persistent socio-economic problems, such as unemployment, high public deficits and/or periodic high rates of inflation, expect that the process of economic integration will provide a spur to accelerate economic growth, ensure the economic catching-up and the reduction of economic crisis phenomena.

Second, *in political terms:* Countries lying behind in terms of «democratic maturity» expect that membership in the European Union will help them to overcome their problems in this regard. Two kinds of problems are relevant here:
– Three Southern European countries experienced dictatorial regimes in the post-war period, until the mid-Seventies. This was the case in *Portugal, Spain* and *Greece*. In fact, it was a condition of admission to the European Union that democratic political regimes were established in these countries, which in turn hope that EU-membership will serve as a kind of guarantee of their democratic maturing.
–   Another country, *Italy,* has been characterized throughout the post-war period by a rather unstable political situation. This is reflected most clearly in the fact that Italy has had over fifty governments between 1945 and 1998; the mean duration of a government in power was less than one year. This instability is also reflected in the fact that Italy is characterized by very high

levels of «anti-civilian» behaviour (including tax evasion, clientelism, corruption and the like) among the elites as well as among the population.[4]
- In Italy, but also in Greece, the danger of a take-over of power by strong communist parties was felt, particularly during the Fifties and Sixties.

Thus, in the case of four members of the European Union, the motives for membership included the expectation that European integration would serve as an economic and political prop or crutch (see also Pfetsch 1997: 77ff.). In Portugal, Spain, Italy, and Greece, membership was also motivated according to official declarations by the desire to strengthen their democratic systems. In the cases of Portugal, Spain and Greece, this desire meant nurturing young democracies after decades of authoritarian rule; in the case of Italy, it meant developing more stable and civilized democratic conditions. A similar factor might also have been significant in the case of *Belgium*.[5] Both Belgium and Italy would certainly not have been able to reduce their budgets significantly if there had not been the strong pressure exerted by the prerequisite conditions for participation in the Euro. A very nice parody on the tendency of the Italians to expect the cure of all national ills from the European Union and the Euro was made by Giorgio Bocca (1998) [in his article «Santa Europa, benedetto Euro» in: *Il Venerdi della Republica, Supplemento del giornale La Republica,* Roma, 27.2.1998, p. 38].

The economic motive was also important for all of these countries. In view of their relative economic backwardness, given a high proportion of relatively poor agrarian populations, countries like Portugal, Greece, and Ireland (and, to a lesser degree, Spain and Italy) expected, and to a large degree obtained, economic support from the Union for their underdeveloped areas. In the case

---

4   By referring to these negative aspects of social and political life in Italy, I would not like to discredit Italy or the Italians in general as being dishonest, inefficient, etc.. Rather, as the Swiss author Victor Willi (1983) has shown in a very nice book – «Surviving in the Italian Way» – most Italians are characterized by high levels of responsibility and efficiency in carrying through their activities, even in spite of adverse circumstances. In my view, the main reason for the high instability of Italian post-war governments, as well as for the high levels of corruption, was the fact that the Communist Party was not considered as a «constitutional party». This had the consequence that the coalitions which were formed between Christian-conservatives, social democrats and a few other small centre parties had a monopoly on government. Until the early Nineties, these coalitions had a clear majority of the votes in parliamentary elections and were therefore able to treat political offices, as well as the broad sector of politically controlled services and industries, as their own private domain, in which posts and privileges were distributed mainly according to party interests. See also Rusconi (1993) for a discussion of the relationship between national and European identity in Italy.

5   Among possible reasons for the relatively low sense of national pride among Belgians, three could be mentioned: the loss of their colonies; their quick defeat by Nazi troops in the Second World War and the partial collaboration of Belgium with Nazi Germany; and the deep internal cleavage along linguistic-ethnic lines between the Flemish and the Wallonian groups. Therese Jacobs (University of Antwerp) suggested in a lecture at the University of Graz (14.4.1998), however, that only the last factor plays a significant role today. Belgians, particularly French-speaking Belgians, might greet European integration as a means of overcoming this division of the country. The country's capital Brussels especially profits directly from being the new capital of Europe.

of Ireland, the reduction of its economic dependence on England was an additional incentive.[6]

If we look at some statistical indicators for the levels of development and the net contributions of the different EU-member-states to the household of the European Union, we can see that a considerable net financial transfer is made to the four peripheral nations Greece, Ireland, Portugal, and Spain (see *Table 1*).[7] These four peripheral nations are also those which in the early Nineties still had over 10% of their active populations employed in the agricultural sector; their general standard of living was clearly below the EU-mean.

Table 1:   Indicators for the economic relevace of membership
in the European Union to the member-states in 1991

Country	% of Persons employed in Agriculture (1986)	GNP in % of the EU-mean	Net contribution to the EU-budget per head in ECU's (1995)
Great Britain with North Ireland)	2,2	98,2	80,7
Denmark	5,2	112,0	−58,6
Germany	3,7	106,7	164,6
Belgium	2,9	110,4	30,6
France	5,9	107,2	29,6
Netherlands	3,7	100,4	129,7
Luxembourg	1,3	128,9	110,6
Italy	7,9	101,7	10,7
Ireland	13,7	85,2	−526,8
Spain	10,1	76,1	−184,0
Portugal	11,5	67,9	−241,8
Greece	21,8	60,6	−333,0
Austria	6,9	109,3	112,9
Sweden	3,4	95,3	105,5
Finnland	8,6	92,5	32,3

Source: Pfetsch (1997: 177, 260)

---

6   The motive of European integration as a prop or crutch to help solve domestic problems is also evident in other nation-states. For example, during the governmental campaign in Austria for EU-membership, it was stated openly, particularly by big industrialists and the conservative party Österreichische Volkspartei, that membership of the Union would oblige the country to open up its ossified institutional structures and to adapt to a more competitive environment (see also Haller 1994).

7   Otherwise only Denmark, with its significant but rather modernized agrarian sector, gains from EU-membership by receiving direct transfers.

Table 2: Indicators for the approval of European Integration among the population of the 12 member-states of the European Union in 1991

Country	Q.13: Thinks of himself/herself often as European	Q.14: A European citizenship would be a good thing	Q.17: In general, very much in favour of European unification	Q.18: My country's membership in the EU is a good thing	Q.19: My country has benefited from being a member of the EU	Q.20: I would be very sorry if the EU had been scrapped	Mean approval of European unification*)
Great Britain	14	53	28	**59**	**55**	**33**	40
Denmark	21	**29**	**25**	63	77	46	44
North Ireland	7	67	29	63	73	36	59
West Germany	17	59	38	74	62	61	52
East Germany	10	64	33	83	83	65	56
Belgium	23	64	28	78	83	50	54
France	26	67	27	73	71	53	53
Netherlands	14	62	26	**90**	**89**	58	57
Luxembourg	**36**	55	33	86	86	**70**	61
Italy	29	80	46	83	81	66	64
Ireland	14	73	47	80	88	58	60
Spain	31	**84**	49	82	70	58	62
Portugal	16	77	**64**	83	81	60	65
Greece	22	80	47	80	86	64	63
Mean**) Difference largest/smallest value***)	20	65	38	77	70	56	56

Source: Eurobarometer 1/1991

*) Aggregate mean
**) Based on individual values
***) Printed in bold figures

It is therefore not difficult to understand why the «official» attitudes toward membership of the European Union were and still are very positive in these five countries. These attitudes are evidently supported by their populations at large. If we look at the findings of the Eurobarometer surveys concerning public approval of European integration, we find that it is precisely the populations of these five countries which are shown to be those most in favour (see *Table 2*). In Ireland, Portugal, Spain, Italy, and Greece, a clear majority of the respective populations – nearly two-thirds in each case – approves of their country being an EU-member; about 80% think that the membership of their country is «a good thing» and has been to their advantage; 70–80% think that European citizenship would be a good thing. These sentiments are statistically significantly higher than the findings for most other European nations.

There is another indication of the convergence between the aims and strategies of these countries at the macro-level, and the micro-level of the very positive attitudes of their individual citizens. This is the fact that the political elites of none of the four South-European countries felt it necessary to put the issue of EC- or EU-membership to a public vote or referendum (see *Synopsis 2*). Had they done so, they would probably have obtained results similar to those in Ireland, where a referendum about the ratification of the Treaty of Maastricht won a two-thirds majority in 1993. Before this vote, Irish political elites were eager to present the advantages of EU-membership to their citizens in the most brilliant colours.

Synopsis 2: Results of Referenda in 9 European countries and regions resp. concerning the joining to the European Community/Union and the acceptation of the Treaties of Maastricht

Year	Country and topic of Referendum	Result
Positive decisions		
02.10.1972	Denmark: joining the EC	majority in favour
05.06.1975	Great Britain: remaining in the EC	68% in favour
26.05.1987	Ireland: ratification of the European Act	majority in favour
18.06.1992	Ireland: ratification of the Treaties of Maastricht	68.7% in favour
1992	France: ratification of the Treaties of Maastricht	majority in favour
18.05.1993	Denmark, second referendum about Treaties of Maastricht	56.8% in favour
12.06.1994	Austria: joining of the EU	66.5% in favour
16.10.1994	Finnland: joining of the EU	57% in favour
13.11.1994	Sweden: joining of the EU	52% in favour
Negative decisions		
26.09.1992	Norway: joining of the EU	majority against
23.02.1982	Greenland (autonomous region of Denmark): remaining in the EU	majority against
02.06.1992	Denmark: acceptation of the Treaties of Maastricht	68.7% against
06.12.1992	Switzerland: joining of the European Economic Area (EWR)	50% against
27./28.11.1994	Norway: joining of the EU	52.2% against

Source:	Pfetsch 1 (997: 290 ff.)

2.2 European integration as a necessary evil

There is at least one large nation-state in which European integration is clearly not seen as a positive goal in and of itself, but as something which nevertheless cannot be avoided in the long run because in that case, negative consequences would have to be accepted. This state is *Great Britain;* to a lesser degree, the *Scandinavian states* also fit into this category. It is well known that the official aims and actions of British European politics have changed several times. There are at least three reasons for this: (1) historically, Britain was at the centre of its own large Commonwealth empire, and it still maintains close ties with Canada, Australia and New Zealand; (2) Britain also maintains particularly close ties with the United States, ties which are based on a common cultural heritage and intensive economic, social, cultural-scientific and political relations; (3) their tradition of economic and political liberalism, as well as their old and well-established democratic system, make Britons suspicious of any strongly centralized political and comprehensive welfare system.

Britain's official policy towards Europe after World War II began with Winston Churchill's famous speech at the University of Zurich in 1947. In this speech, Churchill asked for a united Europe which would secure the peace on the Continent; but Britain was not seen as being part of this alliance. Again, the foundation of the European Economic Community of the Six in the mid-Fifties took place without Britain. It was only in the Sixties that British European policy changed significantly. But even then, it was defined as «a policy of the last resort» (Pfetsch 1997: 74). The European Community was seen as a necessary new partner for trade, because Britain's relationships with the former colonies (or Commonwealth partners) had changed drastically, to the disadvantage of Britain. At the same time, the increasing economic power of the Community made it clear to the British that they would lose influence in Europe if they did not join the EC. However, French President de Gaulle then blocked British entrance to the Community. In 1971, a new vote in the British parliament brought a majority in favour of joining the EC, although the votes of the Commons were rather divided (59% pro). A referendum in 1975 obtained a surprisingly high percentage (68%) in favour. But once more, in the Eighties, many objections were raised to British EC-membership, this time by Prime Minister Margaret Thatcher. She argued strongly for Europe as «a family of nations» as opposed to an integrated federal state. This position led to additional protocols in the Treaties of Maastricht in respect of Britain's special position. As far as social policy and the monetary union are concerned, Britain is not obliged to adhere completely to the integration process. A more pro-European attitude, however, has been evident since 1997 with the new Labour government of Tony Blair.

In the case of Britain, then, EU-membership is not something which Britons think is absolutely necessary for their country. This is clearly reflected in survey data. The British are characterized by a rather high level of national pride; they are particularly proud of the working of democracy in their country, of their armed forces, and of their history (see *Table 3*); and they feel much closer to their nation-state than to Europe *(Table 4)*. In the mean, only a strong minority of 40% of the population – the lowest proportion of any of the EU-member-states – approves of Britain being an EU-member *(Table 2)*.

Table 3: Dimensions of national pride in 12 countries (ISSP-95)

Dimension	AUT	G-W	G-E	GB	ITA	SPA	USA	NOR	SWE	POL	CZECH	HUNG	SLO	Mean	Variation*)
	- Percent of respondents who are «proud» or «very proud» of their country in regard to … -														
Working of Democracy	67	62	32	60	26	52	83	76	61	21	33	20	19	47	64
World political influence	65	54	54	48	22	35	80	72	37	31	45	18	25	45	58
Economic achievements	77	76	77	38	39	38	82	74	16	25	39	9	31	48	73
Social security system	80	68	37	44	27	51	50	59	63	15	18	7	27	42	63
Scientific-technol. achievements	77	74	75	79	80	64	95	70	75	49	47	78	53	70	48
Achievements in sports	83	60	73	70	87	85	88	89	80	39	64	87	87	76	50
Achievements in arts/literature	69	57	69	69	93	81	88	63	59	57	79	89	66	72	36
Armed forces	41	26	22	81	42	55	91	33	26	49	15	28	53	43	76
History	77	30	28	83	88	89	88	72	60	72	87	72	70	70	61
Fair treatment of groups	52	65	21	47	22	57	88	42	40	27	19	44	35	43	69
Mean value	69	57	49	62	53	61	83	65	52	38	45	45	47		
(N)	(1007)	(1282)	(612)	(1078)	(1094)	(1221)	(1367)	(1527)	(1470)	(1603)	(1111)	(965)	(1036)		

Source: ISSP-95

*) Difference between lowest and highest value

Table 4:   Feeling of closeness to different territorial units in 12 countries

Country	Feel «very close» or «close to ...» (in %)				
	Neighbor-hood	Town/City	Province	State (very close)	Europe (America)
Austria	81	51	86	(55) 89	66
Germany (West)	67	48	58	(22) 73	50
Germany (East)	69	45	67	(26) 76	49
Italy	68	82	79	(43) 87	67
Great Britain	60	50	44	(21) 63	19
Slowenia	77	77	94	(49) 92	65
Hungary	79	84	86	(79) 97	94
Czech Republic	78	72	66	(46) 89	73
Poland	69	72	60	(53) 92	63
Sweden	63	63	65	(32) 81	35
Norway	51	69	78	(51) 94	54
Spain	88	92	91	(43) 89	62
USA	57	60	62	(35) 81	59
Mean	70	66	72	(43) 85	58
(N)	(907)	(865)	(936)	(555) (1103)	(756)

Source: ISSP-95.

A somewhat similar attitude toward the European Union can be seen among several *Scandinavian countries.* These countries are today, in economic terms, among the wealthiest countries in the world. At the same time, they are proud of their welfare and social security systems, which have achieved a considerable equalization of life chances and the virtual elimination of open poverty, and these facts are reflected in rather high levels of national pride (see *Table 3).* But Scandinavians are also quite proud of their democracies and history. It is not surprising, therefore, that Norwegians and Swedes are more attached to their nation-state than to Europe as a whole (see *Table 4).* The data for Denmark, which – as an older EU-member – is also found in the Eurobarometer surveys, show the second lowest level of attachment to the European Union among the twelve member-states (see *Table 2).*

Another factor which tended to make Finland and Sweden sceptical for a long time about the European Union was their position of political neutrality in foreign affairs. It was thought, especially as long as Europe was divided into two hostile camps (East versus West), that neutrality was not compatible with membership of the European Community, as the EC maintains close ties with America and the military alliance NATO.[8]

2.3 European integration as the creation of a new kind of bureaucratized super-state

The sort of critical stance towards the European Union displayed by Britain and Scandinavia, is even more pronounced in the cases of two small European nation-states which have so far officially rejected membership of the EC/EU. These two states are *Norway* and *Switzerland*. In Norway, the population has twice rejected joining the European Union, in 1992 and again in 1994. In Switzerland, even the question of joining the European Economic Area was rejected by a small majority in 1992 (see *Synopsis 2*). What were the reasons for the critical attitudes of the populations (not the elites!) in these two countries?

In the case of Norway, the main reasons were probably the same as those which inhibited Finland and Sweden for a long time from joining the European Community (political neutrality, a strong welfare state, a high standard of living). In addition, though, we might mention the high revenues which Norway gets from North Sea oil, providing this country with considerable economic strength, at the very time when Finland and Sweden ran into serious economic difficulties, albeit for different reasons.[9]

In the case of Switzerland, factors similar to those influencing Britain might account for the negative attitudes toward European integration. In the first instance, pride in the history of the country and the well-established federal and democratic system must be taken into account. Unlike Britain, however, Switzerland did not experience an economic decline in the post-war years – rather the opposite. In spite of the small size of this country, the Swiss *Franken* is one of the strongest currencies in the world. We can probably also say that the strong sense of national identity among the Swiss is second to none in Europe.[10] I would argue that the resistance, particularly of the population of the German-speaking rural cantons, was not in the first instance (as many commentators would have it) an expression of backwardness, but a well-founded fear that local democracy and national political autonomy would be signi-

8   A strong attachment to political neutrality was also one of most important reasons for the scepticism of many Austrians about EC-membership. This positive evaluation of neutrality still exists, but is declining in the face of a sustained propaganda campaign against it, perpetrated by the political elites in power (see Haller et al. 1996: 501 ff.). It must be admitted, however, that the meaning and function of political neutrality has changed since the collapse of the Iron Curtain, increasing European integration, and globalization (Kriesi 1998: 27 ff.).

9   Finland because of the collapse of its close economic relations with the former Soviet Union, Sweden because of a sudden change in currency policy and an overloading of the welfare state, due to high increases of wages (see Jochem 1998).

10   Unfortunately, we do not have strictly comparable survey data on this topic, because Switzerland is not a member of the International Social Survey Programme (ISSP), neither are the Eurobarometer surveys conducted there.

ficantly undermined by joining the EU (see Kriesi 1998: 90 ff., for a systematic discussion of the Swiss system of direct democracy).[11]

2.4 European integration as a substitute for a weak sense of national identity

A pattern which is almost the opposite of that in Switzerland can be observed in the case of *Germany.* The present-day Germans are characterized by a comparatively low level of national pride. It is, in fact, the lowest level among the 26 countries examined in the study on National Identity conducted by the International Social Science Survey Programme (ISSP) in 1995, and one of the lowest in the World Value Survey of 1990 (see also Westle 1992). *Table 3* shows that Germans both in the East and the West have by far the lowest pride in their history and armed forces. The low level of German national pride is clearly the product of two historical facts: (1) German responsibility for the outbreak of the Second World War, and their total defeat in this war; (2) German responsibility for the Holocaust, the systematic genocide of nearly six million Jews in the concentration camps. Consciousness of this crime remains a painful trauma for many Germans today. This issue continues to be debated hotly and strongly in the German public arena[12] (for further evidence, see von Krockow 1970; Greiffenhagen 1979; Buruma 1994). We must say, indeed, that Germany is still today an «ashamed nation.»[13] This thesis is supported by the fact that the Italians, who were also defeated in World War II, also have a low sense of pride in their army, but a rather high feeling of pride in their history; the latter is similarly true for Austria.[14]

Looking at the data concerning the identification of Germans with Europe, we cannot say that they are as enthusiastic as the first group of countries discussed above. The data on the identification with different territorial units *(Table 4)* as well as those on their identification with the European Union *(Table 2),*

---

11 This anxiety would be seen to be entirely justified were we to compare the example of Austria after it joined the EU. In the Austrian parliament, hundreds and hundreds of decisions had to be taken almost overnight, in order to enact EU-law in Austria. Today, it is said that 70–80% of all political decisions which affect Austria are taken in Brussels.

12 One of the most recent instances was the publication of Daniel Goldhagen's book on the attitudes and behaviour of ordinary Germans concerning the Holocaust (Goldhagen 1996).

13 In German political science literature, a heated discussion about this designation has taken place during the last few years. The well-known social scientist Elisabeth Noelle-Neumann (Noelle-Neumann/Köcher 1987) has used the term «verletzte Nation» («hurt nation»), which I think is misleading in this regard, however, since Germany was not hurt by others but by its own national socialist regime, which was guilty of committing crimes against the Jews. (See Scheff 1994 about the importance and exact meaning of the concepts of «pride» and «shame».)

14 See Haller et al. 1996 for a systematic comparison between Germany and Italy, and Haller 1999b for a comparison between Austria and Germany.

show that the Germans have only an intermediate level of attachment to Europe. In a comparative analysis of national pride in Germany and Italy, I correlated the feeling of belonging to different geographic-political units (local/regional/national/European identity) with national pride (Haller 1999b). It was found in the case of Germany that those respondents who identified themselves in the first instance with «Europe» or with «the world as a whole» were characterized by a low level of national pride,[15] but the same was not true for Italy. Thus, we can say that at least for a significant subgroup of the German population, the identification with Europe constitutes a substitute for a low sense of national identity and pride.

2.5 European integration as a positive vehicle for the realization of particular economic, political and/or cultural interests

Under this rubric, I would include three kinds of ideas and strategies. The first concerns the realization of positive economic goals and interests. In this connection, it is quite evident from the perspective of contemporary history that the interests of large enterprises and multinational corporations have taken the lead in the breakthrough of European economic integration since the early Eighties. This is clearly shown in a comprehensive recent study by Volker Bornschier and associates (1999; see also Middlemas 1995). The European Round Table of Industrialists, established in 1983, which included all the major European transnational and multinational corporations (Philips, Siemens, Shell, Olivetti, etc.) developed very concrete ideas and proposals about how Europe should meet the challenge presented by the United States and Japan on the world economic scene. The ideas of this Round Table were largely taken over by the EU-Commission and its president, Jacques Delors, in the *White Book for the Internal Market,* published in 1985. In this pamphlet, the future shape of a fully free market in Europe was very clearly laid out in its principal characteristics.

There is one small member-state of the European Union which fits particularly well into this pattern. This is *Luxembourg,* whose entire economy, but especially its banking sector, profits massively from European integration. Due to specific advantageous conditions, the private and corporate moneyed aristocracy from the neighbouring countries prefers to invest money in this small

---

15 In 1988, only 9% of the respondents who identified in the first instance with Europe, were «very proud» of Germany while, in the whole sample, this proportion was about 25%; in this subgroup, the proportion of those with «no pride» in Germany was 56% (in the whole sample about 30%).

country or to establish puppet companies there in order to evade taxes and other public burdens and restrictions.[16]

Besides Luxembourg, this motive of using the EU as a vehicle for the realization of the interests of big enterprises and capital is certainly relevant for every European country which hosts such companies. This applies particularly to Germany, France, the Netherlands, and Italy.

A second positive aim (or group of aims) connected with European integration is political. The dominant aim here was, in the Fifties, clearly that of maintaining internal peace between the member-states, particularly between France and Germany. The close and friendly relationship that was established between these two core European countries was an epochal achievement of several political personalities, including Charles de Gaulle and Konrad Adenauer. In more recent times, this aim has been enlarged to include that of providing the European Union with more concerted power to effect foreign policy and relations with other countries and regions of the world. It is quite evident that, once again, this aim is supported primarily by the larger member-states of the EU, notably Germany, France and, belatedly, Great Britain. By uniting the armed forces of the fifteen member-states, the European Union could, at least in theory, play a significant role in world politics. In this way, it could compensate these middle-sized nations for the loss of their former world power and influence. It should come as no surprise, then, that from time to time politicians from these countries ask for a common military force in the EU, or even attempt to establish a small European corps.

A third and final aim of the European Union may be called the realization of a cultural vision. Here, Europe is seen as a cultural unit, stemming from the Middle Ages when the Roman Catholic church extended over and united almost the whole continent.[17] From that time on, this concept of a Christian Europe («Abendland», as against the pagan Orient) has been a politically contentious but potent symbol (Faber 1979). The success of post-war economic integration can only be fully appreciated if we recognize the fact that the «European Idea» has really been current for centuries (Swedberg 1994).

---

16   This certainly also applies to Switzerland (see Ziegler 1992). Since Switzerland's entry to the EU would bring an end to some of the advantages which it enjoys through these means, this could be another reason for the negative EU-attitudes of some Swiss people.

17   I am aware that this «cultural» or «religious unity» of the European Occident did not preclude many conflicts between the several Christian kings. On occasion, they (notably the French kings, who were consistently in opposition to the German emperors of the Holy Roman Empire) even entered into alliances with pagan rulers, such as the Turkish Sultans.

All of these three concepts and aims associated with European integration are most prominent in the central European nation-states, particularly in France and Germany, and to a lesser extent also in the Benelux nations and in Italy. The largest multinational corporations of the EU are located in these countries. Some of these countries, again most notably France and Germany, have also played central roles in European and world history as major powers, subsequently experiencing decline in this sphere. Moreover, with few exceptions (Netherlands, North and East Germany), Catholic Christians constitute a majority of the population in these countries, and Catholicism can be considered historically as having been the «dominant religion». It is not surprising, therefore, that we find solid majorities approving of European integration in all of these countries (see *Table 2*).

If we consider the role of Catholicism in particular, we find an additional explanation for some surprising findings. It is possible that Catholicism is a religion which can contribute to a more positive attitude toward European integration, because among other things: (1) Catholicism is a universal religion, thus supporting international co-operation and integration; and (2) the Roman Catholic Church is a strongly centralized and hierarchical organization. Both of these facts would suggest that Catholics will be less afraid than Protestants of a new central EU-bureaucracy in Brussels. This effect of religion could also explain the essentially positive attitudes of Austrians and Italians. German Catholics, too, have traditionally had a positive attitude toward European integration (Langner 1985). The thesis that Catholicism predisposes towards a positive integration attitude is also confirmed by the fact that the leading German politicians in European integration were Catholics or came from the South-West Catholic regions of Germany (K. Adenauer, W. Hallstein, H. Kohl).

What would a «Catholic European Union» look like? It would be: (1) strongly centralized, bureaucratized, hierarchically structured; (2) a very well integrated and comprehensive welfare state, effectively reducing inequalities and poverty; (3) a paternalistic-elitist state whose citizens were well provided for in material terms, but had few interests, possibilities, or powers in political terms. In short, it would be a new kind of «mild totalitarian state», as was foreseen by Alexis de Tocqueville (1976).

3   Concluding remarks

In concluding, I shall point out some of the implications of the widely differing
images and expectations concerning the European Union and its identity, in
relation to three of the aforementioned functions of European integration.

European integration as a prop or crutch: Will European integration really
help the Southern and peripheral European nations in economic and political
terms? What will be the consequence of the inclusion of these countries, and
also in the foreseeable future of the former communist nations of East-Cen-
tral Europe (Poland, the Czech Republic, Slovakia, Hungary, Slovenia), for the
European Union as a whole? In economic terms, it is a fact that Ireland has
profited considerably from integration. As far as the peripheral South European nations and regions are concerned, however, the picture is much less clear.
But as a comparison, it might be observed, for example, that almost one hundred years of considerable support by Italian governments for the Mezzo-
giorno have not really brought Southern Italy much closer to the high level of
development in Northern Italy.

This situation in Italy could be replicated in Europe, namely, a spillover of internal problems to the whole Union. The persistence of corruption in Italy is
closely related to central government support for the South (as well as for
state-owned and state-controlled enterprises which are very important in Italy,
but also in France). Corruption in its less openly criminal forms of clientelism,
patronage, favouritism, etc. is an endemic feature of modern societies. It flou-
rishes particularly in market societies where transactions are no longer controlled by primordial units but where an open flow of resources and opportunities exists together with an increasing inequality of access to the market and
socio-political sphere[18] (Roniger 1994: 8; Roniger/Günes-Ayata 1994). Two
tendencies are relevant here: first, the massive increase of the sphere of state
activities in all Western democracies and the increasing complexity of decision-making processes; second, the differential capacities of access to the spon-
soring activities (Fördertöpfe) at the level of the European Union. It was probably not pure chance that in 1998, an Italian and a French EU-Commissioner
were involved in dubious financial transactions and in the haggling for well-
paid jobs within the EU-bureaucracy. Even more problematic in my view is

---

18 «Clientelistic relations» are defined as being «built around asymmetric but mutually beneficial and open-
ended transactions and predicated on the differential control by social actors over the access and flow of resources in stratified societies ... Basically, clientelism creates an inherently contradictory situation.
Asymmetrical power and/or inequality is combined with solidarity, and potential and/or actual coercion co-
exists with an ideological emphasis on the voluntary nature of the attachment.» (Roniger/Günes-Ayata
1994: 3f.)

another fact: the respected British newspaper *Financial Times,* which detected and criticized these practices, was taken to court and charged by EU-bureaucrats for publishing its enquiry!

Europe as a substitute for a weak sense of national identity. This function of membership in the European Union was quite obvious in the case of Germany, but I see two problems here. First, from the democratic point of view, it is disturbing that to date Germans have never had an opportunity to vote in a referendum about such a far-reaching inclusion of their political system within a new, larger unit which in fact considerably undermines their national action potential. As in the case of all the other member-states of the EU, we cannot say whether the possibility of Germans being able to elect deputies to the European Parliament would be an adequate compensation for the significant loss of impact of the Bundestag.

Second, since the high level of integration and stability in present-day Germany ultimately does not depend on the economic prosperity of the country, negative economic events or trends could significantly affect the attitudes of the German population toward European integration. In this respect, the high net financial transfers to other member-states and the high symbolic value of the Deutsche Mark pose particular problems (see Martin 1991). It could become very problematic if Germans began to see that redistribution within the European Union helps to strengthen a bureaucratic and corrupt apparatus. A problem could also arise if the Euro were to become less stable than the DM.

Inherent conflicts between different functions of European integration, and between the interests of elites and people: I have argued that in the cases of some nation-states, social and economic groups, we can say that European integration was in fact more or less consciously planned for and pursued. This raises two questions: have the aims of integration been achieved so far? Do conflicts exist between the different aims or between the actors and the people at large?

Economic integration, the liberalization of markets, and the introduction of the common currency, significantly reduce the potential of the single nation states to pursue autonomous and effective economic and social policies. At the same time, the development of a new welfare state at the EU-level is not yet in sight, nor even imaginable. The American writer John Newhouse has shown in his recent book, *Europe Adrift* (1997/98), that the Maastricht treaty was an incomplete compromise between France and England on the one side, and Germany on the other side. The first two countries and their political representatives (particularly President Mitterand, who was at first openly opposed to German reunification) wanted to introduce monetary union in order to control Germany's economic power. Germany, under Chancellor Kohl, wanted to introduce a political union. Only the first goal was achieved. The consequence is that the European Union in its present form is a torso – a structure with strong economic and market integration, but no corresponding integration of domestic and foreign policy.

A new European technocratic elite is coming into existence which is very remote from the daily life of the citizens in their home nations and regions (Bach 1999). It is not well known that 90% of the political decisions in Brussels are taken not by the Council of Ministers – the direct representatives of the single nation-states – but by a very small committee called COREPER (Comité des Représentants Permanents): this group prepares all the decisions which the Council of Ministers makes. Since the members of the Commission – the «acting government» of the EU – are also appointed by national governments, none of the most influential groups and authorities at the central level of the EU are elected in a democratic process.

Another serious problem exists with the objective of preserving the high degree of cultural differentiation within Europe – in the first instance, the variety of languages – while at the same time attempting to resolve the considerable imbalances caused by the relative sizes and degrees of power of the constituent nation-states within the European Union. No single federal state in the world – from Germany and Switzerland, to Canada and the United States – is characterized by such a high degree of internal differentiation and size and power imbalances between its subunits (Haller 1992). As long as these remain the only constituent units of the European Union – and there is no expectation that they will be replaced as such – a balanced power structure is hardly possible.

All of these facts – the tendency to undermine national political autonomy, the weak development of democratic processes at the level of central authorities in the EU, the large gaps between the national level and the level of European institutions in Brussels, Strasbourg and elsewhere – could help to explain why, throughout most of Europe, there is very little enthusiasm for European integration (Giesen 1993; Immerfall/Sobisch 1997). Nevertheless, I would not like to argue that European integration as a whole is a problematic undertaking. As an example of an integration process that was successful in the long run, we could mention the United States, which were deeply divided between North and South in social and cultural terms until the late 19th Century.[19] I

---

19   One could well ask, though, whether the national unification of the USA (and the according of equal status to the blacks) was worth the extremely bloody civil war of 1861–65, in which over 600000 people died. I would answer this question with a «No».

would argue, however, first, that we must see the European integration process much more critically than the actors involved seem to see it, and second, that we should invest more time and energy in thinking about institutional structures which are appropriate and adapted to this extremely variegated and complex entity which is called «the European Union».

Can we give an answer to the general question whether a truly European identity will develop among the people of this continent? I would be rather sceptical if we were to think here simply of feelings of attachment comparable to those expressive of a national identity. The European Union is obviously a much larger, abstract, and complex entity than any single nation-state. The EU cannot rely on a common history and on shared and venerated symbols, as nation-states can do. None of this necessarily presents a problem, however, as long as the Union keeps clearly to its character as a community of nations which does not seek to regulate the daily lives of its citizens in every detail and to become one of the power-players on the world scene. As a comparatively loose union of relatively independent nation-states, it can fulfil important and useful instrumental functions for its constituent units. An attachment to the Union as an entity which is more instrumental and neutral, but overall positive, could well go hand-in-hand with a stronger emotionally based, but demystified sense of national identity for Europeans.[20]

---

20 For ample evidence showing that chauvinistic forms of national identity are declining in Europe, see Dogan (1994).

References

Arnold, Hans (1993). *Europa am Ende? Die Auflösung von EG und NATO.*
München: Piper.

Bach, Maurizio (1993). «Vom Zweckverband zum technokratischen Regime:
Politische Legitimation und institutionelle Verselbständigung in der Europäischen Gemeinschaft», pp. 288–308 in H. A. Winkler und H. Kaelble
(eds.). *Nationalismus Nationalitäten Supranationalität.* Stuttgart: Klett-
Cotta.

Bach, Maurizio (1999). *Die Bürokratisierung Europas.* Frankfurt: Campus.

Billig; Michael (1995). *Banal Nationalism.* London: Sage

Bornschier, Volker (ed.) (1999). *Statebuilding in Europe. The Revitalization of
Western European Integration.* London: Routledge & Kegan Paul (in press).

Bruckmüller, Ernst (1996). *Nation Österreich. Kulturelles Bewusstsein und ge-
sellschaftlich-geschichtliche Prozesse.* Wien: Böhlau

Buruma, Jan (1994). *The Wages of Guilt. Memories of War in Germany and
Japan.* London: Vintage/Random House (deutsch: *Erbschaft der Schuld.
Vergangenheitsbewältigung in Deutschland und Japan.* München).

Campbell, David F. (1994). «European Nation-State under pressure: National
fragmentation or the evolution of suprastate structures?» *Cybernetics and
Systems* 25: 879–909.

Cutler, Tony et al. (1989). *1992 – The Struggle for Europe. A Critical Evaluation
of the European Community.* New York: Berg.

Deflem, Mathieu and Fred C. Pampel (1996). «The myth of postnational identity: Popular support for European unification», *Social Forces* 75: 119–143.

Delanty, Gerard (1995). *Inventing Europe. Idea, Identity, Reality.* Houndsmills/
London.

Dogan, Mattei (1994). «The erosion of nationalism in the West European
Community», pp. 31–54 in Max Haller and Rudolf Richter (eds.). *Toward a
European Nation? Political Trends in Europe. East and West, Center and
Periphery.* Armonk (N.Y.): M.E. Sharpe.

Elwert, Georg (1999). «Deutsche Nation», in B. Schäfers und W. Zapf, (eds.).
Handwörterbuch zur Gesellschaft Deutschlands. Opladen: Westdeutscher
Verlag (in press).

Estel, Bernd und Tilman Mayer (eds.) (1994). *Das Prinzip Nation in modernen
Gesellschaften. Länderdiagnosen und theoretische Perspektiven.* Opladen:
Westdeutscher Verlag.

Faber, Richard (1979). *Abendland. Ein «politischer Kampfbegriff».* Hildes-
heim: Gerstenberg Verlag.

Francis, Emmerich K. (1965). *Ethnos und Demos,* Berlin: Duncker & Humblot.

Friedrich, Carl J. (1969). *Europe. An Emergent Nation.* New York: Harper &
Row.

Galli, R. (1991). *Globale/Locale.* Milano: ISEDI.

Giesen, Bernhard (1993). «Intellektuelle, Politiker und Experten: Probleme der Konstruktion einer europäischen Identität», pp. 492–504 in B. Schäfers (ed.). *Lebensverhältnisse und soziale Konflikte im neuen Europa, Verhandlungen des 26. Deutschen Soziologentages in Düsseldorf 1992.* Frankfurt: Campus.

Goldhagen, Daniel (1996). *Hitlers willige Vollstrecker. Ganz gewöhnliche Deutsche und der Holocaust.* Berlin: Siedler.

Greiffenhagen, Martin and Sylvia (1979). *Ein schwieriges Vaterland. Zur politischen Kultur Deutschlands.* Frankfurt: Suhrkamp.

Habermas, Jürgen (1976). *Zur Rekonstruktion des Historischen Materialismus.* Frankfurt: Suhrkamp.

Haller, Max (1992). «Zur Rolle von Ethnizität und nationaler Selbstbestimmung im Prozess der Einigung Europas», pp. 25–49 in Hermann Atz und Ornella Buson (eds.). *Interethnische Beziehungen: Leben in einer mehrsprachigen Gesellschaft.* Bozen: Landesinstitut für Statistik.

Haller, Max (1994). «Über die Notwendigkeit einer objektiven und kritischen Aufklärung über den Prozess der europäischen Integration», pp. 11–39 in M. Haller und P. Schachner-Blazizek (eds.). *Europa wohin? Wirtschaftliche Integration, soziale Gerechtigkeit und Demokratie.* Graz: Leykam.

Haller, Max (1995). «Das Vereinte Europa als demokratisch-föderalistische Staatenunion. Soziologische Überlegungen zu Grundlagen und Funktionsprinzipien einer neuen ‹Verfassung› der EU», pp. 196–232 in Josef Langer und Wolfgang Pöllauer (eds.). *Kleine Staaten in grosser Gesellschaft.* Eisenstadt: Verlag für Soziologie und Humanethologie.

Haller, Max (1996). «The dissolution and building of new nations as strategy and process between elites and people. Lessons from historical European and recent Yugoslav experience», *International Review of Sociology* 6: 231–247.

Haller, Max, unter Mitarbeit von Stefan Gruber, Josef Langer, Günter Paier, Albert Reiterer, Peter Teibenbacher (1996). *Identität und Nationalstolz der Österreicher. Gesellschaftliche Ursachen und Funktionen, Herausbildung und Transformation seit 1945, internationaler Vergleich.* Wien: Böhlau Verlag.

Haller, Max (1999a). *Soziologische Theorie im systematisch-kritischen Vergleich.* Opladen: Leske und Budrich/UTB.

Haller, Max (1999b). «Effizienter Staat, beschämte Nation – ineffizienter Staat, stolze Nation? Befunde über nationale Identität und Nationalstolz der Deutschen und Italiener», in H. von Meulemann und R. Gubert (eds.). *Gesellschaftsvergleich Deutschland-Italien.* Annali di Sociologia/Soziologisches Jahrbuch, Universität Trient (in Druck).

Haller, Max and Rudolf Richter (eds.) (1994). *Toward a European Nation? Political Trends in Europe. East and West, Center and Periphery.* Armonk (N.Y.): M. E. Sharpe.

Heller, Hermann (1934). *Staatslehre.* Leiden: A.W. Sijthoffs.

Hondrich, Karl-Otto (1996). «Ethnizität und Wir-Gefühle», in S. Böckler (eds.). *Ritorno dell'Etnico? Etnicità tra decostruzione e ricostruzione/Wiederkehr des Ethnischen? Ethnizität zwischen Dekonstruktion und Rekonstruktion.* Annali di Sociologia/Soziologisches Jahrbuch 12, I–II: 163–178.

Immerfall, Stefan und Andreas Sobisch (1997). «Europäische Integration und europäische Identität. Die Europäische Union im Bewusstsein ihrer Bürger», *Aus Politik und Zeitgeschichte* (Beilage zur *Wochenzeitung Das Parlament*) B 10/97: 25–37.

Jochem, Sven (1998). *Die skandinavischen Wege in die Arbeitslosigkeit.* Opladen: Leske & Budrich.

Knieper, Rolf (1991). *Nationale Souveränität. Versuch über Ende und Anfang einer Weltordnung.* Frankfurt: Fischer Taschenbuch Verlag.

Kohr, Leopold (1983). *Die überentwickelten Nationen. Rückbesinnung auf die Region.* Salzburg: Winter (Goldmann Taschenbuchausgabe).

Kriesi, Hanspeter 1998). *Le Système Politique Suisse.* Paris: Economica.

Langner, Albrecht, (ed.) (1985). *Katholizismus, nationaler Gedanke und Europa seit 1800.* Paderborn: F. Schöningh.

Lepsius, M. Rainer (1988). *Ideen, Interessen und Institutionen.* Opladen: Westdeutscher Verlag.

Lepsius, M. Rainer (1992). *Die europäische Gemeinschaft und die Zukunft des Nationalstaates.* Festvortrag am 28.5.1992 in Regensburg anlässlich der 87. Fortbildungstagung der Ärzte (Sonderdruck).

Martin, Paul C. (1991). *Zahlmeister Deutschland. So verschleudern sie unser Geld.* München: Langen-Müller/Herbig.

Martin, Hans-Peter und Harald Schumann (1996). *Die Globalisierungsfalle. Der Angriff auf Demokratie und Wohlstand,* Reinbek bei Hamburg: Rowohlt.

Middlemas, Keith (1995). *Orchestrating Europe. The Informal Politics of the European Union 1973–95.* London: Fontana Press.

Milward, Alan S. (1992). *The European Rescue of the Nation-State.* London: Routledge & Kegan Paul.

Newhouse, John (1998). *Sackgasse Europa. Der Euro kommt, die EU zerbricht.* München: Droemer (American ed.: Europe Adrift, Pantheon Books, New York 1997).

Noelle-Neumann, Elisabeth und Renate Köcher (eds.) (1987). *Die verletzte Nation. Über den Versuch der Deutschen, ihren Charakter zu ändern.* Stuttgart: Deutsche Verlags-Anstalt.

Pfetsch, Frank (1997). *Die Europäische Union. Geschichte, Institutionen, Prozesse.* München: Wilhelm Fink Verlag.

Puntscher-Riekmann, Sonja (1998). *Die kommissarische Neuordnung Europas.* Berlin: Springer Verlag.

Roniger, Luis (1994). «Civil society, patronage and democracy», *International Journal of Comparative Sociology* XXXV: 1-14.

Roniger, Luis and Ayse Günes-Ayata (eds.) (1994). *Democracy, Clientelism, and Civil Society.* Boulder (Col.): L. Rienner Publ.

Rusconi, Gian Enrico (1993). *Se cessiamo di essere una nazione. Tra etnodemocrazie regionali e cittadinanza europea.* Bologna: il Mulino.

Schauer, Hans (1997). «Nationale und europäische Identität. Die unteschiedlichen Auffassungen in Deutschland, Frankreich und Grossbritannien», *Aus Politik und Zeitgeschichte* (Beilage zur *Wochenzeitung Das Parlament*) B 10/97: 3-13.

Scheff, Thomas (1994). *Bloody Revenge. Emotions, Nationalism, and War.* Boulder: Westview Press.

Scheuch, Erwin K. und Ute Scheuch (1992). *Cliquen, Klüngel und Karrieren. Über den Verfall der politischen Parteien – eine Studie.* Reinbek: Rowohlt.

Scholz, Reiner (1995). *Korruption in Deutschland. Die schmutzigen Finger der öffentlichen Hand.* Reinbek: Rowohlt.

Simmel, Georg (1923). *Soziologie. Untersuchungen über die Formen der Vergesellschaftung.* München: Duncker & Humblot.

Smith, Anthony D. (1991). *National Identity.* London: Penguin.

Swedberg, Richard (1994). «The idea of ‹Europe› and the origin of the European Union – A sociological approach», *Zeitschrift für Soziologie* 23: 378-387.

Therborn, Göran (1995). *European Modernity and Beyond. The Trajectory of European Societies, 1945–2000.* London: Sage

Tocqueville, Alexis de (1976). *Über die Demokratie in Amerika,* München: dtv.

Van Deth, Jan W. (1995). «Comparative politics and the decline of the nation-state in Western Europe», *European Journal of Political Research* 27: 443-462.

Von Krockow, Christian Graf (1970). *Nationalismus als deutsches Problem.* München: Piper.

Weber, Manfred, (ed.) (1991). *Europa auf dem Weg zur Währungsunion,* Darmstadt: Wissenschaftliche Buchgesellschaft.

Weber, Max (1964). *Wirtschaft und Gesellschaft, 2 Bde.* Köln: Kiepenheuer & Witsch.

Wehner, Burkhard (1992). *Nationalstaat, Solidarstaat, Effizienstaat. Neue Staatsgrenzen für neue Staatstypen.* Darmstadt: Wissenschaftliche Buchgesellschaft.

Weidenfeld, Werner (ed.) (1985). *Die Identität Europas.* Bonn

Westle, Bettina (1992). «Strukturen nationaler Identität in Ost- und West-deutschland», *Kölner Zeitschrift für Soziologie u. Sozialpsychologie* 44: 461–488.

Willi, Victor (1983). *Überleben auf Italienisch.* Wien: Europaverlag.

Ziegler, Jean (1992). *Die Schweiz wäscht weisser. Die Finanzdrehscheibe des internationalen Verbrechens.* München: Droemer Knaur.